D0509152

SPELLING THE EASY WAY

SECOND EDITION

JOSEPH MERSAND
Formerly Associate Professor of Education
York College of the City University of New York

FRANCIS GRIFFITH
Emeritus Professor of Education
Hofstra University, Hempstead, New York

BARRON'S EDUCATIONAL SERIES, INC.
New York • Toronto • London • Sydney

© Copyright 1988, 1982 by Barron's Educational Series, Inc.
also entitled *Spelling Your Way to Success*

All rights reserved.
No part of this book may be reproduced
in any form, by photostat, microfilm, xerography,
or any other means, or incorporated into any
information retrieval system, electronic or
mechanical, without the written permission
of the copyright owner.

All inquiries should be addressed to:
Barron's Educational Series, Inc.
250 Wireless Boulevard
Hauppauge, New York 11788

Library of Congress Catalog Card No. 88-6321

Paper Edition
International Standard Book No. 0-8120-3346-9

Library of Congress Cataloging-in-Publication Data

Mersand, Joseph E., 1907–
    Spelling the easy way / Joseph Mersand, Francis
      Griffith. — 2nd ed.

    p. cm. — (Easy way)
    Summary: Discusses the importance of good spelling,
explaining the general rules of English spelling, and
examines some troublesome spelling problems.
    ISBN 0-8120-3346-9
    1. English language—Orthography and spelling.
[1. English language—Spelling.] I. Griffith, Francis J.
II. Title.   III. Title: Barron's spelling the easy way.
IV. Series
PE1145.2.M39   1988   88-6321
428.1—dc19   CIP
                                             AC

PRINTED IN THE UNITED STATES OF AMERICA

012   100   98765

Contents

English as A Second Language

Special Devices

Troublesome Words

Measuring Your Progress

Introduction

Interest in spelling correctly is probably as old as writing. More than 2,000 years ago, The Greek philosopher Aristotle said:

"It is possible to spell a word correctly by chance, or because someone prompts you, but you are a scholar only if you spell it correctly *because you know how*."

Apparently the Greek schoolboy and adult had difficulties with spelling much the same way as so many of us today.

That spelling is troublesome and difficult to many people is obvious from the many complaints that have been made about the poor spelling practices of employees in business as well as students in high school and college. In a recent survey, one hundred presidents of the largest business concerns in the United States were asked their opinions about the competence in English of high school and college graduates of the last five to ten years. Over twenty of these executives indicated that spelling needed great improvement. Here are some typical comments:

"Inability to spell simple words used in business communications, such as *receive, recommend, all right*."

"They cannot spell common every day words."

"Spelling is a lost art that should be revived."

"Their spelling has been atrocious."

"High school graduates exhibit a noticeable deficiency in ability to spell."

These are the opinions held not only by many business executives but by many college teachers and college presidents as well. Parents who compare their own achievements as students with those of their children today are also among the severe critics of today's spellers.

The recent emphasis upon the basics in education implies emphasis on correct spelling. Although all sorts of machines can perform acts more speedily than the human mind, no machine can express a person's thoughts. And if that person is a poor speller, the machine, no matter how costly and intricate, will make the same spelling mistakes.

Of the production of spelling books, there seems to be no end. From the famous blue-backed speller of Noah Webster in 1783 to the ever-increasing number in our own times, books on spelling have been numerous. A new book in this field can be justified if it endeavors to combine the knowledge of the experts in the field of spelling with more effective presentation and better methods for mastering this important subject. If the author by his manner of presenting the important subject of spelling, through clearly stated rules, copious exercises, and numerous examples will make you interested in improving your spelling, then you will be well along the way to becoming a better speller. Like so many other aspects of learning, we learn best what we are interested in and what we really want to learn.

Most chapters in the book have one or more exercises designed to fix in your memory and to make habitual the principles of correct spelling. It is imperative that you do these exercises carefully. Note the errors that you have made and review until you spell these troublesome words effortlessly. A few minutes a day over a period of time should suffice to achieve your objectives. The exercises are of various types, in accordance with the best methods of teaching.

Above all, you must try to use as many of the words you have been studying as soon as and as often as possible. Memorizing the rules will not be of much help unless you apply them.

Lord Chesterfield, who said so many wise things to his son in his famous letters, also considered the subject of spelling.

"Orthography is so absolutely necessary for a man of letters, or a gentleman, that one false spelling may fix ridicule upon him for the rest of his life, and I know a man of quality who never recovered the ridicule of having spelled *wholesome* without the *w*."[1]

His remark about orthography (or correct spelling) which applied to the aristocratic gentleman of his day is now pertinent to everyone who wishes to be considered an educated man.

Even one of our founding fathers, Thomas Jefferson, expressed himself on this subject to his daughter, in whose education he was so interested:

"Take care that you never spell a word wrong. Always before you write a word, consider how it is spelled, and if you do not remember, turn to a dictionary. It produces great praise to a lady to spell well."

Whether from the viewpoint of good social etiquette, success in school and college work or promotion in your chosen profession, you cannot afford to remain a poor speller. This book will help you to become a good one.

The authors wish to express their thanks to Margaret C. Chandler, James W. Connolly, Bidabee Gloster, Kathryn O'D. Griffith, Estelle J. Mersand, Laura and Robert Pagano, Gladys D. Roche, David Sharp, Carol Sullivan, and Jeremiah J. Sullivan for their assistance in preparing and editing the manuscript.

Joseph Mersand
Francis Griffith

---

[1] Lord Chesterfield, *Letters to His Son,* 1750.

10,000 Word
Ready
Reference
Spelling List

10,000 Word Ready Reference Spelling List

How to Use This List

Spelling. The words in this reference list are spelled according to American usage.

When two spellings are valid, both are listed:

dem·a·gogue, dem·a·gog

Dividing words at the end of a line. Centered dots indicate division points at which a hyphen may be put at the end of a line of typing or writing. For example, *baccalaureate* (*bac·ca·lau·re·ate*) may be ended on one line with

bac-
bacca-
baccalau-
baccalaure-

and continued on the next line, respectively, with

-calaureate
-laureate
-reate
-ate

2

Note, however, that a single initial letter or a single terminal letter is not cut off. The following words, for example, are not hyphenated:

abound	icy
o'clock	seamy

Plurals. Most English nouns form their plural by adding *s*. These regular plurals are not shown in the reference list. Irregular plurals are shown:

la·bo·ra·to·ry (–ries)
knife (knives)
lar·ynx (la·ryn·ges *or* lar·ynx·es)
las·so (las·sos *or* las·soes)
la·tex (la·ti·ces *or* la·tex·es)
oc·to·pus (–pus·es *or* –pi)

Definitions. Brief definitions of confusing pairs of words are given:

arc (something arched or curved; see *ark*)
ark (a boat; a repository for Torah scrolls; see *arc*)
af·fect (to influence; see *effect*)
ef·fect (to accomplish; see *affect*)

Brief definitions of foreign words and phrases are also given:

ad va·lo·rem (Latin: according to value)
a pri·o·ri (Latin: reasoning from self-evident proposition)

10,000
Words

A

aback
aba·cus (–cus·es)
aban·don
aban·don·ment
abase
abase·ment
abash
abate·ment
ab·bey
ab·bot
ab·bre·vi·ate
ab·bre·vi·a·tion
ab·di·cate
ab·di·ca·tion
ab·do·men
ab·dom·i·nal
ab·duct
ab·duc·tion
ab·er·ra·tion
abet
abet·ted
ab·hor
ab·hor·rence
abide
abil·i·ty (–ties)
ab·ject
ab·jur·ing
able-bod·ied
ab·lu·tion
ably
ab·ne·ga·tion
ab·nor·mal·i·ty (–ties)
ab·nor·mal·ly
aboard
abol·ish
ab·o·li·tion
A-bomb
abom·i·na·ble
abort
abor·tion
abound
about-face
above·board
above men·tioned
abra·sive
abreast
abridge
abridg·ment, abridge·ment
abroad
ab·ro·gate

abrupt
ab·scess
ab·scond
ab·sence
ab·so·lute
ab·solve
ab·sorb
ab·stain
ab·strac·tion
abun·dant
abut·ment
abys·mal
abyss
ac·cede
ac·cel·er·ate
ac·cent
ac·cept (to receive; see
    except)
ac·ces·so·ry, ac·ces·sa·ry
    (–ries)
ac·ces·si·ble
ac·ci·dent
ac·claim
ac·cli·mate
ac·cli·ma·tize
ac·co·lade
ac·com·mo·date
ac·com·mo·da·tion
ac·com·pa·nist
ac·com·pa·ny
ac·com·plice
ac·com·plish
ac·cord
ac·cost
ac·count
ac·coun·tant
ac·cru·al
ac·cu·mu·late
ac·cu·ra·cy
ac·cuse
ac·e·tate
acet·y·lene
achieve
ac·knowl·edge
acous·tics
ac·quain·tance
ac·qui·esce
ac·quire
ac·qui·si·tion
ac·quit·tal

acre
acre·age
ac·ri·mo·ni·ous
across
ac·tiv·i·ty (–ties)
ac·tu·al
ac·tu·ar·i·al
ac·tu·ary
acu·punc·ture
ad·ap·ta·tion
ad·dict
ad·di·tion·al
ad·dress·ee
ad·duce
ad·e·noid
ad·e·quate
ad·here
ad·he·sive
ad hoc (Latin: pertaining to
    the case at hand)
ad ho·mi·nem (Latin:
    argument based on
    personality)
adieu (adieus *or* adieux)
    (French: farewell)
ad in·fi·ni·tum (Latin:
    without end)
ad·ja·cent
ad·jec·tive
ad·join·ing
ad·journ
ad·journ·ment
ad·ju·di·cate
ad·junct
ad·just·able
ad·ju·tant
ad-lib (Latin: without
    preparation)
ad·min·is·ter
ad·min·is·trate
ad·min·is·tra·tion
ad·min·is·tra·tor
ad·mi·ra·ble
ad·mis·si·ble
ad nau·se·am (Latin: to a
    sickening degree)
ad·o·les·cent
adopt
ad·re·nal
adroit

ad·u·la·tion
ad va·lo·rem (Latin:
  according to value)
ad·van·ta·geous
ad·ven·tur·ous
ad·ver·sary (–sar·ies)
ad·ver·si·ty (–ties)
ad·ver·tise·ment
ad·vice (recommendation;
  see *advise*)
ad·vis·able
ad·vise (to give advice; see
  advice)
ad·vis·er, ad·vi·sor
ad·vo·cate
aer·ate
ae·ri·al (relating to the air)
aer·i·al (antenna)
aero·dy·nam·ics
aero·nau·tics
aero·sol
aes·thet·ics
af·fa·ble
af·fect (to influence; see
  effect)
af·fec·tion·ate
af·fi·da·vit
af·fil·i·ate
af·fin·i·ty (–ties)
af·fir·ma·tive
af·flic·tion
af·flu·ent
af·ford
af·fray
af·front
af·ghan
afore·men·tioned
afraid
af·ter·ward, af·ter·wards
again
agen·cy (–cies)
agen·da
agent
ag·glom·er·ate
ag·gran·dize·ment
ag·gra·vate
ag·gres·sion
ag·gres·sive
ag·grieved
aghast
ag·ile

agil·i·ty (–ties)
ag·i·tate
ag·i·ta·tor
ag·nos·tic
ag·on·ize
agrar·i·an
agree·able
ag·ri·cul·ture
agron·o·my
aid (to give assistance, a
  subsidy; see *aide*)
aide (military assistant; see
  aid)
air-con·di·tion
air con·di·tion·er
air force
air·line
air·port
aisle
a la carte (French: each
  item is priced separately)
alac·ri·ty
al·ba·tross
al·bu·men
al·che·my
al·co·hol
al·ge·bra
al·ga (al·gae)
alias
al·i·bi
alien·ate
align·ment, aline·ment
al·i·men·ta·ry
al·i·mo·ny (–nies)
alive
al·ka·li (–lies *or* –lis)
al·lay (relieve; see *alley,*
  ally)
al·le·ga·tion
al·lege
al·le·giance
al·le·go·ry (–ries)
al·ler·gy (–gies)
al·le·vi·ate
al·ley (narrow passage; see
  allay, ally)
al·li·ance
al·li·ga·tor
al·lit·er·ate
al·lit·er·a·tion
al·lo·cate

al·lot
al·lot·ment
all·over (repeated design;
  see *all over*)
all over (everywhere; see
  allover)
al·low
al·low·able
al·low·ance
al·loy
all right
al·lude (to refer; see *elude*)
al·lure
al·lu·sion
al·ly (an associate; see
  allay, alley)
al·ma·nac
al·mond
al·most
alms
alo·ha
alone
aloud
al·pha·bet
al·pha·bet·ize
al·ready
al·tar (structure used in
  religious ceremonies; see
  alter)
al·ter (to change; see *altar*)
al·ter·a·tion
al·ter·ca·tion
al·ter·nate
al·ter·na·tive
al·though
al·tim·e·ter
al·ti·tude
al·to·geth·er
al·tru·ism
al·um
alu·mi·num
alum·na (–nae)
alum·nus (–ni)
al·ways
amal·gam·ate
am·a·teur
am·a·to·ry
amaze
am·bas·sa·dor
am·bi·dex·trous
am·bi·ence, am·bi·ance

am·bi·gu·ity (–ties)
am·big·u·ous
am·bi·tious
am·biv·a·lence
am·bu·lance
am·bu·la·to·ry
ame·lio·rate
ame·na·ble
amend·ment
ame·ni·ty (–ties)
am·e·thyst
ami·a·ble
am·i·ca·ble
am·i·ty (–ties)
am·mo·nia
am·mu·ni·tion
am·ne·sia
am·nes·ty (–ties)
am·nio·cen·te·sis
amoe·ba (–bas or –bae)
amor·al
am·o·rous
amor·phous
am·or·ti·za·tion
amor·tize
amount
am·phet·amine
am·phib·i·an
am·phi·the·ater
am·pli·fy
am·pu·tate
amuse·ment
anach·ro·nism
an·al·ge·sic
anal·o·gous
anal·o·gy
anal·y·sis
an·a·lyst
an·a·lyze
an·ar·chy
anath·e·ma
anat·o·my
an·ces·tor
an·ces·try
anchor
an·cho·vy (–vies or –vy)
an·cient
an·cil·lary
an·ec·dote
an·es·the·sia
an·eu·rysm, an·eu·rism

an·gel (heavenly
    messenger; see *angle*)
an·gle (geometric figure;
    see *angel*)
an·guish
an·i·mate
an·i·mos·i·ty (–ties)
an·nals
an·neal
an·nex (noun), an·nex
    (verb)
an·ni·hi·late
an·ni·ver·sa·ry (–ries)
an·no·tate
an·nounce·ment
an·nounc·er
an·noy
an·nu·al
an·nu·ity (–ities)
an·nul
an·nun·ci·ate
anoint
anom·a·ly (–lies)
anon·y·mous
an·swer
ant (insect; see *aunt*)
an·tag·o·nize
an·te·ced·ent
an·te·date
an·te·lope
an·ten·na
an·te·ri·or
an·te·room
an·them
an·thol·o·gy (–gies)
an·thra·cite
an·thro·pol·o·gy
an·ti·bi·ot·ic
an·tic
an·tic·i·pate
an·ti·cli·max
an·ti·dote
an·ti·his·ta·mine
an·ti·pas·to
an·tip·a·thy (thies)
an·ti·pol·lu·tion
an·ti·quar·i·an
an·tique
an·tiq·ui·ty (–ties)
an·ti·sep·tic
an·ti·so·cial

an·tith·e·sis (–e·ses)
ant·onym
anx·i·ety (–eties)
anx·ious
aor·ta
apart·heid
apart·ment
ap·a·thy
aper·i·tif
ap·er·ture
apex
aph·o·rism
aph·ro·dis·i·ac
aplomb
apoc·a·lypse
apoc·ry·phal
apo·gee
apol·o·gize
apol·o·gy (–gies)
ap·o·plec·tic
ap·o·plexy
apos·tle
apos·tro·phe
apo·the·o·sis (–ses)
ap·pall, ap·pal
ap·pa·ra·tus (–tus·es or
    –tus)
ap·par·el
ap·par·ent
ap·pa·ri·tion
ap·peal
ap·pear·ance
ap·pease
ap·pel·lant
ap·pe·late
ap·pend·age
ap·pen·dec·to·my (–mies)
ap·pen·di·ci·tis
ap·pen·dix (–dix·es or
    –di·ces)
ap·per·tain
ap·pe·tite
ap·pe·tiz·er
ap·plaud
ap·plause
ap·pli·ance
ap·pli·ca·ble
ap·pli·ca·tion
ap·pli·ca·tor
ap·plied
ap·ply

ap·point·ment
ap·por·tion
ap·pose
ap·praise
ap·pre·ci·ate
ap·pre·hend
ap·pren·tice
ap·prise
ap·proach
ap·pro·ba·tion
ap·pro·pri·ate
ap·pro·pri·a·tion
ap·prov·al
ap·prox·i·mate
apri·cot
a pri·o·ri (Latin: reasoning
   from self-evident
   propositions)
ap·ro·pos
ap·ti·tude
apt·ly
aquar·i·um
aquat·ic
aq·ue·duct
ar·bi·ter
ar·bi·trary
ar·bi·trate
ar·bi·tra·tor
ar·bor
arc (curved line; see *ark*)
ar·cade
arch
ar·chae·ol·o·gy
ar·cha·ic
ar·chery
ar·che·type
ar·chi·pel·a·go (–goes)
ar·chi·tect
ar·chi·tec·tur·al
ar·chi·tec·ture
ar·chive
arc·tic
ar·dent
ar·dor
ar·du·ous
ar·ea
are·na
ar·gue
aria
ar·id

ar·is·toc·ra·cy (–cies)
aris·to·crat
arith·me·tic
ark (boat; see *arc*)
ar·ma·ment
ar·ma·ture
ar·mi·stice
ar·moire
ar·mor
ar·my (ar·mies)
aro·ma
arouse
ar·raign
ar·range
ar·ray
ar·rears
ar·rest
ar·riv·al
ar·rive
ar·ro·gance
ar·se·nic
ar·son
ar·te·ri·al
ar·te·rio·scle·ro·sis
ar·tery (–ter·ies)
ar·thri·tis
ar·ti·choke
ar·ti·cle
ar·tic·u·late
ar·ti·fact
ar·ti·fice
ar·ti·fi·cial
ar·ti·san
ar·tis·tic
as·bes·tos, as·bes·tus
as·cend
as·cen·sion
as·cent (climb; see *assent*)
as·cer·tain
as·cet·ic
as·cribe
asep·tic
askew
as·par·a·gus (–gus·es)
as·pect
as·per·i·ty (–ties)
as·per·sion
as·phalt
as·phyx·i·ate
as·pire

as·pi·rin
as·sail
as·sas·sin
as·sas·si·na·tion
as·sault
as·sem·ble
as·sem·bly (–blies)
as·sent (to agree; see
   ascent)
as·sert
as·sess·ment
as·set
as·sid·u·ous
as·sign·ment
as·sim·i·late
as·sis·tant
as·so·ci·a·tion
as·so·nance
as·sort·ment
as·suage
as·sump·tion
as·sur·ance
as·ter·isk
as·ter·oid
asth·ma
astig·ma·tism
as·trin·gent
as·trol·o·gy
as·tro·naut
as·tron·o·mer
as·tro·nom·i·cal,
   as·tro·nom·ic
as·tron·o·my (–mies)
as·tute
asun·der
asy·lum
asym·met·ric,
   asym·met·ri·cal
at·a·vism
athe·ist
ath·lete
ath·let·ic
at·mo·sphere
atom·ic
aton·al
atone·ment
atro·cious
at·ro·phy
at·tach
at·ta·ché

at·tack
at·tain
at·tempt
at·ten·dance
at·ten·tive
at·ten·u·ate
at·test
at·tic
at·tire
at·ti·tude
at·tor·ney
at·trac·tive
at·tri·bute
at·tri·tion
at·tune
atyp·i·cal
au·burn
auc·tion·eer
au·da·cious
au·dac·i·ty (–ties)
au·di·ble
au·di·ence
au·dio·vi·su·al
au·dit
au·di·tion
au·di·to·ri·um
au·ger
aug·ment
auld lang syne (Scottish:
   the good old times)
aunt (relative; see *ant*)
au·ral (relating to the ear;
   see *oral*)
au re·voir (French: good-
   bye)
au·ri·cle

aus·pic·es
aus·pi·cious
aus·tere
aus·ter·i·ty (–ties)
au·then·tic
au·then·ti·cate
au·then·tic·i·ty
au·thor
au·thor·i·ta·tive
au·thor·i·ty (–ties)
au·tho·ri·za·tion
au·tho·rize
au·to·bio·graph·i·cal,
   au·to·bio·graph·ic
au·to·bi·og·ra·phy (–phies)
au·toc·ra·cy (–cies)
au·to·crat
au·to·graph
au·to·mat·ed
au·to·mat·ic
au·to·mat·i·cal·ly
au·to·ma·tion
au·tom·a·ton
au·to·mo·bile
au·to·mo·tive
au·ton·o·mous
au·ton·o·my (–mies)
au·top·sy (–sies)
au·to·sug·ges·tion
au·tumn
aux·il·ia·ry (–ries)
avail·abil·i·ty (–ties)
avail·able
av·a·lanche
av·a·rice
av·a·ri·cious

avenge
av·e·nue
av·er·age
averse
aver·sion
avert
avi·ary (–ar·ies)
avi·a·tion
avi·a·tor
av·id
av·o·ca·do (–dos *or* –does)
av·o·ca·tion
avoid·able
avoid·ance
av·oir·du·pois (French:
   weight)
await
awake
awak·en·ing
award
aware
away
awe·some
aw·ful
awhile
awk·ward
aw·ning
awoke
ax·i·al
ax·i·om
ax·i·om·at·ic
ax·is (ax·es)
ax·le
aza·lea
az·i·muth
azure

B

bab·ble
ba·by (ba·bies)
ba·boon
bac·ca·lau·re·ate
bach·e·lor
ba·cil·lus (–li)
back·bone
back·fire
back·log
back·stop
back·ward
ba·con
bac·te·ri·al
bac·te·ri·ol·o·gy
bac·te·ri·um (–ria)
bad·ger
bad·i·nage
bad·min·ton
baf·fle
bag·gage
bail (security for due
    appearance; see *bale*)
bai·liff
bai·li·wick
bak·ery (–er·ies)
bak·ing
bal·ance
bal·co·ny (–nies)
bale (large bundle; see *bail*)
balk
bal·lad
bal·last
bal·le·ri·na
bal·let
bal·lis·tics
bal·loon
bal·lot
balm
ba·lo·ney, bo·lo·ney
bal·sa
bam·boo
ba·nal
ba·nana
ban·dage
ban·dan·na
ban·di·try
bane·ful
ban·ish
ban·is·ter
bank·rupt

bank·rupt·cy (–cies)
ban·ner
ban·quet
ban·ter
bap·tism
bap·tize
bar·be·cue
bare (exposed; see *bear*)
ba·rom·e·ter
ba·ron (a lord of the realm;
    see *barren*)
bar·rack
bar·rel
bar·ren (not reproducing;
    see *baron*)
bar·rette (hair pin; see
    beret)
bar·ri·cade
bar·ri·er
bar·room
base (bottom; see *bass*)
bash·ful
ba·sic
ba·si·cal·ly
ba·sil·i·ca
ba·sis (ba·ses)
bas·ket·ry (–ries)
bass (a deep tone; see
    base)
bas·si·net
bas·soon
bas·tard
baste
bas·tion
bathe
bat·tal·ion
bat·tle
bau·ble
baux·ite
bay·o·net
bay·ou
ba·zaar (market; see
    bizarre)
beach (shore; see *beech*)
bea·con
beady
bear (an animal, to endure,
    to give birth; see *bare*)
beard
beast

beau
beau·ti·ful
beau·ti·fy
beau·ty (–ties)
be·cause
bed·lam
bed·ou·in, bed·u·in
    (bed·ou·ins, bed·u·ins)
    often in CAPS
beech (tree; see *beach*)
beer (alcoholic beverage;
    see *bare, bier*)
be·fore
be·fud·dle
beg·gar
be·gin·ning
be·go·nia
be·grudge
be·guile
be·hav·ior
be·he·moth
be·hest
be·hold·en
be·hoove
beige
be·ing
be·la·bor
be·lat·ed
bel·fry (–fries)
be·lie
be·lief
be·lieve
bell (chime; see *belle*)
belle (beauty; see *bell*)
bel·lig·er·ent
bel·lows
be·neath
bene·dic·tion
bene·fac·tor
be·nef·i·cence
ben·e·fi·cial
ben·e·fi·cia·ry (–ries)
be·nev·o·lence
be·nign
ben·zene, ben·zine
be·queath
be·quest
be·reave
be·ret (woolen cap; see
    barrette)

ber·serk
berth (place; see *birth*)
be·siege
bes·tial
be·stow
be·tray
be·tween
be·twixt
bev·el
bev·er·age
bevy (bev·ies)
be·wail
bi·an·nu·al
bi·as (–es)
bi·ble
bib·li·cal
bib·li·og·ra·phy (–phies)
bib·lio·phile
bib·u·lous
bi·cam·er·al
bi·car·bon·ate
bi·cen·ten·ni·al
bi·ceps
bi·cy·cle
bi·en·ni·al
bier
bi·fo·cal
big·a·my
big·ot
big·ot·ry (–ries)
bi·ki·ni
bi·lat·er·al
bi·lin·ear
bi·lin·gual
bil·ious
bil·let
bil·let-doux (French: a love
    letter)
bil·liards
bil·lion
bi·na·ry
bin·au·ral
bind·ery (–er·ies)
bin·oc·u·lar
bio·chem·is·try
bio·de·grad·able
bio·graph·i·cal
bi·og·ra·phy (–phies)
bi·o·log·i·cal
bi·ol·o·gy

bi·op·sy
bi·par·ti·san
bi·ra·cial
birth (originate; see *berth*)
bis·cuit
bi·son
bisque
bit·ter
bi·tu·mi·nous
biv·ouac
bi·zarre (out of the
    ordinary; see *bazaar*)
black·mail
blar·ney
bla·sé
blas·phe·my (–mies)
bla·tant
bla·zon
blem·ish
blight
blind·ly
blithe
blitz·krieg (German: war
    conducted with great
    speed)
bliz·zard
bloc (group; see *block*)
block (hinder; see *bloc*)
block·ade
blos·som
blotch
blown
blud·geon
blue
blurb
boar (wild pig; see *bore*)
board (a piece of wood; see
    bored)
bod·ily
bo·gey
bog·gle
bo·lo·gna
bo·lo·ney, ba·lo·ney
bol·ster
bom·bard
bona fide (Latin: in good
    faith)
bo·nan·za
bond·age
bon·fire

bo·nus
bon voy·age (French:
    farewell)
book·keep·ing
boo·mer·ang
boon·dog·gle
boor·ish
bo·rax
bor·der
bore (to drill; past of *bear*;
    dull person; see *boar*)
bored (past of *bore*; see
    board)
born (from birth; see
    borne)
borne (past participle of
    bear; see *born*)
bor·ough (town; see
    borrow)
bor·row (to receive with
    intention of returning;
    see *borough*)
borscht (Russian: soup of
    beets and sour cream)
bo·som
bos·sy
bot·a·ny (–nies)
bot·tle
bot·tom
bou·doir (French: bedroom,
    private sitting room)
bough (tree limb; see *bow*)
bouil·la·baisse (French: fish
    stew)
bouil·lon
boul·der
bou·le·vard
bound·ary (–aries)
boun·te·ous
bou·quet
bour·bon
bour·geois (plural also
    bourgeois) (French:
    middle class)
bou·ton·niere (French:
    flower worn in
    buttonhole)
bo·vine
bow (to bend; see *bough*)
bow·el

boy·cott
brace·let
braid
braille
braise
brake (to stop; see *break*)
bram·ble
bras·siere
bra·va·do
brav·ery
bra·vo (bra·vos)
brawny
bra·zen
breach
breadth
break (to tear; see *brake*)
break·fast
breathe
breath·less
breech·es
breeze
breth·ren
bre·via·ry (–ries)
brev·i·ty
brib·ery
bric-a-brac
brid·al (relating to a bride; see *bridle*)
bridge
bri·dle (horse's headgear; see *bridal*)
brief
bri·gade
brig·a·dier
brig·and
bright
bril·liant
brine
bri·quette, bri·quet

bris·tle
brit·tle
broach (to open up a subject for discussion; see *brooch*)
broad·cast
bro·cade
bro·co·li, broc·o·li
bro·chure
brogue
bro·ker·age
bro·mide
bron·chi·al
brooch (ornament; see *broach*)
broth·er·ly
brow·beat
browse
bruise
brunet, brun·ette
brusque
bru·tal
bub·ble
buc·ca·neer
buck·et
bu·col·ic
bud·get
buf·fa·lo
buf·fet (verb: a blow with the hand)
buf·fet (noun: meal set out for self-service)
buf·foon
bug·a·boo
bu·gle
build
bul·le·tin
bul·lion
bul·wark

bump·kin
bump·tious
bun·ga·low
bun·gle
buoy·an·cy
bur·den
bu·reau
bu·reau·cra·cy (–cies)
bu·reau·crat
bur·geon
bur·glar
buri·al
bur·lesque
bur·ly
burnt
bur·ro (donkey; see *burrow*)
bur·row (a hole made in the ground by an animal; see *burro*)
bur·sar
bush·el
busi·ness
bus·tle
busy
butch·er
butte
but·tock
but·ton
but·tress
bux·om
buy (purchase; see *by*)
buzz
buz·zard
by (near; see *buy*)
by·pass
by-pro·duct
by·stand·er
by·way

ca·bal
ca·bana
cab·a·ret
cab·bage
cab·i·net
ca·ble
ca·boose
cache
ca·chet
ca·coph·o·ny (–nies)
cac·tus
ca·dav·er
ca·dence
caf·e·te·ria
caf·feine
ca·gey
cais·son
ca·jole
ca·lam·i·ty (–ties)
cal·ci·fy
cal·ci·um
cal·cu·late
cal·cu·la·tor
cal·cu·lus (–lus·es)
cal·en·dar (a system for fixing divisions of time in order; see *calender*)
cal·en·der (to press between rollers or plates)
cal·i·ber, cal·i·bre
cal·i·brate
cal·i·co
cal·is·then·ics
cal·lig·ra·pher
cal·lig·ra·phy
cal·lous (feeling no emotion; see *callus*)
cal·lus (hard, thickened area of skin; see *callous*)
cal·o·rie, cal·o·ry (–ries)
cal·um·ny (–nies)
ca·lyp·so
ca·ma·ra·de·rie
ca·mel·lia, ca·me·lia
cam·eo (cam·eos)
cam·i·sole
cam·ou·flage
cam·paign
cam·phor

ca·nal
can·a·pé (French: type of appetizer)
ca·nard
ca·nas·ta
can·cel
can·cel·la·tion, can·cel·ation
can·cer
can·des·cence
can·di·da·cy (–cies)
can·di·date
can·dle
can·dor
ca·nine
can·is·ter
can·ker
can·ni·bal
can·non (gun; see *canon*)
can·not
ca·noe
canon (dogma; see *cannon*)
can·o·py (–pies)
can·ta·loupe
can·tan·ker·ous
can·ta·ta
can·teen
can·ter (horse's gait; see *cantor*)
can·ti·cle
can·ti·le·ver
can·to
can·tor (synagogue official who sings liturgy; see *canter*)
can·vas (closely woven cloth; see *canvass*)
can·vass (examine votes; see *canvas*)
can·yon
ca·pa·bil·i·ty (–ties)
ca·pa·ble
ca·pa·cious
ca·pac·i·ty (–ties)
ca·per
cap·il·lary (–lar·ies)
cap·i·tal (seat of government; see *capitol*)
cap·i·tal·ism

cap·i·tol (building in which legislature meets; see *capital*)
ca·pit·u·late
ca·pon
ca·price
ca·pri·cious
cap·sule
cap·tain
cap·tion
cap·ti·vate
car·a·mel
car·at, kar·at (unit of weight; see *caret, carrot*)
car·a·van
car·bine
car·bo·hy·drate
car·bon
car·bun·cle
car·bu·re·tor
car·cass
car·cin·o·gen
car·di·ac
car·di·gan
car·di·nal
car·dio·gram
car·di·ol·o·gist
ca·reen
ca·reer
care·ful
ca·ress
car·et (printing symbol; see *carat, carrot*)
car·go
car·i·ca·ture
car·ies
car·il·lon
car·nage
car·nal
car·ni·val
car·niv·o·rous
car·ol
car·pen·ter
carp·ing
car·rel
car·riage
car·ri·er
car·ri·on

C

car·rot (vegetable; see
   carat, caret)
carte blanche (French: full
   discretionary power)
car·tog·ra·pher
car·ton
car·toon
car·tridge
cas·cade
case·work
cash·ier
cash·mere
ca·si·no
cas·ket
cas·se·role
cas·sette, ca·sette
cas·sock
cast (direct; see *caste*)
cas·ta·net
caste (class; see *cast*)
cas·ti·gate
cas·tle
cas·tor
ca·su·al·ty (–ties)
cat·a·clysm
cat·a·comb
cat·a·lep·sy (–sies)
cat·a·log, cat·a·logue
cat·a·lyst
cat·a·pult
cat·a·ract
ca·tarrh
ca·tas·tro·phe
cata·ton·ic
cat·e·chism
cat·e·go·rize
cat·e·go·ry (–ries)
ca·ter
cat·er·cor·ner, kit·ty-
   cor·ner
cat·er·pil·lar
ca·thar·sis
ca·the·dral
cath·e·ter
cath·o·lic (universal; see
   Catholic)
Cath·o·lic (member of a
   Catholic church; see
   catholic)
cat·sup, ketch·up

cau·cus
caught
caul·dron
cau·li·flow·er
caulk
caus·al
caus·tic
cau·tion
cau·tious
cav·al·cade
cav·a·lier
cav·al·ry (–ries)
cav·i·ar
cav·il
cav·i·ty (–ties)
ca·vort
cease
ce·dar
cede
ceil·ing
cel·e·brate
ce·leb·ri·ty (–ties)
ce·ler·i·ty
cel·ery (–er·ies)
ce·les·tial
cel·i·ba·cy
cell (microscopic mass; see
   sell)
cel·lar (basement; see
   seller)
cel·lo
cel·lo·phane
cel·lu·loid
ce·ment
cem·e·tery (–ter·ies)
cen·ser (incense burner;
   see *censor*)
cen·sor (supervisor of
   conduct and morals; see
   censer)
cen·sure
cen·sus
cent (monetary unit; see
   sent)
cen·te·na·ry (–ries)
cen·ten·ni·al
cen·ter·piece
cen·ti·grade
cen·ti·me·ter
cen·trif·u·gal

cen·trip·e·tal
cen·tu·ry (–ries)
ce·phal·ic
ce·ram·ic
ce·re·al (prepared grain;
   see *serial*)
cer·e·bel·lum
ce·re·bral
cer·e·mo·ny (–nies)
ce·rise
cer·tain
cer·tif·i·cate
cer·ti·fy
cer·ti·tude
ces·sa·tion
ces·sion
cess·pool
chafe
chaff
cha·grin
chair·man
cha·let
chal·ice
chalk
chal·lenge
chal·lis (chal·lises)
cham·ber·lain
cham·bray
cha·me·leon
cham·ois
cham·pagne
cham·pi·on
chan·cel·lor
chan·cery (–cer·ies)
chan·de·lier
change
chan·nel
chan·tey, chan·ty
   (chan·teys, chan·ties)
Cha·nu·kah, Ha·nuk·kah
cha·os
chap·ar·ral
cha·peau (French: hat)
cha·pel
chap·er·on, chap·er·one
chap·lain
chap·ter
char·ac·ter
cha·rade
char·coal

charge
char·gé d'af·faires (French: a diplomat who substitutes for an ambassador)
char·i·ot
cha·ris·ma
char·i·ty (–ties)
char·la·tan
char·treuse
chary
chasm
chas·sis
chaste
chas·tise
chas·ti·ty
châ·teau (French: mansion)
chat·tel
chat·ty
chauf·feur
chau·vin·ism
check
chee·tah
chef
chem·i·cal
che·mise
che·mo·ther·a·py
che·nille
cher·ish
cher·ub
chess
che·va·lier
chev·ron
chic
chi·ca·nery (–ner·ies)
chick·a·dee
chic·o·ry (–ries)
chief
chif·fon
child (chil·dren)
chime
chim·ney
chim·pan·zee
chin·chil·la
chintz
chi·ro·prac·tor
chis·el
chiv·al·ry (–ries)
chlo·rine
chlo·ro·form

chlo·ro·phyll
choc·o·late
choir (group of singers; see *quire*)
chol·era
cho·les·ter·ol
chord
cho·re·og·ra·phy (–phies)
chorus
chor·tle
chris·ten
chro·mat·ic
chrome
chro·mo·some
chron·ic
chron·i·cle
chro·no·log·i·cal
chro·nol·o·gy (–gies)
chrys·a·lis (chry·sal·i·des, chrys·a·lis·es)
chry·san·the·mum
church
chute
ci·gar
cig·a·rette, cig·a·ret
cin·der
cin·e·ma
cin·na·mon
ci·pher
cir·cle
cir·cuit
cir·cu·lar
cir·cu·la·tion
cir·cum·cise
cir·cum·fer·ence
cir·cum·lo·cu·tion
cir·cum·scribe
cir·cum·spect
cir·cum·stance
cir·cum·stan·tial
cir·cum·vent
cir·rho·sis
cis·tern
cit·a·del
ci·ta·tion
cite (to quote; see *site*)
cit·i·zen
city
civ·ic
ci·vil·i·ty (–ties)

civ·i·li·za·tion
claim·ant
clair·voy·ance
clam·my
clam·or
clan·des·tine
clan·gor
claque
clar·et
clar·i·fy
clar·i·net
clar·i·on
clar·i·ty
clas·sic
clas·si·cal
clas·si·cist
clas·si·fied
class·less
clause
claus·tro·pho·bia
clav·i·chord
clav·i·cle
cleanse
clear·ance
cleave
clef
clem·en·cy (–cies)
cler·i·cal
cli·ché (French: trite expression)
click (slight sharp noise; see *clique*)
cli·en·tele
cliff
cli·mate
climb (to go upward; see *clime*)
clime (climate; see *climb*)
clin·ic
clique (exclusive group; see *click*)
clob·ber
clois·ter
clos·et
cloth
clothe
cloud
clout
clus·ter
clutch

co·ag·u·late
co·alesce
co·ali·tion
coarse (rough; see *course*)
coax
co·bra
co·caine
cock·le·shell
cock·ney
co·coa
co·coon
cod·dle
co·de·fen·dant
co·deine
cod·ger
cod·i·cil
cod·i·fy
co·ed·u·ca·tion
co·ef·fi·cient
co·erce
cof·fers
cof·fin
co·gent
cog·i·tate
co·gnac
cog·ni·tion
cog·ni·zant
co·here
co·he·sive·ness
coif·fure
co·in·cide
col·an·der
col·ic
col·i·se·um
col·lab·o·rate
col·lapse
col·late
col·lat·er·al
col·league
col·lec·tive
col·lege
col·lide
col·lie
col·li·sion
col·lo·qui·al
col·lo·quy (–quies)
col·lu·sion
co·logne
co·lon

col·o·nel (army officer; see
   kernel)
co·lo·nial
col·on·nade
col·o·ny (–nies)
co·lo·phon
col·or
co·los·sal
col·umn
co·ma
comb
com·bat n., com·bat vb.
com·bi·na·tion
com·e·dy (–dies)
com·et
come·up·pance
com·fort·able
com·ma
com·man·deer
com·mand·ment
com·man·do
com·mem·o·rate
com·mence
com·mend
com·men·da·tion
com·men·su·rate
com·men·tary (–tar·ies)
com·men·ta·tor
com·merce
com·mer·cial
com·min·gle
com·mis·er·ate
com·mis·sar
com·mis·sary (–sar·ies)
com·mis·sion
com·mit
com·mit·tee
com·mode
com·mo·di·ous
com·mod·i·ty (–ties)
com·mo·dore
com·mon
com·mo·tion
com·mu·nal
com·mune
com·mu·ni·ca·ble
com·mu·ni·cate
com·mu·nion
com·mu·ni·qué

com·mu·nism
com·mu·nist
com·mu·ni·ty (–ties)
com·mute
com·pa·ny (–nies)
com·pan·ion
com·par·a·tive
com·pas·sion·ate
com·pat·i·ble
com·pel
com·pen·sate
com·pete
com·pe·tence
com·pe·ti·tion
com·pet·i·tor
com·pi·la·tion
com·pla·cent (self-satisfied;
   see *complaisant*)
com·plain
com·plais·ant (obliging; see
   complacent)
com·ple·ment (something
   that completes; see
   compliment)
com·plete
com·plex·i·ty (–ties)
com·pli·ant
com·pli·cate
com·plic·i·ty (–ties)
com·pli·ment (expression of
   praise; see *complement*)
com·ply
com·po·nent
com·pos·ite
com·po·si·tion
com·pos·i·tor
com·pound
com·pre·hend
com·pre·hen·sive
com·press
com·prise
com·pro·mise
comp·trol·ler, con·trol·ler
com·pul·sion
com·punc·tion
com·put·er
com·rade
con·ceal
con·cede

con·ceit
con·ceive
con·cen·trate
con·cen·tric
con·cept
con·cern
con·cert (noun), con·cert
  (verb)
con·cer·to
con·ces·sion
con·cil·i·ate
con·cise
con·clude
con·coct
con·com·i·tant
con·cord
con·course
con·crete
con·cu·bine
con·cu·pis·cent
con·cur·rent
con·cus·sion
con·dem·na·tion
con·dense
con·de·scend
con·di·ment
con·di·tion·al
con·do·lence
con·do·min·i·um
con·done
con·du·cive
con·duct (noun), con·duct
  (verb)
con·duit
con·fer·ence
con·fes·sion
con·fet·ti
con·fi·dant (one to whom
  secrets are entrusted;
  see *confident*)
con·fi·dante (a female
  confidant)
con·fi·dence
con·fi·dent (assured; see
  confidant)
con·fig·u·ra·tion
con·fine
con·firm
con·fis·cate

con·fla·gra·tion
con·flict
con·form
con·frere
con·fron·ta·tion
con·fu·sion
con·geal
con·ge·nial
con·gest
con·glom·er·ate
con·grat·u·late
con·gre·gate
con·gres·sio·nal
con·gru·ent
con·ic
co·ni·fer
con·jec·ture
con·ju·gal
con·ju·gate
con·junc·tion
con·jure
con·nect
con·nive
con·nois·seur
con·no·ta·tion
con·nu·bi·al
con·quer
con·quis·ta·dor (Spanish:
  one that conquers)
con·san·guin·i·ty (−ties)
con·science
con·sci·en·tious
con·scious
con·script (noun),
  con·script (verb)
con·se·crate
con·sec·u·tive
con·sen·sus
con·sent
con·se·quence
con·ser·va·tion
con·ser·va·tive
con·ser·va·to·ry (−ries)
con·sid·er
con·sign
con·sis·tent
con·sole (noun), con·sole
  (verb)
con·sol·i·date

con·som·mé
con·so·nance
con·spic·u·ous
con·spir·a·cy (−cies)
con·spir·a·tor
con·spire
con·sta·ble
con·stab·u·lary
con·stant
con·stel·la·tion
con·ster·na·tion
con·sti·pa·tion
con·stit·u·ent
con·sti·tute
con·sti·tu·tion
con·sti·tu·tion·al·i·ty
con·strain
con·strict
con·struc·tive
con·strue
con·sul
con·sul·ta·tion
con·sume
con·sum·er
con·sum·mate
con·sump·tion
con·tact
con·ta·gious
con·tain·er
con·tam·i·na·tion
con·tem·plate
con·tem·po·ra·ne·ous
con·tem·po·rary
con·tempt·ible
con·temp·tu·ous
con·tend
con·tent (noun), con·tent
  (verb, adjective)
con·tes·tant
con·text
con·tig·u·ous
con·ti·nence
con·ti·nent
con·tin·gen·cy (−cies)
con·tin·u·al
con·tin·u·um
con·tort
con·tour
con·tra·band

con·tra·cep·tion
con·trac·tion
con·trac·tu·al
con·tra·dict
con·tral·to
con·trary (–trar·ies)
con·trast (noun), con·trast (verb)
con·tra·vene
con·trib·ute
con·trite
con·trive
con·trol·ler, comp·trol·ler
con·tro·ver·sy (–sies)
con·tro·vert
con·tu·ma·cious
con·tu·me·li·ous
con·tu·sion
co·nun·drum
con·va·lesce
con·vene
con·ven·tion
con·ve·nience
con·verge
con·ver·sa·tion
con·ver·sion
con·vert·er
con·vey
con·vic·tion
con·vince
con·viv·ial
con·vo·ca·tion
con·vo·lu·tion
con·vulse
coo·lie
co·op·er·ate
co·or·di·nate
co·pi·ous
cop·u·late
co·quette
cor·dial
cor·don
cor·do·van
cor·du·roy
cor·nea
cor·ner
cor·net
cor·nu·co·pia
cor·ol·lary (–lar·ies)
cor·o·nary

cor·o·na·tion
cor·o·ner
cor·po·ral
cor·po·rate
cor·po·ra·tion
cor·po·re·al
corps (group; see *corpse*)
corpse (dead body; see *corps*)
cor·pu·lent
cor·pus·cle
cor·pus de·lic·ti (New Latin: fact necessary to prove a crime)
cor·ral
cor·rect
cor·rec·tion
cor·re·late
cor·re·la·tion
cor·re·spon·dence
cor·ri·dor
cor·rob·o·rate
cor·rode
cor·ro·sion
cor·rupt
cor·sage
cor·set
cor·tege, cor·tège
cor·ti·sone
co·sign·er
cos·met·ic
cos·mo·pol·i·tan
cos·mos
cos·tume
cost·ly
co·te·rie
cot·tage
cou·gar
could
coun·cil (advisory group; see *counsel*)
coun·sel (advice; see *council*)
coun·sel·or, coun·sel·lor
coun·te·nance
coun·ter·feit
coun·try
coup
coupe
cou·ple

cou·pon
cou·ra·geous
cou·ri·er
course (direction, customary procedure; see *coarse*)
cour·te·ous
cous·in
cou·tu·ri·er
cov·e·nant
co·vert
coy·ote
crab·by
cra·dle
cra·ni·al
cra·vat
cray·on
crease
cre·ativ·i·ty
crea·ture
crèche
cre·dence
cre·den·tial
cred·i·ble
cred·it
cre·do
cre·du·li·ty
cre·du·lous
cre·mate
cre·ole
cre·o·sote
crepe, crêpe
cre·scen·do
cres·cent
cre·tin
cre·vasse
crev·ice
cri·er
crim·i·nal
crim·i·nol·o·gy
cringe
crin·kle
crip·ple
cri·sis (–ses)
cris·py
cri·te·ri·on (–ria *or* –rions)
crit·i·cal
crit·i·cism
cri·tique
cro·chet

crotch·ety
crock·ery
croc·o·dile
cro·cus
crois·sant
cro·ny (–nies)
cro·quet
cross·road
crouch
crou·ton
crowd
cru·cial
cru·ci·fix (–fix·es)
cru·el
cruise
cru·sade
crutch
crux
cry
cryp·tic
crys·tal
cu·bi·cal (shaped like a cube; see *cubicle*)
cu·bi·cle (sleeping compartment; see *cubical*)

cud·dle
cud·gel
cui·sine
cul-de·sac (culs-de-sac) (French: street closed at one end)
cu·li·nary
cul·mi·nate
cul·pa·ble
cul·ti·vate
cul·tur·al
cum·ber·some
cu·mu·la·tive
cun·ning
cup·board
cu·po·la
cu·rate
cu·ra·tor
cur·few
cu·ri·ous
cur·rant (berry; see *current*)
cur·ren·cy (–cies)
cur·rent (present; see *currant*)
cur·ric·u·lum

cur·so·ry
cur·tail·ment
cur·tain
cur·te·sy (–sies)
curt·sy, curt·sey (curt·sies *or* curt·seys)
cur·va·ture
curve
cush·ion
cus·tard
cus·to·di·an
cus·to·dy (–dies)
cus·tom
cus·tom·ary
cus·tom·er
cu·ti·cle
cut·lery
cy·cle
cy·clone
cyl·in·der
cym·bal
cyn·ic
cy·press
cyst
czar, tsar

D

dab·ble
dad·dy (daddies)
daf·fo·dil
dag·ger
da·guerre·o·type (French: an early photograph produced in a special manner)
dahl·ia
dai·ly
dai·ry
dai·sy (daisies)
dam·age
dam·ask
dam·sel
dance
dan·de·li·on
dan·druff
dan·ger·ous
dan·gle
dash·board
da·ta
date
daugh·ter
daunt·less
daw·dle
daz·zle
dea·con
dear (expensive; expression of endearment; see *deer*)
de·ba·cle
de·base·ment
de·bat·able
de·bauch
de·ben·ture
de·bil·i·tate
deb·it
deb·o·nair
de·brief
de·bris (plural also debris)
debt
debt·or
de·but
de·cade
dec·a·dence
de·caf·fein·ate
de·cal
de·cap·i·tate
de·cath·lon
de·cay

de·ceased
de·cree
de·ceit
de·ceive
de·cent
de·cen·tral·iza·tion
de·cep·tion
deci·bel
de·cide
de·cid·u·ous
dec·i·mal
dec·i·mate
de·ci·pher
de·ci·sion
dec·la·ma·tion
dec·la·ra·tion
de·clas·si·fy
de·clen·sion
dec·li·na·tion
de·cliv·i·ty (–ties)
dé·col·le·tage (French: low neckline)
de·com·pose
de·con·tam·i·nate
de·cor, dé·cor (French: decoration)
dec·o·rate
dec·o·rous
de·co·rum
de·coy (noun), de·coy (verb)
de·crease
de·crep·it
de·cry
ded·i·cate
de·duc·tion
deer (an animal; see *dear*)
de fac·to (New Latin: in reality)
def·a·ma·tion
de·fault
de·fec·tive
de·fen·dant
de·fense, de·fence
def·er·ence
de·fi·ance
de·fi·cien·cy (–cies)
def·i·cit
de·fine
def·i·nite

def·i·ni·tion
de·fo·li·ant
de·for·mi·ty (–ties)
de·fraud
de·fray
deft
de·fy
de·gen·er·ate
de·gree
de·hy·drate
de·i·fy
deign
de·i·ty (–ties)
de·lay
de·lec·ta·ble
del·e·gate
de·lete
del·e·te·ri·ous
de·lib·er·ate
del·i·cate
de·li·cious
de·light
de·lin·eate
de·lin·quent
de·lir·i·ous
de·liv·ery (–er·ies)
de·lude
del·uge
de·lu·sion
de·luxe
dem·a·gogue, dem·a·gog
de·mand
de·mean·or
de·mil·i·ta·rize
de·mise
demi·tasse
de·moc·ra·cy (–cies)
de·mol·ish
dem·on·strate
de·mor·al·ize
de·mur
de·mure
de·ni·al
den·i·grate
den·im
de·nom·i·na·tion
de·nom·i·na·tor
de·noue·ment (French: outcome)
de·nounce

dense
den·tal
den·tist·ry
de·odor·ant
de·part·ment
de·par·ture
de·pen·dent
de·pict
de·pil·a·to·ry (–ries)
de·plete
de·plor·able
de·por·ta·tion
de·pos·it
de·pos·i·to·ry (–ries)
de·pot
dep·re·cate
de·pre·ciate
dep·re·da·tion
de·pres·sion
de·pri·va·tion
depth
dep·u·ty (–ties)
de·reg·u·la·tion
der·e·lict
der·i·va·tion
der·ma·tol·o·gy
de·rog·a·to·ry
der·rick
de·scend·ant, de·scend·ent
de·scen·sion
de·scent
de·scribe
de·scrip·tion
des·e·crate
de·seg·re·ga·tion
de·sert (arid barren tract;
   see *dessert*)
des·ic·cate
de·sid·er·a·tum (–ta)
de·sign
des·ig·nate
de·sir·able
de·sist
des·o·la·tion
des·per·ate
de·spi·ca·ble
de·spise
de·spite
de·spon·dent
des·pot

des·sert (course served at
   end of meal; see *desert*)
des·ti·ny (–nies)
des·ti·tute
de·stroy
de·struc·tion
de·sue·tude
des·ul·to·ry
de·tach
de·tail
de·tect
de·ter·gent
de·te·ri·o·rate
de·ter·mi·na·tion
de·ter·rent
det·o·na·tion
de·tour
de·tract
det·ri·ment
deuce
de·val·u·a·tion
dev·as·tate
de·vel·op
de·vi·ate
de·vice (mechanism; see
   devise)
de·vi·ous
de·vise (to invent; see
   device)
de·void
de·vour
de·vout
dew (moisture; see *due*)
dex·ter·i·ty (–ties)
di·a·be·tes
di·a·bol·ic
di·a·dem
di·ag·no·sis (–no·ses)
di·ag·o·nal
di·a·gram·ing,
   di·a·gram·ming
di·a·lect
di·a·logue
di·am·e·ter
di·a·mond
di·a·per
di·a·phragm
di·ar·rhea
di·a·ry (–ries)
di·a·ther·my

di·a·tribe
di·chot·o·my (–mies)
dic·tate
dic·ta·tion
dic·ta·tor
dic·tio·nary (–nar·ies)
dic·tum (dic·ta, dic·tums)
di·dac·tic
die (to expire; see *dye*)
die·sel
di·etary
dif·fer·ence
dif·fer·en·tial
dif·fi·cult
dif·fi·dence
dif·fuse
di·gest·ible
dig·it
dig·i·tal·is
dig·ni·fy
dig·ni·tary (–tar·ies)
di·gress
di·lap·i·dat·ed
di·late
dil·a·tory
di·lem·ma
dil·et·tante
dil·i·gence
dil·ly·dal·ly
di·lute
di·men·sion
di·min·ish
di·min·u·tive
din·er (restaurant; see
   dinner)
di·nette
din·ghy (dinghies)
din·ner (meal; see *diner*)
di·no·saur
di·o·cese
di·ora·ma
diph·the·ria
diph·thong
di·plo·ma
di·plo·ma·cy
di·rec·tion
di·rec·tor·ate
dirge
dis·abil·i·ty
dis·ad·van·tage

dis·agree
dis·al·low
dis·ap·pear
dis·ap·point
dis·ap·prove
dis·ar·ma·ment
dis·arm·ing
dis·ar·range
dis·ar·ray
dis·as·so·ci·ate
dis·as·ter
dis·as·trous
dis·avow
dis·burse
disc, disk
dis·cern
dis·cern·ible, dis·cern·able
dis·ci·ple
dis·ci·pline
dis·claim·er
dis·clo·sure
dis·com·fort
dis·con·cert·ing
dis·con·nect
dis·con·so·late
dis·con·tin·ue
dis·cor·dant
dis·count
dis·cour·age
dis·cour·te·ous
dis·cov·ery (–er·ies)
dis·creet (showing
　discernment in speech;
　see *discrete*)
dis·crep·an·cy (–cies)
dis·crete (individually
　distinct; see *discreet*)
dis·cre·tion
dis·crim·i·nate
dis·cur·sive
dis·cus (disk; see *discuss*)
dis·cuss (to talk about; see
　discus)
dis·cus·sion
dis·dain
dis·ease
dis·em·bark
dis·en·chant
dis·en·fran·chise
dis·en·gage

dis·en·tan·gle
dis·gorge
dis·grace
dis·guise
dis·gust·ing
dis·har·mo·ny
dis·heart·en
di·shev·el
dis·hon·es·ty
dis·il·lu·sion
dis·in·cline
dis·in·fec·tant
dis·in·her·it
dis·in·te·grate
dis·in·ter
disk, disc
dis·lodge
dis·mal
dis·miss
dis·obe·di·ent
dis·obey
dis·or·ga·nized
dis·par·age
dis·pa·rate
dis·pas·sion·ate
dis·patch
dis·pel
dis·pens·able
dis·pen·sa·ry (–ries)
dis·pen·sa·tion
dis·perse
dis·plea·sure
dis·pose
dis·pos·sess
dis·pute
dis·pro·por·tion
dis·re·gard
dis·re·pair
dis·re·pute
dis·rupt
dis·sat·is·fy
dis·sect
dis·sem·ble
dis·sem·i·nate
dis·sen·sion, dis·sen·tion
dis·sent
dis·ser·ta·tion
dis·ser·vice
dis·si·dent
dis·sim·i·lar

dis·sim·u·late
dis·si·pate
dis·so·ci·ate
dis·so·lute
dis·solve
dis·so·nance
dis·suade
dis·taff
dis·tain
dis·tance
dis·taste·ful
dis·tem·per
dis·tinct
dis·tin·guish
dis·tor·tion
dis·tract
dis·traught
dis·tress
dis·tri·bu·tion
dis·tur·bance
dis·uni·ty
di·verge
di·verse
di·ver·si·fy
div·i·dend
di·vine
di·vis·i·ble
di·vi·sion
di·vi·sive
di·vorce
div·ot
di·vulge
doc·ile
dock·et
doc·tor
doc·trine
doc·u·ment
dod·der·ing
dodge
doe (female deer; see
　dough)
dog·ger·el
dog·ma
doi·ly
dole·ful
dol·lar
do·lor·ous
dol·phin
do·main
do·mes·tic

do·mi·cile
dom·i·nance
dom·i·neer
do·min·ion
dom·i·no
do·nate
don·key
do·nor
doo·dle
dor·mant
dor·mi·to·ry (–ries)
dor·sal
dos·age
dos·sier
dou·ble
doubt
douche
dough (flour mixture; money; see *doe*)
dough·nut
dour
douse, dowse
dow·a·ger
down·ward
dow·ry (dowries)
dox·ol·o·gy (–gies)

doz·en
draft
drag·net
drag·on
drain
dra·ma
drap·ery (–er·ies)
drawl
drea·ry
dredge
driv·el
driz·zle
droll
drom·e·dary (–dar·ies)
drought, drouth
drowsy
drudge
drug·gist
drunk·ard
dry
du·al (two parts; see *duel*)
du·bi·ous
duc·tile
dud·geon
due (owing; see *dew*)
du·el (combat; see *dual*)

du·et
duf·fel, duf·fle
dul·cet
dul·ci·mer
dumb·bell
dumb·found, dum·found
dun·ga·ree
dun·geon
du·plex
du·pli·cate
du·plic·i·ty (–ties)
du·ra·ble
du·ra·tion
du·ress
du·ti·ful
dwarf
dwin·dle
dye (color; see *die*)
dy·nam·ic
dy·na·mite
dy·nas·ty (–ties)
dys·en·tery (–ter·ies)
dys·lex·ia
dys·pha·sia
dys·tro·phy (–phies)

E

ea·ger
ea·gle
ear·ache
early
ear·nest
earn·ings
ear·ring
earth
ea·sel
ease·ment
eas·i·ly
east·ern
easy
eau de co·logne (French: cologne)
eaves·drop
eb·o·ny (–nies)
ebul·lient
ec·cen·tric
ec·cle·si·as·tic
ech·e·lon
echo (ech·oes)
éclair
eclec·tic
eclipse
ecol·o·gy
eco·nom·ic
ec·sta·sy (–sies)
ec·stat·ic
ec·u·men·i·cal
ecu·me·nism
ec·ze·ma
edge
ed·i·ble
edict
ed·i·fi·ca·tion
ed·i·fice
edi·tion
ed·i·tor
ed·u·ca·tion
ee·rie, ee·ry
ef·face
ef·fect (to accomplish; see *affect*)
ef·fem·i·nate
ef·fer·ves·cence
ef·fi·ca·cious
ef·fi·ca·cy (–cies)
ef·fi·cien·cy (–cies)
ef·fi·gy (–gies)

ef·fort·less
ef·fron·tery
ef·fu·sion
egal·i·tar·i·an
ego·cen·tric
ego·tist
egre·gious
eighth
ei·ther
ejac·u·late
elab·o·rate
elapse
elas·tic
ela·tion
el·bow
el·der·ly
elec·tion
elec·tor·al
elec·tric
elec·tro·car·dio·gram
elec·tro·cute
elec·trode
elec·trol·y·sis
elec·tron
el·ee·mos·y·nary
el·e·gance
ele·gi·ac
el·e·gy (–gies)
el·e·men·ta·ry
el·e·phant
el·e·va·tion
elev·en
elic·it (draw out; see *illicit*)
el·i·gi·ble
elim·i·nate
eli·sion
elite
elix·ir
el·lipse
el·o·cu·tion
elon·gate
elope
el·o·quence
elu·ci·date
elude (avoid; see *allude*)
elu·sive
ema·ci·at·ed
em·a·nate
eman·ci·pate
emas·cu·late

em·bar·go
em·bar·ka·tion
em·bar·rass
em·bas·sy (–sies)
em·bel·lish
em·ber
em·bez·zle
em·bit·ter
em·bla·zon
em·blem
em·body
em·brace
em·broi·der
em·broi·dery (–der·ies)
em·broil
em·bryo
em·bry·ol·o·gy
em·bry·on·ic
em·cee (also M.C.)
emend
em·er·ald
emerge
emer·gen·cy (–cies)
emer·i·tus (–ti)
em·ery (–er·ies)
emet·ic
em·i·grate (to leave one's country; see *immigrate*)
émi·gré, emi·gré
em·i·nence
em·is·sary
emis·sion
emol·lient
emol·u·ment
emo·tion
em·pa·thy
em·per·or
em·pha·sis
em·pha·size
em·phat·ic
em·pire
em·pir·i·cal
em·place·ment
em·ploy·able
em·ploy·ee, em·ploye
em·ploy·ment
em·po·ri·um
emp·ty
em·py·re·an
em·u·late

emul·si·fy
en·able
en·act·ment
enam·el
en·camp·ment
en·ceph·a·li·tis
  (en·ceph·a·lit·i·des)
en·chant
en·cir·cle
en·close, in·close
en·clo·sure
en·code
en·co·mi·um
en·com·pass
en·core
en·coun·ter
en·cour·age
en·croach
en·cum·ber
en·cum·brance
en·cyc·li·cal
en·cy·clo·pe·dia
en·dan·ger
en·dear·ment
en·deav·or
en·dem·ic
en·dive
end·less
en·do·crine
en·do·cri·nol·o·gy
en·dorse
en·dow·ment
en·dur·ance
en·dure
en·e·ma
en·e·my (–mies)
en·er·get·ic
en·er·gize
en·er·gy
en·er·vate
en·fran·chise
en·gage
en·gage·ment
en·gen·der
en·gi·neer
en·grave
en·gross
en·gulf
en·hance
enig·ma

en·join
en·joy·ment
en·large·ment
en·light·en·ment
en·list
en·liv·en
en masse
en·mesh
en·mi·ty (–ties)
en·no·ble
en·nui (French: boredom)
enor·mous
enough
en·plane
en·rage
en·rap·ture
en·rich
en·roll·ment
en route
en·sem·ble
en·shrine
en·sign
en·slave
en·sue
en·tail
en·tan·gle
en·ter·prise
en·ter·tain
en·thrall
en·throne
en·thu·si·asm
en·tice
en·tire·ly
en·tire·ty (–ties)
en·ti·tle
en·ti·ty (–ties)
en·tomb
en·to·mol·o·gy
en·tou·rage
en·trails
en·trance
en·trant
en·treat
en·trée, en·tree
en·trench
en·tre·pre·neur
en·trust
en·try
en·twine
enu·mer·ate

enun·ci·ate
enun·ci·a·tion
en·vel·op (enclose
  completely; see
  envelope)
en·ve·lope (container for
  letter; see *envelop*)
en·vi·able
en·vi·ous
en·vi·ron·ment
en·vi·rons
en·vi·sion
envoi (final stanza of
  ballade; see *envoy*)
en·voy (government
  representative; see *envoi*)
en·vy
en·zyme
eon
ep·au·let, ep·au·lette
  (French: shoulder
  ornament)
ephem·er·al
ep·ic
ep·i·cure
ep·i·dem·ic
epi·der·mis
ep·i·gram
ep·i·gram·mat·ic
ep·i·lep·sy
ep·i·logue
ep·i·sode
epis·tle
ep·i·thet
epit·o·me
ep·och·al
equa·ble
equal
equal·ize
equa·nim·i·ty (–ties)
equate
equa·tion
equa·tor
eques·tri·an
equi·dis·tant
equi·lat·er·al
equi·lib·ri·um
equine
equi·noc·tial
equi·nox

equip

equip·ment

eq·ui·ta·ble

eq·ui·ty (–ties)

equiv·a·lent

equiv·o·cate

era

erad·i·cate

eras·er (a device to remove marks; see *erasure*)

era·sure (act of erasing; see *eraser*)

ere

erec·tion

er·go (Latin: therefore, hence)

er·mine

erode

erog·e·nous

ero·sion

erot·ic

err

er·rand

er·rant

er·rat·ic

er·ro·ne·ous

er·ror

er·satz

erst·while

er·u·dite

erup·tion

es·ca·late

es·ca·la·tor

es·ca·pade

es·cape

es·ca·role

es·chew

es·cort

es·crow

esoph·a·gus

es·o·ter·ic

es·pe·cial·ly

es·pi·o·nage

es·pla·nade

es·pouse

espres·so

es·prit de corps (French: a common enthusiasm for the group)

es·quire

es·say (noun), es·say (verb)

es·sence

es·sen·tial

es·tab·lish

es·tate

es·teem

es·thet·ic

es·ti·ma·ble

es·ti·mate

es·trange

es·tu·ary (–ar·ies)

et cet·era (Latin: and so forth)

etch·ing

eter·nal

eter·ni·ty (–ties)

ether

ethe·re·al

eth·i·cal

eth·ics

eth·nic

ethos

eth·yl

eti·ol·o·gy

et·i·quette

étude

et·y·mol·o·gy (–gies)

eu·ca·lyp·tus (–ti)

eu·chre

eu·gen·ic

eu·lo·gy (–gies)

eu·nuch

eu·phe·mism

eu·phon·ic

eu·pho·ria

eu·re·ka

eu·tha·na·sia

evac·u·ate

evade

eval·u·ate

ev·a·nes·cence

evan·ge·list

evap·o·rate

eva·sion

even·tu·al·i·ty (–ties)

ev·ery·where

evict

ev·i·dent

evil

evince

evis·cer·ate

evoc·a·tive

evoke

evo·lu·tion

evolve

ex·ac·er·bate

ex·act

ex·act·ly

ex·ag·ger·ate

ex·alt

ex·am·i·na·tion

ex·am·ple

ex·as·per·ate

ex·ca·va·tion

ex·ceed

ex·cel

ex·cel·lent

ex·cel·si·or

ex·cept (leave out; see *accept*)

ex·cep·tion·al

ex·cerpt

ex·cess

ex·change

ex·che·quer

ex·cise (noun), ex·cise (verb)

ex·cite·ment

ex·claim

ex·cla·ma·tion

ex·clude

ex·clu·sive

ex·com·mu·ni·cate

ex·co·ri·ate

ex·cre·ment

ex·cru·ci·at·ing

ex·cur·sion

ex·cus·ably

ex·e·cra·ble

ex·e·cute

ex·e·cut·able

ex·ec·u·tive

ex·ec·u·tor

ex·e·ge·sis

ex·em·pla·ry

ex·em·pli·fy

ex·empt

ex·emp·tion

ex·er·cise

ex·ert

ex·ha·la·tion
ex·haust
ex·hib·it
ex·hil·a·rate
ex·hort
ex·hume
ex·i·gen·cy (–cies)
ex·ig·u·ous
ex·ile
ex·is·tence
ex·is·ten·tial·ism
ex·it
ex·o·dus
ex·on·er·ate
ex·or·bi·tant
ex·or·cise
ex·o·ter·ic
ex·ot·ic
ex·pand
ex·panse
ex·pa·tri·ate
ex·pec·tan·cy (–cies)
ex·pec·to·rate
ex·pe·di·en·cy (–cies)
ex·pe·dite
ex·pe·di·tion
ex·pe·di·tious
ex·pel
ex·pend·able
ex·pen·di·ture
ex·pense
ex·pe·ri·ence
ex·per·i·ment
ex·pert
ex·per·tise
ex·pi·ate

ex·pi·ra·tion
ex·plain
ex·plan·a·tory
ex·ple·tive
ex·pli·ca·ble
ex·plic·it
ex·plode
ex·ploi·ta·tion
ex·plore
ex·plor·ato·ry
ex·plo·sion
ex·po·nent
ex·port (noun), ex·port (verb)
ex·pose (to disclose; see *exposé*)
ex·po·sé (a statement; see *expose*)
ex·po·si·tion
ex post fac·to (Latin: after the foot)
ex·pos·tu·late
ex·po·sure
ex·pound
ex·press
ex·press·way
ex·pro·pri·ate
ex·pul·sion
ex·punge
ex·pur·gate
ex·qui·site
ex·tant
ex·tem·po·ra·ne·ous
ex·tem·po·rize
ex·tend
ex·ten·sion

ex·ten·sive
ex·tent
ex·ten·u·ate
ex·te·ri·or
ex·ter·mi·nate
ex·ter·nal
ex·tinct
ex·tin·guish
ex·tir·pate
ex·tol
ex·tort
ex·tra
ex·tract (noun), ex·tract (verb)
ex·tra·cur·ric·u·lar
ex·tra·dite
ex·tra·mar·i·tal
ex·tra·ne·ous
ex·traor·di·nary
ex·trap·o·late
ex·tra·sen·so·ry
ex·tra·ter·res·tri·al
ex·tra·ter·ri·to·ri·al
ex·trav·a·gance
ex·tra·vert, ex·tro·vert
ex·treme
ex·trem·i·ty (–ties)
ex·tri·cate
ex·trin·sic
ex·tru·sion
ex·u·ber·ant
ex·ude
ex·ult
ex·ul·tant
eye
eyre

F

fa·ble	far·ci·cal	fe·ral
fab·ric	fare·well	fer·ment (noun), fer·ment
fab·ri·cate	fa·ri·na	(verb)
fab·u·lous	farm·er	fe·ro·cious
fa·cade, fa·çade	far·ther	fer·ret
face	fas·ci·nate	fer·ry (–ries)
fac·et	fas·cism	fer·tile
fa·ce·tious	fash·ion·able	fer·til·ize
fa·cial	fas·ten	fer·vent
fac·ile	fas·tid·i·ous	fer·vid
fa·cil·i·tate	fa·tal	fer·vor
fa·cil·i·ty (–ties)	fate	fes·ti·val
fac·sim·i·le	fa·ther	fes·toon
fac·tion	fath·om	fe·tal
fac·to·ry (–ries)	fa·tigue	fet·id
fac·tu·al	fat·ten	fe·tus
fac·ul·ty (–ties)	fat·u·ous	feud
fad·dist	fau·cet	feu·dal
Fahr·en·heit	fault·less	fe·ver
fail·ure	faun (mythological being;	few
faint (lose consciousness;	see *fawn*)	fi·an·cé (French: engaged
see *feint*)	fau·na	man)
fairy	faux pas (French: a social	fi·an·cée (French: engaged
fait ac·com·pli (French:	blunder)	woman)
accomplished fact)	fa·vor·able	fi·as·co
faith·ful	fawn (young deer; see	fi·ber·glass
fak·er	*faun*)	fic·tion
fal·con	fear·ful	fic·ti·tious
fall	fea·si·ble	fid·dle
fal·la·cious	feast	fi·del·i·ty (–ties)
fal·la·cy (–cies)	feat (deed; see *feet*)	fid·get
fal·li·ble	feath·er	fi·du·cia·ry (–ries)
fal·low	fea·ture	field
fal·set·to	fe·cund	fiend
fal·si·fy	fed·er·al	fierce
fal·ter	fee	fi·ery
fa·mil·iar	fee·ble	fi·es·ta
fam·i·ly (–lies)	feet (plural of foot; see	fifth
fam·ine	*feat*)	fif·ti·eth
fam·ish	feign	fight
fa·mous	feint (something feigned;	fig·ment
fa·nat·ic	see *faint*)	fig·ure
fan·ci·ful	fe·lic·i·tate	fig·u·rine
fan·fare	fe·line	fil·a·ment
fan·tasm, phan·tasm	fel·low·ship	fil·ial
fan·tas·tic	fel·o·ny	fil·i·bus·ter
fan·ta·sy (–sies)	fe·male	fil·i·gree
farce	fem·i·nine	fil·let, fi·let
far·away	fence	fil·ly (fillies)

film
fil·ter
fi·nal
fi·na·le
fi·nance
fi·nan·cier
fine
fi·nesse
fin·ger·print
fi·nis
fin·ish
fi·nite
fire
fiord, fjord
fir·ma·ment
first
fis·cal
fis·sure
fix·ture
flac·cid
flag·el·late
flag·on
flag·pole
fla·grant
flair (natural aptitude; see
   flare)
flak
flam·boy·ant
fla·min·go
flam·ma·ble
flan·nel
flap·per
flare (unsteady glaring
   light; see *flair*)
flat·tery (–ter·ies)
flaunt
fla·vor
flaw·less
flax·en
flea (insect; see *flee*)
fledg·ling
flee (to run from; see *flea*)
fleece
fleur-de-lis, fleur-de-lys
   (fleurs-de-lis *or* fleur-de-
   lis, fleurs-de-lys *or* fleur-
   de-lys)
flew (past tense of fly; see
   flue)

flex·i·ble
fli·er
flight
flir·ta·tion
float·ing
floc·cu·lent
flock
flog
flood·light
floor·board
flor·al
flo·res·cence
flo·ri·cul·ture
flor·id
flo·rist
flo·ta·tion
flo·til·la
flot·sam
flounce
floun·der
flour (grain; see *flower*)
flow·chart
flow·er (blossom; see *flour*)
fluc·tu·ate
flue (air channel; see *flew*)
flu·ent
flu·id
flu·o·res·cent
flu·o·ri·date
flu·o·ri·nate
flu·o·ro·scope
flute
fly (flies)
fo·cal
fo·cus (–cus·es *or* –ci)
foe
foi·ble
fold·er
fo·liage
fo·lio
folk
fol·li·cle
fol·low
fol·ly (follies)
fo·ment
fon·dle
fon·due
food
fool·ish

foot·age
foot·note
for·age
for·ay
for·bear·ance
for·bid·den
force
for·ceps
forc·ible
fore·bear, for·bear
fore·cast
fore·clo·sure
for·eign
fore·man
fo·ren·sic
for·est·ry
fore·word (preface; see
   forward)
for·ev·er
for·feit
for·gery (er·ies)
for·get·ful
for·giv·ing
for·go, fore·go
for·got·ten
fork
for·lorn
for·mal·i·ty (–ties)
for·mal·ly (following
   established custom; see
   formerly)
for·mat
for·ma·tive
for·mer·ly (at an earlier
   time; see *formally*)
for·mi·da·ble
for·mu·la (–las *or* –lae)
for·mu·late
for·syth·ia
fort (fortified place; see
   forte)
forte (one's strong point;
   see *fort*)
forth (forward; see *fourth*)
forth·right
for·ti·eth
for·ti·fi·ca·tion
for·tis·si·mo
for·ti·tude

fort·night
for·tress
for·tu·itous
for·tu·nate
fo·rum
for·ward (in front; see
   foreword)
fos·sil
fos·ter
foul (offensive to the
   senses; see *fowl*)
foun·da·tion
found·ry (–ries)
foun·tain
four
fourth (musical interval;
   see *forth*)
fowl (bird; see *foul*)
foy·er
fra·cas (–cas·es)
frac·tion
frac·ture
frag·ile
frag·ment
fra·grant
frail
fran·chise
frank·fur·ter
frank·in·cense
fran·tic
frap·pe, frap·pé
fra·ter·ni·ty (–ties)
fraud

fraud·u·lent
fraught
free·dom
freeze (turn into ice; see
   frieze)
freight
fre·net·ic, phre·net·ic
fren·zy (fren·zies)
fre·quent (adjective),
   fre·quent (verb)
fresh·man (–men)
Freud·ian
fri·ar (monk; see *fryer*)
fric·as·see
fric·tion
friend
frieze (architectural
   decoration; see *freeze*)
frig·ate
fright·en
fringe ben·e·fit
frisky
frit·ter
friv·o·lous
frol·ic
front·age
fron·tier
fron·tis·piece
fro·zen
fru·gal
fru·ition
fruit·ful
frus·trate

fry·er (something intended
   for frying; see *friar*)
fuch·sia
fu·el
fu·gi·tive
fugue
ful·crum
ful·fill, ful·fil
ful·some
fu·mi·gate
func·tion·al
fun·da·men·tal
fu·ner·al
fu·ne·re·al
fun·nel
fu·ri·ous
furl
fur·lough
fur·nace
fur·ni·ture
fu·ror
fur·ri·er
fur·row
fur·ther
fur·tive
fuse
fu·se·lage
fus·ible
fu·sil·lade
fu·sion
fu·tile
fu·til·i·ty (–ties)
fu·ture

G

gab·er·dine
gad·get
gai·ety (–eties)
gain·ful·ly
gait (manner of walking;
  see *gate*)
gal·axy (gal·ax·ies)
gal·lant
gal·le·on
gal·lery (–ler·ies)
gal·ley
gall·ing
gal·lon
gal·lop
ga·lore
ga·losh (–es)
gal·lows
gal·va·nize
gam·bit
gam·ble (bet on an
  uncertain outcome; see
  gambol)
gam·bol (skip about; see
  gamble)
game·keep·er
gam·ut
gan·der
gan·gli·on (gan·glia)
gan·grene
ga·rage
gar·bage
gar·ble
gar·den·er
gar·de·nia
gar·gan·tuan
gar·goyle
gar·ish
gar·land
gar·ment
gar·ner
gar·nish
gar·nish·ee
gar·ri·son
gar·ru·lous
gas·eous
gas·ket
gas·o·line
gas·tric
gas·tron·o·my

gate (opening in wall or
  fence; see *gait*)
gath·er·ing
gauche
gaudy
gauge
gaunt
gaunt·let
gauze
gav·el
ga·ze·bo
ga·zelle
ga·zette
gei·sha
gel·a·tin
gen·darme
gene
ge·ne·al·o·gy (–gies)
gen·er·al·i·ty (–ties)
gen·er·ate
gen·er·a·tion
gen·er·ic
gen·er·ous
gen·e·sis (–e·ses)
ge·net·ic
ge·nial
gen·i·tal
ge·nius (–nius·es or –nii)
gen·o·cide
genre
gen·teel
gen·tile
gen·til·i·ty (–ties)
gen·tle·man (–men)
gen·try
gen·u·flect
gen·u·ine
ge·og·ra·phy (–phies)
ge·ol·o·gy
ge·om·e·try (–tries)
ge·ra·ni·um
ge·ri·at·rics
ger·mane
ger·mi·cide
ger·mi·na·tion
ger·on·tol·o·gy
ger·ry·man·der
gest
ges·ta·tion

ges·tic·u·late
ges·ture
gey·ser
ghast·ly
gher·kin
ghet·to (ghettos *or*
  ghettoes)
ghoul·ish
gi·ant
gib·ber·ish
gibe
gib·lets
gi·gan·tic
gig·o·lo
gild (to overlay with a thin
  covering of gold or
  something similar; see
  gilt)
gift
gilt (covered with gold, or
  with something that
  resembles gold; see *gild*)
gim·mick
gin·ger
ging·ham
gi·raffe
gird·er
gir·dle
girth
gist
give
giz·zard
gla·cial
gla·cier
glad·i·a·tor
glad·i·o·la
glam·or·ous
glam·our, glam·or
glan·du·lar
glas·nost (openness)
glass·ware
glau·co·ma
gla·zier
glib
glim·mer
glimpse
glis·ten
glob·al
glob·u·lar

gloomy

glo·ri·ous

glos·sa·ry (–ries)

glossy (gloss·ies)

glove

glu·cose

glue

glut·ton

glyc·er·in

gnarl

gnash

gnat

gnaw

gnome

gnu (African antelope; see *knew* and *new*)

goal

gob·let

gog·gles

goi·ter

gold·en

golf (a game; see *gulf*)

gon·do·la

good·will

go·pher

gor·geous

go·ril·la (an ape; see *guerrilla*)

gos·sa·mer

gos·sip

gouge

gou·lash

gourd

gour·met

gout

gov·ern·ment

gov·er·nor

gra·cious

gra·da·tion

gra·di·ent

grad·u·al

grad·u·ate

grad·u·a·tion

grain

gram·mar

gra·na·ry (–ries)

gran·deur

grand·fa·ther

gran·di·ose

grand·mo·ther

gran·ite

grant

gran·u·late

graph·ic

graph·ite

grap·ple

grate (rasp noisily; see *great*)

grate·ful

grat·i·fy

grat·i·tude

gra·tu·ity (–i·ties)

grav·i·tate

grav·i·ty (–ties)

great (large; see *grate*)

greedy

gre·gar·i·ous

grem·lin

gre·nade

gren·a·dine

grey·hound

grid·dle

grid·iron

griev·ance

griev·ous

gri·mace

grime

grippe

gris·ly (inspiring horror; see *grizzly*)

griz·zly (bear; see *grisly*)

groan

gro·cery (–cer·ies)

gro·tesque

grot·to (–toes)

group

grouse (grouse *or* grouses)

grov·el

grudge

gru·el

grue·some

grum·ble

guar·an·tee (assurance of quality; see *guaranty*)

guaranty (something given as security; see *guarantee*)

guard·ian

gu·ber·na·to·ri·al

guer·ril·la (one who engages in irregular warfare; see *gorilla*)

guess

guest

guid·ance

guild

guile

guil·lo·tine

guilt

guise

gui·tar

gulf (part of an ocean, a chasm; see *golf*)

gul·li·ble

gul·ly (–lies)

gur·gle

gu·ru

gut·tur·al

guz·zle

gym·na·si·um

gym·nast

gy·ne·col·o·gy

gyp·sum

gyp·sy

gy·rate

gy·ro·scope

ha·be·as cor·pus (Latin: legal writ to bring a person before a court)
hab·er·dash·ery (–er·ies)
ha·bil·i·ment
hab·it·able
hab·i·tat
ha·bit·u·al
ha·bi·tué
hack·ney
had·dock
hag·gard
hag·gle
hail (greet; see *hale*)
hair (threadlike outgrowth on skin; see *hare*)
hal·cy·on
hale (free from disease; see *hail*)
half
hal·i·but
hal·i·to·sis
hal·le·lu·jah
hal·low
Hal·low·een
hal·lu·ci·na·tion
hal·lu·ci·no·gen
halve
hal·yard
ham·burg·er
ham·mer
ham·mock
ham·per
hand·i·cap
hand·i·craft
hand·ker·chief
han·dle
hand·some (pleasing appearance; see *hansom*)
handy
han·gar (place for housing aircraft; see *hanger*)
hang·er (device on which something is hung; see *hangar*)
han·som (cab; see *handsome*)
Ha·nuk·kah, Cha·nu·kah
hap·haz·ard
hap·pen

hap·pi·ness
hap·py
hara-kiri, hari-kari (Japanese: suicide by disembowelment)
ha·rangue
ha·rass
har·bin·ger
har·bor
hard·ly
hard·ship
har·dy
hare (animal resembling rabbit; see *hair*)
hare·brained
har·em
har·lot
harm·less
har·mon·ic
har·mo·ni·ous
har·mo·ny (nies)
har·ness
har·poon
harp·si·chord
har·row·ing
har·ry
hart (male of red deer; see *heart*)
har·vest
hash·ish
has·sock
hatch·et
hate·ful
ha·tred
haugh·ty
haul
haunch
haunt
haute cou·ture (French: fashions created by famous designers)
haute cui·sine (French: elaborate style of cooking)
ha·ven
hav·oc
haw·thorn
haz·ard·ous
haze
ha·zel

head·ache
heal (restore to health; see *heel*)
health·ful
hear (listen; see *here*)
hear·ken
hearse
heart (bodily organ; see *hart*)
hearth
heart·i·ly
heat
heath
hea·then
heath·er
heav·en
heavy
heck·le
hec·tic
hedge
he·do·nism
heed·less
heel (part of foot; see *heal*)
hefty
he·ge·mo·ny
heif·er
height
hei·nous
heir
heist
he·li·cop·ter
he·li·um
help·ful
hemi·sphere
hem·lock
he·mo·phil·ia
hem·or·rhage
hem·or·rhoid
hence·forth
hen·na
hep·a·ti·tis
her·ald
herb
Her·cu·le·an
here (in this place; see *hear*)
he·red·i·tary
her·e·sy (–sies)
her·e·tic
her·i·tage

her·maph·ro·dite
her·met·ic
her·mit
her·nia
her·o·in (drug; see *heroine*)
her·o·ine (central figure in drama; see *heroin*)
her·on
her·ring·bone
hes·i·tate
het·ero·dox
het·er·o·ge·neous
het·ero·sex·u·al
heu·ris·tic
hew (to cut by blows; see *hue*)
hexa·gon
hex·am·e·ter
hi·a·tus
hi·ba·chi
hi·ber·nate
hi·bis·cus
hic·cough, hic·cup
hid·eous
hi·er·ar·chy (–chies)
hi·ero·glyph·ic
high·er (more elevated, taller; see *hire*)

hi·jack
hi·lar·i·ous
hin·drance
hinge
hip·po·drome
hip·po·pot·a·mus (–mus·es or –mi)
hire (employ, wage; see *higher*)
his·ta·mine
his·to·ri·an
his·tor·i·cal
his·to·ry (–ries)
his·tri·on·ic
hith·er·to
hives
hoar (frost; see *whore*)
hoard
hoarse
hoax
hob·ble
hock·ey
ho·cus-po·cus
hodge·podge
hoe
hoist
ho·li·ness
hol·lan·daise

hol·low
holo·caust
ho·lo·gram
ho·lo·graph
hol·ster
hom·age
home·ly
ho·mi·cide
hom·i·ly (–lies)
ho·mo·ge·neous
ho·mog·e·nize
hom·onym
ho·mo·sex·u·al
hon·es·ty (–ties)
hon·ey
hon·or
hon·o·rar·i·um
hon·or·ary (–ar·ies)
hood·lum
hoo·li·gan
hope
hop·ing (longing for; see *hopping*)
hop·ping (jumping; see *hoping*)
horde
ho·ri·zon
hor·i·zon·tal

hor·mone
horo·scope
hor·ren·dous
hor·ri·ble
hor·rid
hor·ror
hors d'oeuvre (French:
    appetizers)
horse
hor·ti·cul·ture
ho·siery
hos·pi·tal
hos·tage
hos·tel
host·ess
hos·tile
ho·tel
hour (time; see *our*)
house·hold
hov·el
hov·er
howl
huck·le·ber·ry (–ries)
huck·ster
hue (complexion, see *hew*)
huge
hu·man·i·tar·i·an

hum·ble
hu·mid
hu·mi·dor
hu·mil·i·ate
hu·mil·i·ty
hu·mor
hu·mor·ous
hu·mus
hun·dredth
hun·ger
hur·dle
hur·dy-gur·dy (–dies)
hurl
hur·ri·cane
hur·ried
hur·tle
hus·band
hus·ky (–kies)
hus·tle
hy·a·cinth
hy·brid
hy·dran·gea
hy·drant
hy·drate
hy·drau·lic

hy·dro·chlo·ric
hy·dro·elec·tric
hy·dro·gen
hy·drom·e·ter
hy·dro·pho·bia
hy·drox·ide
hy·giene
hy·gien·ic
hy·men
hymn
hy·per·bo·la
hy·per·bo·le
hy·per·ten·sion
hy·phen
hyp·no·sis (–ses)
hyp·no·tism
hy·po·chon·dria
hy·poc·ri·sy (–sies)
hy·po·crite
hy·po·der·mic
hy·pot·e·nuse,
    hy·poth·e·nuse
hy·poth·e·sis (–ses)
hy·poth·e·size
hy·po·thet·i·cal
hys·ter·ec·to·my (–mies)
hys·te·ria

I

ice·berg
ice floe
ici·cle
ic·ing
icy
icon, ikon
icon·o·clast
idea
ide·al
iden·ti·cal
iden·ti·fi·ca·tion
iden·ti·fy
ide·ol·o·gy, ide·al·o·gy
   (–gies)
id·i·o·cy (–cies)
id·i·om
id·i·om·at·ic
id·io·syn·cra·sy (–sies)
id·i·ot
idle (not occupied; see *idol*,
   idyll)
idol (false god; see *idle*,
   idyll)
idol·a·try (–tries)
idol·ize
idyll, idyl (narrative poem;
   see *idle, idol*)
ig·loo
ig·ne·ous
ig·nite
ig·ni·tion
ig·no·ble
ig·no·min·i·ous
ig·no·rance
ig·nore
igua·na
ikon, icon
il·le·gal
il·leg·i·ble
il·le·git·i·mate
ill-got·ten
il·lib·er·al
il·lic·it (not permitted; see
   elicit)
il·lim·it·able
il·lit·er·ate
ill·ness
il·lu·mi·na·tion
il·lu·sion (misleading
   image; see *allusion*)

il·lu·so·ry
il·lus·trate
il·lus·tra·tion
il·lus·tri·ous
im·age
imag·in·able
imag·i·na·tive
imag·ine
im·bal·ance
im·be·cile
im·bibe
im·bro·glio
im·bue
im·i·ta·tion
im·i·ta·tive
im·mac·u·late
im·ma·nent (inherent; see
   imminent)
im·ma·te·ri·al
im·ma·ture
im·mea·sur·able
im·me·di·ate
im·me·mo·ri·al
im·mense
im·merse
im·mer·sion
im·mi·grate (to come into a
   country; see *emigrate*)
im·mi·nent (ready to take
   place; see *immanent*)
im·mo·bile
im·mod·er·ate
im·mod·est
im·mo·late
im·mor·al
im·mor·tal
im·mov·able
im·mune
im·mu·ni·ty (–ties)
im·pact (noun), im·pact
   (verb)
im·pair
im·pale
im·pal·pa·ble
im·par·tial
im·pass·able
im·passe
im·pas·sioned
im·pas·sive
im·pa·tience

im·peach
im·pec·ca·ble
im·pe·cu·nious
im·pede
im·ped·i·ment
im·pel
im·pend·ing
im·pen·e·tra·ble
im·pen·i·tence
im·per·a·tive
im·per·cep·ti·ble
im·per·fect
im·pe·ri·al
im·pe·ri·ous
im·per·ish·able
im·per·ma·nence
im·per·me·able
im·per·mis·si·ble
im·per·son·al
im·per·son·ate
im·per·ti·nent
im·per·turb·able
im·per·vi·ous
im·pet·u·ous
im·pe·tus
im·pi·ety (–eties)
im·pinge
im·pi·ous
imp·ish
im·pla·ca·ble
im·plau·si·ble
im·ple·ment
im·pli·cate
im·plic·it
im·plore
im·ply
im·po·lite
im·pol·i·tic
im·pon·der·a·ble
im·port (noun), im·port
   (verb)
im·por·tance
im·por·tu·nate
im·pose
im·po·si·tion
im·pos·si·bil·i·ty (–ties)
im·pos·si·ble
im·pos·tor, im·pos·ter
im·pos·ture
im·po·tent

im·pound
im·pov·er·ish
im·prac·ti·ca·ble
im·prac·ti·cal
im·pre·cate
im·pre·cise
im·preg·na·ble
im·pre·sa·rio
im·press
im·pres·sive
im·pri·ma·tur
im·print
im·pris·on·ment
im·prob·a·ble
im·promp·tu
im·prop·er
im·pro·pri·ety (–eties)
im·prove·ment
im·prov·i·dent
im·pro·vise
im·pru·dent
im·pu·dent
im·pugn
im·pulse
im·pu·ni·ty (–ties)
im·pu·ri·ty (–ties)
im·pute
in·abil·i·ty (–ties)
in ab·sen·tia
in·ac·ces·si·ble
in·ac·cu·ra·cy (–cies)
in·ac·tive
in·ad·e·qua·cy (–cies)
in·ad·e·quate
in·ad·mis·si·ble
in·ad·ver·tent
in·ad·vis·able
in·alien·able
in·al·ter·able
in·amo·ra·ta
inane
in·an·i·mate
in·ap·pli·ca·ble
in·ap·pre·cia·tive
in·ap·proach·able
in·ap·pro·pri·ate
in·ar·tic·u·late
in·ar·tis·tic
in·as·much
in·at·ten·tive

in·au·di·ble
in·au·gu·ral
in·au·gu·rate
in·aus·pi·cious
in·born
in·cal·cu·la·ble
in·can·des·cent
in·can·ta·tion
in·ca·pa·ble
in·ca·pac·i·tate
in·car·cer·ate
in·car·nate
in·cau·tious
in·cen·di·ary (–ar·ies)
in·cense (noun), in·cense
  (verb)
in·cen·tive
in·cep·tion
in·ces·sant
in·cho·ate
in·ci·den·tal·ly
in·cin·er·ate
in·cip·i·ent
in·cise
in·ci·sion
in·ci·sive
in·cite (to stir up; see
  insight)
in·clem·ent
in·cli·na·tion
in·cline
in·close, en·close
in·clude
in·cog·ni·to
in·co·her·ent
in·com·bus·ti·ble
in·come
in·com·men·su·ra·ble
in·com·pa·ra·ble
in·com·pat·i·ble
in·com·pe·tence
in·com·plete
in·com·pre·hen·si·ble
in·con·ceiv·able
in·con·clu·sive
in·con·gru·ous
in·con·se·quen·tial
in·con·sid·er·ate
in·con·sist·tent
in·con·sol·able

in·con·spic·u·ous
in·con·stant
in·con·test·able
in·con·tro·vert·ible
in·con·ve·nient
in·cor·por·ate
in·cor·rect
in·cor·ri·gi·ble
in·cor·rupt·ible
in·crease (noun), in·crease
  (verb)
in·creas·ing·ly
in·cred·i·ble
in·cred·i·bly
in·cre·du·li·ty
in·cred·u·lous
in·cre·ment
in·crim·i·nate
in·cu·bate
in·cu·ba·tor
in·cu·bus (–bus·es *or* –bi)
in·cul·cate
in·cum·bent
in·cur
in·cur·able
in·debt·ed
in·de·cent
in·de·ci·pher·able
in·de·ci·sion
in·de·fat·i·ga·ble
in·de·fen·si·ble
in·de·fin·able
in·def·i·nite
in·del·i·ble
in·del·i·cate
in·dem·ni·fy
in·den·ta·tion
in·den·ture
in·de·pen·dent
in·de·scrib·able
in·de·struc·ti·ble
in·de·ter·min·able
in·dex (in·dex·es *or*
  in·di·ces)
In·di·an
in·di·cate
in·dict (charge with
  offence; see *indite*)
in·dif·fer·ent
in·dig·e·nous

in·di·gent
in·di·gest·ible
in·di·ges·tion
in·dig·nant
in·dig·ni·ty (–ties)
in·di·go (–gos *or* –goes)
in·di·rect
in·dis·creet
in·dis·cre·tion
in·dis·crim·i·nate
in·dis·pens·able
in·dis·pose
in·dis·put·able
in·dis·sol·u·ble
in·dis·tinct
in·dis·tin·guish·able
in·dite (to put down in
    writing; see *indict*)
in·di·vid·u·al
in·di·vid·u·al·i·ty
in·di·vis·i·ble
in·doc·tri·nate
in·do·lence
in·dom·i·ta·ble
in·du·bi·ta·ble
in·duce
in·duct
in·dulge
in·dul·gence
in·dus·tri·al·ist
in·dus·try (–tries)
ine·bri·ate
in·ed·i·ble
in·ef·fa·ble
in·ef·fec·tive
in·ef·fec·tu·al
in·ef·fi·cien·cy (–cies)
in·elas·tic
in·el·i·gi·ble
in·eluc·ta·ble
in·ept
in·ep·ti·tude
in·equal·i·ty (–ties)
in·eq·ui·ta·ble
in·eq·ui·ty
in·ert
in·er·tia
in·es·cap·able
in·es·ti·ma·ble
in·ev·i·ta·ble

in·ex·cus·able
in·ex·haust·ible
in·ex·o·ra·ble
in·ex·pe·di·ent
in·ex·pen·sive
in·ex·pe·ri·enced
in·ex·pert
in·ex·pli·ca·ble
in·ex·press·ible
in·ex·tin·guish·able
in·ex·tri·ca·ble
in·fal·li·ble
in·fa·mous
in·fan·cy (–cies)
in·fan·ti·cide
in·fan·tile
in·fan·try (–tries)
in·fat·u·a·tion
in·fec·tion
in·fec·tious
in·fer
in·fer·ence
in·fe·ri·or·i·ty (–ties)
in·fer·nal
in·fer·no
in·fer·tile
in·fi·del·i·ty (–ties)
in·field
in·fil·trate
in·fi·nite
in·fin·i·tes·i·mal
in·fin·i·tive
in·fin·i·ty (–ties)
in·fir·ma·ry (–ries)
in·fir·mi·ty (–ties)
in·flame
in·flam·ma·ble
in·flam·ma·tion
in·flate
in·fla·tion
in·flec·tion
in·flex·i·ble
in·flict
in·flu·ence
in·flu·en·za
in·flux
in·for·mal
in·for·ma·tion
in·form·er
in·frac·tion

in·fra·red
in·fre·quent
in·fringe
in·fu·ri·ate
in·fuse
in·fu·sion
in·ge·nious (clever; see
    ingenuous)
in·ge·nu·ity (–ities)
in·gen·u·ous (showing
    childlike simplicity; see
    ingenious)
in·gest
in·glo·ri·ous
in·got
in·grained
in·grate
in·gra·ti·ate
in·grat·i·tude
in·gre·di·ent
in·gress
in·hab·it
in·hab·it·ant
in·ha·la·tion
in·hale
in·her·ent
in·her·i·tance
in·hib·it
in·hos·pi·ta·ble
in·hu·man
in·hu·mane
in·im·i·cal
in·im·i·ta·ble
in·iq·ui·ty (–ties)
ini·tial
ini·tiate
ini·tia·tive
in·jec·tion
in·ju·di·cious
in·junc·tion
in·jure
in·ju·ri·ous
in·ju·ry (–ries)
in·jus·tice
in·kling
in·land
in·let
in·mate
in me·mo·ri·am
in·nate

in·ning
in·no·cent
in·noc·u·ous
in·no·vate
in·no·va·tor
in·nu·en·do (–dos *or* –does)
in·nu·mer·able
in·oc·u·late
in·of·fen·sive
in·op·er·a·ble
in·op·er·a·tive
in·op·por·tune
in·or·di·nate
in·or·gan·ic
in per·so·nam (Latin:
   against a person)
in·quest
in·quire
in·qui·si·tion
in·quis·i·tive
in·road
in·sane
in·san·i·ty (–ties)
in·sa·tia·ble
in·scribe
in·scrip·tion
in·scru·ta·ble
in·sec·ti·cide
in·se·cure
in·sem·i·na·tion
in·sen·sate
in·sen·si·ble
in·sen·si·tive
in·sep·a·ra·ble
in·sert (noun), in·sert (verb)
in·side
in·sid·i·ous
in·sight (act of
   apprehending inner
   nature of things; see
   incite)
in·sig·nia, in·sig·ne (–nia *or*
   –ni·as)
in·sig·nif·i·cant
in·sin·cere
in·sin·u·ate
in·sip·id
in·sist
in·sis·tence
in·sole

in·so·lent
in·sol·u·ble
in·solv·able
in·sol·vent
in·som·nia
in·sou·ci·ance
in·spec·tor
in·spi·ra·tion
in·sta·bil·i·ty
in·stall, in·stal
in·stant
in·stan·ta·neous
in·stead
in·step
in·sti·gate
in·stinct
in·sti·tute
in·struct
in·stru·ment
in·sub·or·di·nate
in·sub·stan·tial
in·suf·fer·able
in·suf·fi·cient
in·su·lar
in·su·late
in·su·lin
in·sult (noun), in·sult (verb)
in·su·per·a·ble
in·sup·port·able
in·sup·press·ible
in·sur·ance
in·sur·gent
in·sur·mount·able
in·sur·rec·tion
in·tact
in·tan·gi·ble
in·te·ger
in·te·gral
in·te·grate
in·teg·ri·ty
in·tel·lect
in·tel·li·gence
in·tel·li·gen·tsia
in·tel·li·gi·ble
in·tem·per·ate
in·tend
in·tense
in·ten·tion·al
in·ter
in·ter·ac·tion

in·ter·cede
in·ter·cept
in·ter·ces·sion
in·ter·change·able
in·ter·com·mu·ni·ca·tion
in·ter·con·nect
in·ter·course
in·ter·de·part·men·tal
in·ter·dict
in·ter·est
in·ter·fere
in·ter·fer·ence
in·ter·im
in·te·ri·or
in·ter·ject
in·ter·lard
in·ter·line
in·ter·lin·ear
in·ter·lock
in·ter·lop·er
in·ter·lude
in·ter·mar·ry
in·ter·me·di·ary (–ar·ies)
in·ter·me·di·ate
in·ter·mez·zo (–zi *or* –zos)
in·ter·mi·na·ble
in·ter·mis·sion
in·ter·mit·tent
in·ter·mix
in·tern (noun), in·tern
   (verb)
in·ter·nal
in·ter·nal·ize
in·ter·na·tion·al
in·ter·ne·cine
in·tern·ee
in·tern·ment
in·ter·po·late
in·ter·pose
in·ter·pret
in·ter·ra·cial
in·ter·ro·gate
in·ter·rupt
in·ter·sect
in·ter·ses·sion
in·ter·sperse
in·ter·state
in·ter·stel·lar
in·ter·stice
in·ter·val

in·ter·vene

in·ter·view

in·tes·tate

in·tes·tine

in·ti·ma·cy (–cies)

in·ti·mate

in·tim·i·date

in·tol·er·a·ble

in·tol·er·ant

in·to·na·tion

in·tox·i·cate

in·trac·ta·ble

in·tra·mu·ral

in·tran·si·gent

in·tran·si·tive

in·tra·ve·nous

in·trep·id

in·tri·ca·cy (–cies)

in·tri·cate

in·trigue

in·trin·sic

in·tro·duce

in·tro·spec·tion

in·tro·ver·sion

in·tro·vert

in·tru·sion

in·tu·ition

in·tu·itive

in·un·date

in·val·id (adjective), invalid
(noun)

in·valu·able

in·vari·able

in·va·sion

in·vec·tive

in·veigh

in·ven·tion

in·ven·to·ry (–ries)

in·verse

in·ver·te·brate

in·ves·ti·ga·tor

in·ves·ti·ture

in·ves·tor

in·vet·er·ate

in·vid·i·ous

in·vig·o·rate

in·vin·ci·ble

in·vi·o·la·ble

in·vis·i·ble

in·vi·ta·tion

in·vo·ca·tion

in·voice

in·voke

in·vol·un·tary

in·volve

in·vul·ner·a·ble

in·ward

io·dine

ion

io·ta

iras·ci·ble

irate

ire

ir·i·des·cence

iris (iris·es *or* iri·des)

irk·some

iron

ir·ra·di·a·tion

ir·ra·tio·nal

ir·rec·on·cil·able

ir·re·cov·er·able

ir·re·deem·able

ir·re·duc·ible

ir·re·fut·able

ir·reg·u·lar

ir·rel·e·van·cy (–cies)

ir·rel·e·vant

ir·re·li·gious

ir·re·me·di·a·ble

ir·rep·a·ra·ble

ir·re·place·able

ir·re·proach·able

ir·re·sist·ible

ir·res·o·lute

ir·re·spec·tive

ir·re·spon·si·ble

ir·re·triev·able

ir·rev·er·ent

ir·re·vers·ible

ir·rev·o·ca·ble

ir·ri·gate

ir·ri·ta·ble

ir·ri·tate

is·land

isle

iso·late

isos·ce·les

iso·tope

is·sue

isth·mus

ital·ic

item·ize

itin·er·ary (–ar·ies)

ivo·ry (–ries)

ivy (ivies)

J

jab·ber
jack·et
jade
jag·ged
jag·uar
jail·er, jail·or
ja·lopy (jalopies)
jam·bo·ree
jan·gle
jan·i·tor
jar·gon
jas·mine
jaun·dice
jaunt
jav·e·lin
jeal·ous
jeans
jeer
jel·ly (jel·lies)
jeop·ar·dize
jer·sey
jest
jet-pro·pelled
jet·ti·son
jet·ty (jetties)
jew·el·ry)

jibe, gibe
jig·ger
jit·ney
jock·ey
jo·cose
joc·u·lar
jo·cund
jodh·pur
jog·ging
join·ing
joint
jos·tle
jounce
jour·nal
jour·ney
joust
jo·vial
joy·ful
joy·ous
ju·bi·lant
ju·bi·lee
judge
judg·ment, judge·ment
ju·di·ca·ture
ju·di·cial
ju·di·cia·ry
ju·di·cious

jug·gler
juicy
ju·jit·su, ju·jut·su
juke·box
ju·lep
ju·li·enne
jum·ble
jum·bo
jump
junc·tion
junc·ture
jun·gle
ju·nior
ju·ni·per
jun·ket
jun·ta
ju·ris·dic·tion
ju·ris·pru·dence
ju·rist
ju·ror
jus·tice
jus·ti·fi·able
jus·ti·fi·ca·tion
jute
ju·ve·nile
jux·ta·pose

ka·lei·do·scope
kan·ga·roo
ka·pok
kar·a·kul
kar·at, car·at
ka·ra·te
ka·ty·did
kay·ak
kayo
keel
keen
keen·ness
keep·sake
kelp
ken·nel
kept
ker·chief
ker·nel (inner part of a
   seed; see *colonel*)
ker·o·sene, ker·o·sine
ketch
ketch·up, cat·sup
ket·tle
kha·ki
kib·butz
ki·bitz·er

ki·bosh
kid·nap
kid·nap·per, kid·nap·er
kid·ney
kiln
kilo·cy·cle
ki·lo·gram
kilo·li·ter
ki·lo·me·ter
kilo·watt
kil·ter
ki·mo·no
kin·der·gar·ten
kin·dle
kind·li·ness
kin·dling
kin·dred
kin·e·scope
kin·es·thet·ic
ki·net·ic
ki·osk
kitch·en·ette
kit·ty-cor·ner, cat·er-
   cor·ner
klep·to·ma·ni·ac

knack
knap·sack
knave (tricky fellow; see
   nave)
knead (press into a mass;
   see *need*)
knee
kneel
knell
knew (past tense of know;
   see *gnu*, *new*)
knick·knack
knife (knives)
knight (feudal nobleman;
   see *night*)
knob
knoll
knot
knowl·edge
knowl·edge·able
knuck·le
ko·ala
kohl·ra·bi (–bies)
ko·sher
ku·dos
kum·quat

L

la·bel
la·bor
lab·o·ra·to·ry (–ries)
la·bo·ri·ous
lab·y·rinth
lac·er·ate
lach·ry·mose
lack·ey
lack·lus·ter
la·con·ic
lac·quer
la·cu·na (–nae or –nas)
lad·der
la·den
lad·ing
la·dle
la·dy·ship
la·ger
lag·gard
la·gniappe
la·goon
la·icize
lair
lais·sez-faire (French: doctrine of individual freedom)
la·ity
lam·baste, lam·bast
lame (cripple; see lamé)
lamé (fabric; see lame)
la·men·ta·ble
lam·i·nate
lamp·light
lam·poon
lance
lan·dau
land·lord
lan·guage
lan·guid
lan·guish
lan·guor
lan·o·lin
lan·tern
lan·yard
la·pel
lap·i·dary (–dar·ies)
lapse
lar·ce·ny (–nies)
lar·der
large

lar·gess, lar·gesse
lar·i·at
lar·va (–vae)
lar·yn·gi·tis
lar·ynx (lar·ynxes)
la·sa·gna
las·civ·i·ous
la·ser
las·si·tude
las·so (las·sos or las·soes)
la·tent
lat·er·al
la·tex (la·ti·ces or la·tex·es)
lath (thin strip of wood; see lathe)
lathe (shaping machine; see lath)
lat·i·tude
la·trine
lat·ter
laud
lau·da·to·ry
laugh
laugh·able
launch
laun·der
laun·dry (–dries)
lau·re·ate
lau·rel
la·va·liere, la·val·liere (French: type of pendant worn as a necklace)
lav·a·to·ry (–ries)
lav·en·der
lav·ish
law·ful
law·ful·ly
lawn
law·yer
lax·a·tive
lax·ity
lay·ette
lay·man (–men)
la·zy
leach (to dissolve out; see leech)
lead
lead·er
leaf·let
league

leak (to escape through an opening; see leek)
lean (to incline; see lien)
learn
lease
leash
least
leath·er
leave
leav·en
lech·er
lech·er·ous
lec·tern
lec·ture
led·ger
leech (bloodsucking worm; see leach)
leek (herb; see leak)
leer
leery
lee·ward
lee·way
left
leg·a·cy (–cies)
le·gal
le·gal·i·ty (–ties)
leg·ate
le·ga·to
leg·end
leg·end·ary
leg·er·de·main
leg·gings, leg·gins
leg·gy
leg·horn
leg·i·ble
le·gion
le·gion·naire
leg·is·late
leg·is·la·tive
leg·is·la·ture
le·git·i·ma·cy
le·git·i·mate
le·gume
lei·sure
lem·ming
length
length·en
le·nient
len·i·ty
len·til

leop·ard

le·o·tard

lep·er

lep·re·chaun

lep·ro·sy

les·bi·an

le·sion

les·see

les·son

les·sor

le·thal

le·thar·gic

let·ter

let·tuce

leu·ke·mia

lev·ee (embankment; see *levy*)

lev·el

lev·i·ty

levy (assessment; see *levee*)

lewd

lex·i·cog·ra·phy

lex·i·con

li·a·ble

li·ai·son

li·ar

li·ba·tion

li·bel

lib·er·al

lib·er·ate

lib·er·tar·i·an

lib·er·tine

lib·er·ty (–ties)

li·bid·i·nous

li·brar·i·an

li·brary (–brar·ies)

li·bret·to (–tos *or* –ti)

li·cense, li·cence

li·cen·tious

li·chen

lic·it

lic·o·rice

lie (untruth; see *lye*)

lien (payment of debt; see *lean*)

lieu

lieu·ten·ant

life (lives)

lig·a·ment

lig·a·ture

light·ning

like·li·hood

li·lac

lily (lil·ies)

limb

lim·bo

lime·light

lim·er·ick

lim·i·ta·tion

limn

lim·ou·sine

lim·pid

lin·eal

lin·ear

lines·man (linesmen)

lin·ge·rie

lin·go (lingoes)

lin·gual

lin·guis·tic

lin·i·ment

lin·ing

li·no·leum

lin·seed

lin·tel

li·on·ize

liq·ue·fac·tion

liq·ue·fy

li·queur

liq·ui·date

li·quor

lisle

lis·some

lis·ten

lit·a·ny (–nies)

li·ter

lit·er·a·cy

lit·er·al

lit·er·ary

lit·er·ate

lit·er·a·ture

lithe

litho·graph

lit·i·gant

lit·i·gate

lit·mus

lit·tle

li·tur·gi·cal

lit·ur·gy (–gies)

liv·able

live·li·hood

live·li·ness

live·ly

liv·er

liv·er·wurst

live·stock

liv·id

liz·ard

lla·ma

loan

loath (unwilling, reluctant; see *loathe*)

loathe (dislike greatly; see *loath*)

lob·by (lobbies)

lob·ster

lo·cal (not general or widespread; see *locale*)

lo·cale (place related to a particular event; see *local*)

lo·cate

lock·et

lo·co·mo·tion

lo·cust

lodge

log·a·rithm

log·i·cal

lo·gis·tics

lo·gy, log·gy

loi·ter

lol·li·pop, lol·ly·pop

lone·li·ness

lone·ly

lon·gev·i·ty

lon·gi·tude

lore

loose

loot (something taken by force; see *lute*)

lop·sid·ed

lo·qua·cious

lo·tion

lot·tery (–ter·ies)

lo·tus, lo·tos

loud

lounge

lou·ver, lou·vre

lov·able, love·able

loy·al

loz·enge
lu·bri·cate
lu·cid
luck·i·ly
lu·cra·tive
lu·cre
lu·di·crous
lug·gage
lum·ba·go
lum·ber
lu·mi·nary (–nar·ies)

lum·mox
lu·na·cy (–cies)
lu·nar
lu·na·tic
lun·cheon
lun·cheon·ette
lunge
lurch
lu·rid
lurk
lus·cious
lus·trous

lute (musical instrument;
   see *loot*)
lux·u·ri·ous
lux·u·ry (–ries)
ly·ce·um
lymph
lynch
lynx (lynx *or* lynx·es)
ly·on·naise
lyre
lyr·ic

ma·ca·bre
mac·ad·am
mac·a·ro·ni
mac·a·roon
mac·er·ate
ma·chete
mach·i·na·tion
ma·chine
ma·chin·ist
mack·er·el
mack·i·naw
mack·in·tosh, mac·in·tosh
mac·ro·cosm
mac·ro·scop·ic
mad·am, ma·dame
mad·den·ing
ma·de·moi·selle
    (ma·de·moi·selles or
    mes·de·moi·selles)
ma·dras
mad·ri·gal
mael·strom
mae·stro (mae·stros or
    mae·stri)
mag·a·zine
ma·gen·ta
mag·got
mag·i·cal
ma·gi·cian
mag·is·trate
mag·nan·i·mous
mag·nate (person of rank
    and power; see magnet)
mag·ne·sia
mag·ne·sium
mag·net (something that
    attracts; see magnate)
mag·nif·i·cent
mag·ni·fy
mag·ni·tude
mag·no·lia
mag·pie
ma·ha·ra·ja, ma·ha·ra·jah
ma·hog·a·ny (–nies)
maid·en
mail (letters; see male)
maim
main (chief; see mane)
main·tain

maî·tre d'hô·tel (maî·tres
    d'hô·tel)
maize (Indian corn; see
    maze)
ma·jes·tic
ma·jor·i·ty (–ties)
mal·ad·just·ment
mal·a·dy (–dies)
mal·aise (French: indefinite
    feeling of ill health)
ma·lar·ia
mal·con·tent
mal de mer (French:
    seasickness)
male (masculine; see mail)
male·fac·tor
ma·lev·o·lent
mal·fea·sance
mal·formed
mal·func·tion
mal·ice
ma·li·cious
ma·lign
ma·lig·nan·cy (–cies)
ma·lin·ger
ma·lin·ger·er
mall
mal·lard
mal·lea·ble
mal·let
mal·nour·ished
mal·nu·tri·tion
mal·prac·tice
malt
mam·mal
mam·moth
man·age·ment
man·da·mus
man·da·rin
man·date
man·da·to·ry
man·di·ble
man·do·lin, man·do·line
mane (long, heavy hair on
    neck of horses; see main)
ma·neu·ver
man·gle
man·go (man·gos or
    man·goes)

mangy
ma·nia
ma·ni·ac
man·ic
ma·ni·cot·ti (plural also
    ma·ni·cot·ti)
man·i·cure
man·i·fest
man·i·fes·to
man·i·fold
ma·nip·u·late
man·li·ness
man·ne·quin
man·ner
man·or
man·sion
man·tel (shelf; see mantle)
man·tle (cloak; see mantel)
man·u·al
man·u·fac·ture
man·u·mit
ma·nure
manu·script
mar·a·schi·no
mar·a·thon
ma·raud·er
Mar·di Gras (French:
    Shrove Tuesday,
    celebration prior to Lent)
mar·ble
mare
mar·ga·rine
mar·gin
mar·gin·al
mari·gold
mar·i·jua·na, mar·i·hua·na
ma·rim·ba
mar·i·nate
ma·rine
mar·i·o·nette
mar·i·tal
mar·i·time
mar·jo·ram
mar·ket·able
mar·lin
mar·ma·lade
ma·roon
mar·quee
mar·quise

mar·qui·sette
mar·riage
mar·row
mar·shal, mar·shall (officer;
    see *martial*)
marsh·mal·low
mar·su·pi·al
mar·tial (relating to war;
    see *marshall*)
mar·ti·net
mar·tyr
mar·vel
marl·vel·ous, mar·vel·lous
mar·zi·pan
mas·cara
mas·cot
mas·cu·line
mas·och·ism
mas·och·ist
ma·son·ry (–ries)
mas·quer·ade
mas·sa·cre
mas·sage
mas·seur
mas·seuse
mas·sive
mas·ter·piece
mast·head
mas·ti·cate
mas·tiff
mas·toid
mat·a·dor
ma·te·ri·al (substance; see
    matériel)
ma·te·ri·al·ism
ma·té·ri·el, ma·te·ri·el
    (equipment and supplies;
    see *material*)
ma·ter·nal
ma·ter·ni·ty (–ties)
math·e·mat·ics
mat·i·nee
ma·tri·arch
ma·tric·u·late
mat·ri·mo·ny
ma·trix (ma·tri·ces *or*
    ma·trix·es)
ma·tron·ly
mat·ter

mat·tress
ma·ture
ma·tu·ri·ty
maud·lin
maul
mau·so·le·um
    (mau·so·le·ums *or*
    mau·so·lea)
mauve
mav·er·ick
max·i·mum (–ma *or*
    –mums)
may·hem
may·on·naise
may·or·al·ty
maze (network of passages;
    see *maize*)
mead·ow
mea·ger, mea·gre
me·an·der
mean·ing·ful
mea·sles
mea·sure
meat (flesh of domestic
    animals; see *mete*)
me·chan·ic
mech·a·nism
med·al (metal disk; see
    meddle)
med·dle (interfere; see
    medal)
me·dia (–di·ae)
me·di·an
me·di·ate
med·i·cal
med·i·ca·tion
me·dic·i·nal
med·i·cine
me·di·eval, me·di·ae·val
me·di·o·cre
me·di·oc·ri·ty (–ties)
med·i·tate
me·di·um (me·di·ums *or*
    me·dia)
med·ley
mega·cy·cle
mega·phone
mega·ton
mel·an·choly (–chol·ies)

mé·lange (French:
    incongruous elements)
me·lee (French: fight)
mel·lif·lu·ent
mel·lif·lu·ous
mel·low
me·lo·di·ous
melo·dra·ma
mel·o·dy (–dies)
mem·ber·ship
mem·brane
me·men·to
mem·oir
mem·o·ra·bil·ia
mem·o·ra·ble
mem·o·ran·dum
me·mo·ri·al
mem·o·ry (–ries)
men·ace
mé·nage (French:
    household)
me·nag·er·ie
men·da·cious
men·di·cant
me·nial
meno·pause
me·no·rah
men·stru·ate
men·su·ra·tion
men·tal
men·thol
men·tion
men·tor
menu
mer·can·tile
mer·ce·nary (–nar·ies)
mer·chan·dise
mer·chant
mer·cy (mer·cies)
mer·e·tri·cious
merge
merg·er
me·rid·i·an
me·ringue
mer·i·to·ri·ous
mer·maid
mes·dames
mes·mer·ize
mes·sage

mes·sen·ger
me·tab·o·lism
me·tal·ic
met·al·lur·gy
meta·mor·pho·sis (–ses)
met·a·phor
meta·phys·ics
mete (allot; see *meat*)
me·te·or·ic
me·ter
meth·a·done, meth·a·don
meth·od
meth·od·ol·o·gy (–gies)
me·tic·u·lous
mé·tier (French: an area of expertise)
met·ric
met·ro·nome
me·trop·o·lis
met·ro·pol·i·tan
met·tle
mez·za·nine
mez·zo-so·pra·no
mi·as·ma (–mas *or* –ma·ta)
mi·ca
mi·cro·anal·y·sis
mi·crobe
mi·cro·cosm
mi·crom·e·ter
mi·cro·phone
mi·cro·scope
mid·dle
midg·et
mid·night
mid·riff
midst
mien
might (power; see *mite*)
mi·graine
mi·grate
mi·gra·to·ry
mi·ka·do
mil·dew
mile·age
mi·lieu (mi·lieus *or* mi·lieux)
mil·i·tan·cy
mil·i·ta·rist
mil·i·tary
mil·i·tate

mi·li·tia
mil·len·ni·um
mil·li·gram
mil·li·li·ter
mil·li·me·ter
mil·li·nery
mil·lion·aire
mim·eo·graph
mi·met·ic
mim·ic
min·a·ret
mi·na·to·ry
minc·ing·ly
mind·less
min·er (mine worker; see *minor*)
min·er·al·o·gy
min·gle
min·ia·ture
min·i·mum
min·i·mize
min·ion
min·is·cule, mi·nus·cule
min·is·te·ri·al
mi·nor (comparatively unimportant; see *miner*)
mi·nor·i·ty (–ties)
min·strel
min·u·et
mi·nus·cule, min·is·cule
min·ute (space of time)
mi·nute (of small importance)
minx
mi·rac·u·lous
mi·rage
mire
mir·ror
mirth·ful
mis·al·li·ance
mis·an·thrope
mis·car·riage
mis·ce·ge·na·tion
mis·cel·la·neous
mis·cel·la·ny (–nies)
mis·chie·vous
mis·con·ceive
mis·con·strue
mis·de·mean·or
mis·er·a·ble

mi·ser·ly
mis·fea·sance
mis·han·dle
mis·in·ter·pret
mis·judge
mis·man·age
mis·no·mer
mi·sog·y·nist
mis·rep·re·sent
mis·sal (prayer book; see *missile*)
mis·shap·en
mis·sile (object or weapon thrown; see *missal*)
mis·sion·ary (–ar·ies)
mis·sive
mis·spell
mis·state
mis·take
mis·tle·toe
mis·tress
mis·tri·al
mite (small object or creature; see *might*)
mit·i·gate
mix·ture
mne·mon·ic
moat (trench; see *mote*)
mo·bile
mo·bi·li·za·tion
moc·ca·sin
mod·el
mod·er·ate
mod·er·a·tor
mod·ern·iza·tion
mod·es·ty
mod·i·fi·er
mod·ish
mod·u·late
mo·gul
mo·hair
moist·en
mo·lar
mo·las·ses
mo·lec·u·lar
mol·e·cule
mo·les·ta·tion
mol·li·fy
mol·ten
mo·men·tary

mo·men·tum
mon·arch
mon·as·tery (–ter·ies)
mon·e·tary
mon·ey (moneys *or*
   mon·ies)
Mon·gol·oid
mon·grel
mon·i·tor
mon·key
mono·chro·mat·ic
mon·o·cle
mo·nog·a·my
mono·gram
mono·logue, mono·log
mono·logu·ist,
   mo·no·lo·gist
mo·nop·o·ly (–lies)
mono·the·ism
mono·tone
mo·not·o·nous
mon·si·gnor (–gnors *or*
   –gno·ri)
mon·soon
mon·stros·i·ty (–ties)
mon·tage
mon·u·men·tal
moon·light
mo·raine
mor·al
mo·rale
mo·rass
mor·a·to·ri·um
   (mor·a·to·ri·ums *or*
   mor·a·to·ria)
mor·bid
mor·dant
mo·res
morgue
mor·i·bund
morn·ing (time from sunrise
   to noon; see *mourning*)
mo·ron·ic
mor·phine

mor·sel
mor·tal·i·ty
mort·gage
mor·ti·cian
mor·ti·fy
mor·tu·ary (–ar·ies)
mo·sa·ic
mosque
mos·qui·to (–tos *or* –toes)
mote (speck; see *moat*)
moth·er
mo·tif
mo·tion
mo·ti·va·tion
mo·tor
mot·tled
mot·to (mot·tos *or*
   mot·toes)
moun·tain·ous
mourn
mourn·ing (act of
   sorrowing; see *morning*)
mousse
mouth·ful
mou·ton
mov·able, move·able
mov·ie
moz·za·rel·la
mu·ci·lage
mu·cous
mug·ger
mug·gy
mu·lat·to (–toes *or* –tos)
mul·ber·ry (–ries)
mulct
mul·ti·eth·nic
mul·ti·fac·et·ed
mul·ti·far·i·ous
mul·ti·lat·er·al
mul·ti·me·dia
mul·ti·mil·lion·aire
mul·ti·na·tion·al
mul·ti·ple
mul·ti·tude

mum·ble
mum·bo jum·bo
mum·my (mummies)
mun·dane
mu·nic·i·pal
mu·nif·i·cent
mu·ni·tion
mu·ral
mur·der·ous
mus·cle (body tissue; see
   mussel)
mus·cu·lar
muse
mu·se·um
mu·si·cal
mu·si·cian
mus·ke·teer
musk·rat
mus·lin
mus·sel (mollusk; see
   muscle)
mus·tache
mus·tard
mu·ta·ble
mu·ta·tion
mu·ti·late
mu·ti·neer
mut·ter
mut·ton
mu·tu·al
muz·zle
my·o·pic
myr·i·ad
myrrh
myr·tle
mys·te·ri·ous
mys·tery (–ter·ies)
mys·tic
mys·ti·cism
mys·tique
myth·i·cal
my·thol·o·gy (–gies)

N

na·ive (na·ïve)
na·ive·té (na·ïve·té)
na·ked·ness
na·palm
naph·tha
nap·kin
nar·cis·sism
nar·cis·sus
nar·cot·ic
nar·rate
nar·ra·tor
nar·row
na·sal·i·ty (–ties)
na·scent
nas·tur·tium
nas·ty
na·ta·to·ri·um
na·tion·al·i·ty (–ties)
na·tive
na·tiv·i·ty (–ties)
nat·u·ral·ize
naugh·ti·ness
nau·se·ate
nau·seous
nau·ti·cal
na·val (relating to ships;
    see *navel*)
nave (church aisle; see
    knave)
na·vel (depression in
    abdomen; see *naval*)
nav·i·gate
nav·i·ga·tor
near·by
neb·u·lous
nec·es·sary (–saries)
ne·ces·si·tate
neck·lace
nec·tar·ine
nee·dle·work
ne'er-do-well
ne·far·i·ous
ne·gate
neg·a·tive
ne·glect
neg·li·gee, neg·li·gé
neg·li·gent
neg·li·gi·ble
ne·go·ti·a·tion
neigh

neigh·bor·hood
nei·ther
nem·e·sis (–ses)
ne·on
neo·phyte
neph·ew
nep·o·tism
ner·vous·ness
nes·tle
net·ting
net·tle
net·work
neu·ral·gia
neu·ro·sis (–ses)
neu·rot·ic
neu·ter
neu·tral·ize
neu·tron
new (recent; see *gnu* and
    knew)
news·stand
nib·ble
nice·ty (–ties)
niche
nick·el, nick·le
nick·nack, knick·knack
nic·o·tine
niece
night (time from dusk to
    dawn; see *knight*)
night·in·gale
night·mare
nim·ble
nine·teen
nine·ty (nineties)
ninth
nip·ple
ni·trate
ni·tro·gen
ni·tro·glyc·er·in,
    ni·tro·glyc·er·ine
no·bil·i·ty
no·ble
noc·tur·nal
noc·turne
nod·ule
noi·some
noisy
no·mad

nom de plume (French: pen
    name, pseudonym)
no·men·cla·ture
nom·i·nal
nom·i·na·tion
nom·i·nee
non·al·co·hol·ic
non·be·liev·er
non·bel·lig·er·ent
non·cha·lance
non·com·ba·tant
non·com·mis·sioned
non·com·mit·tal
non·com·pli·ance
non·con·duc·tor
non·con·form·ist
non·de·script
non·en·ti·ty (–ties)
non·es·sen·tial
non·fic·tion
non·in·ter·ven·tion
non·pa·reil (French: having
    no equal)
non·par·ti·san
non·poi·son·ous
non·pro·duc·tive
non·prof·it
non·re·new·able
non·sec·tar·i·an
non·sense
non se·qui·tur
non·tax·able
non·vi·o·lence
noo·dle
noose
nor·mal
north·ern
nose
nos·tal·gia
nos·tril
nos·trum
no·ta·bly
no·ta·rize
no·ta·ry public (no·ta·ries
    public *or* no·ta·ry
    publics)
no·ta·tion
notch
note·wor·thy
no·tice·able

no·ti·fy
no·tion
no·to·ri·ety (–eties)
no·to·ri·ous
nou·gat
nought
noun
nour·ish·ment
nov·el·lette
nov·el·ty (–ties)
no·ve·na
nov·ice
no·vi·tiate

nox·ious
noz·zle
nu·ance
nu·bile
nu·cle·us (–clei or
   –cle·us·es)
nu·di·ty
nug·get
nui·sance
nul·li·fy
numb
number
nu·mer·al

nu·mer·a·tor
nu·mer·ous
nu·mis·mat·ic
nup·tial
nurse
nurs·ery (–er·ies)
nur·ture
nu·tri·tion
nu·tri·tious
nuz·zle
ny·lon
nymph
nym·pho·ma·ni·ac

oak·en
oa·sis (–ses)
oath
oat·meal
ob·bli·ga·to
ob·du·rate
obe·di·ence
obei·sance
obe·lisk
obese
obe·si·ty
obey
ob·fus·cate
obit·u·ary (–ar·ries)
ob·jec·tion
ob·jec·tor
ob·jet d'art (ob·jets d'art)
ob·li·gate
ob·li·ga·tion
oblig·a·to·ry
oblige
oblique
oblit·er·ate
obliv·i·on
obliv·i·ous
ob·long
ob·lo·quy (–quies)
ob·nox·ious
oboe
obo·ist
ob·scene
ob·scen·i·ty (–ties)
ob·scure
ob·scu·ri·ty (–ties)
ob·se·qui·ous
ob·se·quy (–quies)
ob·ser·vant
ob·ser·va·to·ry (–ries)
ob·ses·sion
ob·so·les·cence
ob·so·lete
ob·sta·cle
ob·ste·tri·cian
ob·stet·rics
ob·sti·nate
ob·strep·er·ous
ob·struc·tion
ob·tain
ob·trude
ob·tru·sive

ob·tuse
ob·vi·ate
ob·vi·ous
oc·ca·sion
oc·cip·i·tal
oc·clu·sion
oc·cult
oc·cu·pan·cy (–cies)
oc·cu·pant
oc·cu·pa·tion
oc·cu·py
oc·cur
oc·curred
oc·cur·rence
ocean
ocean·og·ra·phy
oce·lot
ocher, ochre
oc·ta·gon
oc·tag·o·nal
oc·tane
oc·tave
oc·tet
oc·to·ge·nar·i·an
oc·to·pus (–pus·es or –pi)
oc·u·list
odd·i·ty (–ties)
odd·ly
odi·ous
odi·um
odom·e·ter
odor·ant
odor·ous
od·ys·sey
of·fend·er
of·fense, of·fence
of·fer·to·ry (–ries)
off·hand
of·fi·cer
of·fi·cial
of·fi·ci·ate
of·fi·cious
off·set
off·spring (off·spring or
    off·springs)
ohm
oil·er
oily
oint·ment
okra

old-fash·ioned
old·ster
ole·ag·i·nous
ol·fac·to·ry
oli·gar·chy (–chies)
ol·ive
olym·pi·ad
om·elet, om·elette
om·i·nous
omis·sion
omit
om·ni·bus
om·nip·o·tence
om·ni·science
om·niv·o·rous
on·com·ing
one-night stand
oner·ous
on·ion
on·o·mato·poe·ia
on·set
on·shore
on·side
on·slaught
on·tol·o·gy
onus
on·ward, on·wards
on·yx
oo·long
opal·es·cent
opaque
open
op·er·a·ble
op·er·ate
op·er·at·ic
op·er·a·tion
op·er·et·ta
oph·thal·mol·o·gist
opi·ate
opin·ion
opin·ion·at·ed
opi·um
opos·sum
op·po·nent
op·por·tune
op·por·tu·nis·tic
op·por·tu·ni·ty (–ties)
op·po·site
op·pres·sion
op·pro·bri·ous

op·pro·bri·um
op·ti·cal
op·ti·cian
op·ti·mism
op·ti·mum (–ma *or* –mums)
op·tion
op·tom·e·trist
op·tom·e·try
op·u·lent
opus (opera *or* opus·es)
or·a·cle
oral (relating to the mouth;
   see *aural*)
or·ange
orate
or·a·to·rio (–ri·os)
or·a·to·ry (–ries)
or·bit·al
or·chard
or·ches·tra
or·chid
or·dain
or·deal
or·der
or·di·nance
or·di·nary (-nar·ies)
or·di·nari·ly
or·di·na·tion
ord·nance
or·dure
ore
oreg·a·no
or·gan
or·gan·ic
or·gan·ism
or·ga·ni·za·tion
or·ga·niz·er
or·gasm
or·gi·as·tic

or·gy (or·gies)
ori·en·tal
ori·en·ta·tion
or·i·fice
orig·i·nal·i·ty
orig·i·na·tor
ori·ole
or·i·son
or·na·men·tal
or·na·men·ta·tion
or·nate
or·nery
or·ni·thol·o·gy (–gies)
or·phan·age
orth·odon·tist
or·tho·dox
or·tho·pe·dic,
   or·tho·pae·dic
os·cil·late
os·mo·sis
os·prey
os·si·fi·ca·tion
os·si·fy
os·ten·si·ble
os·ten·ta·tious
os·teo·path
os·tra·cize
os·trich
oti·ose
ot·to·man
ought
ounce
our (relating to us; see
   hour)
oust
out·age
out·break
out·dis·tance
out·fit·ter

out·land·ish
out·pour·ing
out·ra·geous
ou·tré (French: bizarre)
out·ward
out·weigh
out·wit
oval
ova·ry (–ries)
ova·tion
over·alls
over·bear·ing
over·board
over·cast
over·con·fi·dent
over·dose
over·draft
over·ex·pose
over·haul
over·joyed
over·lap
over·rate
over·seas
over·seer
over·sight
overt
over·ture
over·whelm
over·wrought
ovu·late
ow·ing
own·er
ox·i·da·tion
ox·ide
ox·i·dize
ox·tail
ox·y·gen
oys·ter
ozone

pab·u·lum
pace·mak·er
pac·er
pachy·derm
pa·cif·ic
pac·i·fi·er
pack·age
pack·et
pact
pad·ding
pad·dle
pad·dock
pad·lock
pae·an (hymn; see *paeon,
    peon*)
pae·on (metrical foot; see
    paean, peon)
pa·gan
page
pag·eant·ry
pag·i·nate
pa·go·da
paid
pail (container; see *pale*)
pain (suffering; see *pane*)
pains·tak·ing
paint
pair (two; see *pare, pear*)
pa·ja·mas
pal·ace
pal·at·able
pal·ate (roof or mouth; see
    palette, pallet)
pa·la·tial
pa·la·ver
pale (deficient in color; see
    pail)
Pa·leo·lith·ic
pal·ette (painter's board;
    see *palate, pallet*)
pal·frey
pal·in·drome
pal·i·sade
pal·la·di·um (–la·dia)
pall·bear·er
pal·let (straw mattress; see
    palate, palette)
pal·li·ate
pal·lid
pal·lor

pal·met·to
palm·ist
pal·o·mi·no
pal·pa·ble
pal·pi·tate
pal·sy (palsies)
pal·try
pam·pa
pam·per
pam·phle·teer
pan·a·cea
pan·cre·as
pan·da
pan·de·mo·ni·um
pan·der
pane (sheet of glass; see
    pain)
pan·e·gy·ric
pan·el
pan·han·dle
pan·ic
pan·icked
pan·o·ply (–plies)
pan·ora·ma
pan·sy (pansies)
pan·the·ism
pan·ther
pan·ties
pant·ing
pan·to·mime
pan·try (pantries)
panty·waist
pa·pa·cy (–cies)
pa·pal
pa·pa·ya
pa·pier-mâ·ché
pa·poose
pa·pri·ka
pa·py·rus (pa·py·rus·es *or*
    pa·py·ri)
par·a·ble
pa·rab·o·la
para·chute
pa·rade
par·a·digm
par·a·dise
par·a·dox
par·af·fin
par·a·gon
para·graph

par·a·keet
par·al·lax
par·al·lel
par·al·lel·o·gram
pa·ral·y·sis
par·a·lyt·ic
par·a·lyze
pa·ram·e·ter
par·a·mount
par·amour
para·noia
para·noid
par·a·pet
par·a·pher·na·lia
para·phrase
para·ple·gic
par·a·site
para·sol
para·troop·er
par·boil
par·cel
parch
Par·chee·si
parch·ment
par·don·able
pare (shave off; see *pear,
    pair*)
pa·ren·tal
pa·ren·the·sis (–ses)
par·en·thet·i·cal·ly
pa·ri·etal
pa·rish·io·ner
par·i·ty (–ties)
par·ka
park·way
par·lay (two or more bets
    in advance; see *parley*)
par·ley (conference; see
    parlay)
par·lia·ment
par·lia·men·ta·ry
par·lor
par·mi·gia·na, par·mi·gia·no
pa·ro·chi·al
par·o·dy (–dies)
pa·role
par·ox·ysm
par·quet (French: type of
    flooring)
par·ri·cide

par·rot
par·ry
parse
par·si·mo·ni·ous
pars·ley
pars·nip
par·son·age
par·terre
par·tial
par·tic·i·pate
par·ti·cip·i·al
par·ti·ci·ple
par·ti·cle
par·tic·u·lar·ly
par·ti·san, par·ti·zan
par·ti·tion
par·ti·tive
part·ner
par·tridge
par·ve·nu (French: one
   with new wealth, lacking
   social standing)
pas·chal
pass·able
pas·sage
pas·sé (French: behind the
   times)
pas·sen·ger
pass·er·by (pass·ers·by)
pas·sion·ate
pas·sive
pass·port
past
paste
pas·tel
pas·teur·ize
pas·tille, pas·til
pas·time
pas·to·ral
past·ry (pastries)
pas·tur·age
pas·ty (pasties)
patch·work
patchy
pâ·té de foie gras (pâ·tés de
   foie gras)
pat·en
pat·ent
pa·ter·nal·ism
pa·ter·ni·ty

pa·ter·nos·ter
pa·thet·ic
pa·thol·o·gy (–gies)
pa·thos
path·way
pa·tience
pa·tient
pa·ti·na (–nas or –nae)
pa·tio
pa·tois (plural also pa·tois)
pa·tri·arch
pa·tri·cian
pat·ri·cide
pat·ri·mo·ny
pa·tri·ot·ic
pa·trol
pa·tron
pa·tron·age
pat·ro·nym·ic
pat·ter
pat·tern
pau·ci·ty
paunch
pau·per
pause
pave·ment
pa·vil·ion
pawn
pay·able
peace (state of tranquillity;
   see *piece*)
peace·ful
peachy
pea·cock
peak (sharp or pointed end;
   see *peek, pique*)
peal (loud ringing of bells;
   see *peel*)
pea·nut
pear (fruit; see *pair, pare*)
pearl
peas·ant·ry
peb·ble
pe·can
pec·ca·dil·lo
pec·to·ral
pe·cu·liar·i·ty (–ties)
pe·cu·ni·ary
ped·a·gogue, ped·a·gog
ped·a·go·gy

ped·al (foot lever; see
   peddle)
pe·dan·tic
ped·dle (travel with wares
   to sell; see *pedal*)
ped·es·tal
pe·des·tri·an
pe·di·a·tri·cian
pe·di·at·rics
ped·i·cure
ped·i·gree
ped·i·ment
pe·dom·e·ter
peek (look furtively; see
   peak, pique)
peel (strip off; see *peal*)
peer (equal; see *pier*)
peer·age
pee·vish
pei·gnoir
pe·jo·ra·tive
pe·koe
pe·lag·ic
pel·i·can
pel·let
pell-mell
pel·vic
pel·vis (pel·vis·es or
   pel·ves)
pe·nal·ize
pen·al·ty (–ties)
pen·ance
pen·chant
pen·ciled
pen·dant, pen·dent
pen·du·lous
pen·du·lum
pen·e·trate
pen·guin
pen·i·cil·lin
pen·in·su·la
pen·i·tence
pen·i·ten·tial
pen·i·ten·tia·ry (–ries)
pen·man·ship
pen·nant
pen·ni·less
pe·nol·o·gy
pen·sion
pen·ta·gon

pen·tam·e·ter
Pen·ta·teuch
pen·tath·lon
pent·house
pen·ul·ti·mate
pe·nu·ri·ous
pe·on (landless laborer; see
   paean, paeon)
pe·on·age
pe·o·ny (–nies)
peo·ple (peo·ple *or*
   peo·ples)
pep·per
per·ad·ven·ture
per·am·bu·late
per an·num
per·cale
per cap·i·ta
per·ceive
per·cent
per·cent·age
per·cen·tile
per·cept
per·cep·ti·ble
per·cep·tive
per·cep·tu·al
perch
per·chance
per·cip·i·ent
per·co·late
per·co·la·tor
per·cus·sion
per di·em
per·di·tion
per·e·gri·nate
pe·remp·to·ry
pe·ren·ni·al
per·fect (adjective),
   per·fect (verb)
per·fec·ta
per·fid·i·ous
per·fi·dy
per·fo·rate
per·force
per·for·mance
per·fume (noun), per·fume
   (verb)
per·func·to·ry
per·go·la
per·haps

per·i·gee
per·il·ous
pe·rim·e·ter
pe·ri·od·ic
peri·pa·tet·ic
pe·riph·ery (–er·ies)
peri·scope
per·ish·able
peri·to·ni·tis
per·i·win·kle
per·jure
per·ju·ry
per·ma·frost
per·ma·nent
per·me·able
per·me·ate
per·mis·si·ble
per·mis·sion
per·mit·ted
per·mu·ta·tion
per·ni·cious
per·ora·tion
per·ox·ide
per·pen·dic·u·lar
per·pe·tra·tor
per·pet·u·al
per·pe·tu·ity (–ities)
per·plex
per·qui·site
per·se·cu·tion
per·se·ver·ance
per·sis·tence
per·snick·e·ty
per·son·able
per·son·age
per·son·al (private, relating
   to a person; see
   personnel)
per·son·al·i·ty (–ties)
per·so·na non gra·ta (Latin:
   being unwelcome)
per·son·i·fi·ca·tion
per·son·nel (body of
   employees; see *personal*)
per·spec·tive
per·spi·ca·cious
per·spic·u·ous
per·spi·ra·tion
per·sua·sion
per·tain

per·ti·na·cious
per·ti·nent
per·tur·ba·tion
pe·ruse
per·vade
per·verse
per·vert (noun), per·vert
   (verb)
pes·si·mism
pes·ter
pes·tif·er·ous
pes·ti·lence
pes·tle
pet·al
pe·tard
pet·cock
pe·tit four (pe·tits fours *or*
   pe·tit fours) (French:
   small cake)
pe·ti·tion
pet·it jury
pe·tit mal
pet·it point
pe·trel (sea bird; se *petrol*)
pet·ri·fy
pet·rol (gasoline; see
   petrel)
pe·tro·leum
pet·ti·coat
pet·ti·fog·ger
pet·ti·ness (–ness·es)
pet·ty
pet·u·lant
pe·tu·nia
pew·ter
pha·lanx (pha·lanx·es *or*
   pha·lan·ges)
phan·tasm, fan·tasm
phan·tas·ma·go·ria
phan·tom
phar·i·sa·ical
phar·ma·ceu·ti·cal
phar·ma·cist
phar·ma·cy (–cies)
phar·ynx (pha·rynx·es *or*
   pha·ryn·ges)
phase
pheas·ant
phe·nom·e·nal
phi·lan·der·er

phi·lan·thro·py (–pies)
phi·lat·e·list
phi·lip·pic
philo·den·dron
phi·lol·o·gy
phi·los·o·pher
phlegm
phleg·mat·ic
pho·bia
phoe·be
phoe·nix
pho·nate
pho·net·ics
pho·nics
pho·no·graph
phony, phoney (phonies)
phos·phate
phos·pho·res·cent
pho·to·copy (–cop·ies)
pho·to·elec·tric
pho·to·graph·ic
pho·to·stat
phot·to·syn·the·sis
phrase
phrase·ol·o·gy (–gies)
phre·net·ic, fre·net·ic
phre·nol·o·gy
phys·i·cal
phy·si·cian
phys·i·cist
phys·ics
phys·i·ol·o·gy
phys·io·ther·a·py
phy·sique
pi·a·nist
pi·az·za
pi·ca
pic·a·dor (picadors or –es)
pic·ca·resque
pic·ca·lil·li
pic·co·lo
pick·a·back, pig·gy·back
pick·er·el
pick·et
pick·le
pic·nic
pic·nicked
pic·to·graph
pic·to·ri·al
pic·ture (painting, drawing

or photograph; see
    pitcher)
pic·tur·esque
pid·dle
pid·gin (simplified speech;
    see *pigeon*)
pie·bald
piece (part of a whole; see
    peace)
pièce de ré·sis·tance
    (pièces de ré·sis·tance)
    (French: outstanding
    item)
pier (dock; see *peer*)
pierce
pi·ety (pi·eties)
pi·geon (bird; see *pidgin*)
pig·ment
pil·fer
pil·grim·age
pil ing
pil·lage
pil·lar
pil·low
pi·lot
pi·men·to
pim·ple
pin·afore
pince-nez (plural also
    pince-nez) (French:
    eyeglasses without
    sidepieces, clipped to
    nose)
pin·cer
pin·cush·ion
pine·ap·ple
pin·na·cle
pi·noch·le
pi·o·neer
pi·ous
pipe
pip·ing
pi·quant (French:
    charming)
pique (to wound vanity; see
    peak, peek)
pi·ra·cy (–cies)
pir·ou·ette (French: ballet
    turn)
pis·ca·to·ry

pis·ta·chio
pis·til (plant organ; see
    pistol)
pis·tol (gun; see *pistil*)
pitch·er (container for
    liquids; see *picture*)
pitch·fork
pit·e·ous
pit·fall
pithy
piti·able
piti·ful
piti·less
pi·ton
pit·tance
piv·ot·al
pix·ie, pixy (pix·ies)
pix·i·lat·ed
piz·ze·ria
plac·ard
pla·cate
pla·ce·bo
place·ment
plac·id
plack·et
pla·gia·rize
plague
plaid
plain (level country;
    lacking ornament; see
    plane)
plain·tiff
plait
plane (tool; geometric
    surface; see *plain*)
plan·et
plan·e·tar·i·um
plan·tain
plan·ta·tion
plaque
plas·ma
plas·ter
plas·tic
plas·ti·cize
pla·teau
plat·en
plat·form
plat·i·num
plat·i·tude
pla·ton·ic

pla·toon
plat·ter
plau·dit
plau·si·ble
play·go·er
play·mate
play·wright
pla·za
plead
pleas·ant·ry (–ries)
plea·sure
pleat
plebe
ple·be·ian
pleb·i·scite
pledge
ple·na·ry
pleni·po·ten·tia·ry (–ries)
plen·te·ous
plen·ti·ful
ple·o·nas·tic
pleu·ri·sy
pli·able
pli·ers
plight
plim·soll
plo·ver
plow, plough
plow·share
plum·age
plumb·er
plume
plum·met
plump
plun·der
plunge
plu·per·fect
plu·ral
plu·ral·i·ty (–ties)
plu·toc·ra·cy (–cies)
plu·to·ni·um
ply·wood
pneu·mat·ic
pneu·mo·nia
poach·er
pock·et·book
po·di·a·trist
po·di·um
po·em
po·et·i·cal

po·grom
poi·gnan·cy (–cies)
poi·gnant
poin·set·tia
point
poi·son·ous
po·lar·i·ty (–ties)
po·lar·ize
pole (long slender object;
    see *poll*)
po·lem·ic
po·lice (plural also po·lice)
pol·i·cy (–cies)
po·lio
pol·ish
po·lit·bu·ro
po·lit·i·cal
pol·i·ti·cian
pol·i·tics
pol·ka
poll (receive and record
    votes; see *pole*)
pol·len
pol·li·nate
pol·lu·tion
pol·troon
poly·clin·ic
poly·es·ter
po·lyg·a·my
poly·glot
poly·gon
pol·yp
poly·tech·nic
pome·gran·ate
pom·mel
pom·pon
pom·pos·i·ty (–ties)
pomp·ous
pon·cho
pon·der
pon·gee
pon·tiff
pon·tif·i·cal
pon·toon
po·ny·tail
poo·dle
pop·corn
pop·lar (tree; see *popular*)
pop·lin
pop·py (pop·pies)

pop·u·lace
pop·u·lar (commonly liked;
    see *poplar*)
pop·u·la·tion
pop·u·list
por·ce·lain
por·cu·pine
por·nog·ra·phy
po·ros·i·ty (–ties)
po·rous
por·poise
por·ridge
por·ta·ble
por·tend
por·tent
por·ten·tous
por·ter·house
port·fo·lio
por·ti·co (–coes *or* –cos)
por·tiere
por·tion
por·trait
por·tray
pos·it
po·si·tion
pos·i·tive·ly
pos·se
pos·sess·or
pos·ses·sion
pos·si·bil·i·ty (–ties)
post·age
pos·te·ri·or
pos·ter·i·ty
post·hu·mous
post·mor·tem
post·pone
post·script
pos·tu·late
pos·tur·ing
po·ta·ble
po·tage, pot·tage
po·ta·to (–toes)
po·ten·cy (–cies)
po·tent
po·ten·tate
po·ten·tial
po·tion
pot·pour·ri
pot·shot
pot·tery (–ter·ies)

poul·tice
poul·try
pounce
pound
pov·er·ty
pow·der
pow·er·ful
prac·ti·ca·ble
prac·ti·cal
prac·tice, prac·tise
prac·ti·tio·ner
prag·mat·ic
prai·rie
prate
prat·tle
prax·is (prax·es)
prayer·ful
preach
preachy
pre·am·ble
pre·ar·range
pre·car·i·ous
pre·cau·tion
pre·cede
pre·ce·dence
pre·ce·dent (noun),
   pre·ce·dent (adjective)
pre·cept
pre·cinct
pre·ci·os·i·ty (–ties)
pre·cious
prec·i·pice
pre·cip·i·tate
pré·cis
pre·cise
pre·ci·sion
pre·clude
pre·co·cious
pre·con·ceive
pre·con·cep·tion
pre·con·di·tion
pre·cur·sor
pred·a·tor
pre·dawn
pre·de·cease
pre·des·ti·na·tion
pre·de·ter·mine
pre·dic·a·ment
pred·i·cate
pre·dict

pre·di·lec·tion
pre·dis·pose
pre·doc·tor·al
pre·dom·i·nant
pre·em·i·nence
pre·empt
preen
pre·ex·is·tence
pre·fab·ri·cate
pref·ace
pref·a·to·ry
pre·fect
pre·fec·ture
pre·fer
pref·er·a·ble
pref·er·ence
pre·fig·ure
preg·na·ble
preg·nan·cy (–cies)
preg·nant
pre·heat
pre·hen·sile
pre·his·tor·ic
pre·in·duc·tion
prej·u·dice
prel·ate
pre·lim·i·nary (–nar·ies)
pre·lude
pre·mar·i·tal
pre·ma·ture
pre·med·i·cal
pre·med·i·tate
pre·mier (prime minister;
   see *premiere*)
pre·miere (first public
   performance; see
   premier)
pre·mise
pre·mi·um
pre·mo·ni·tion
pre·mon·i·to·ry
pre·oc·cu·pa·tion
prep·a·ra·tion
pre·pa·ra·to·ry
pre·pared·ness
pre·pon·der·ance
prep·o·si·tion
pre·pos·sess
pre·pos·ter·ous
pre·po·tent

pre·pran·di·al
pre·req·ui·site
pre·rog·a·tive
pres·age
pre·sanc·ti·fied
pres·by·ter
pre·scind
pre·scribe
pre·scrip·tion
pre·sent·able
pre·sen·ta·tion
pre·sent·ly
pres·er·va·tion·ist
pre·ser·va·tive
pre·shrunk
pres·i·den·cy (–cies)
pre·sid·i·um
pres·sure
pres·sur·ize
pres·tige
pres·ti·gious
pre·sume
pre·sump·tion
pre·sump·tu·ous
pre·tend·er
pre·ten·sion
pre·ten·tious
pre·ter·nat·u·ral
pre·test
pre·text
pret·ti·fy
pret·ti·ness
pret·ty
pret·zel
pre·vail
prev·a·lent
pre·var·i·cate
pre·vent·able
pre·view
pre·vi·ous
prey
prick·ly
priest·ly
prig·gish
pri·ma ballerina
pri·ma·cy
pri·ma don·na
pri·ma fa·cie
pri·mar·i·ly
pri·mate

prime
prim·er
pri·me·val
prim·ing
prim·i·tive
pri·mo·gen·i·ture
pri·mor·di·al
prim·rose
prince·ly
prin·ci·pal (head of school;
   see *principle*)
prin·ci·ple (fundamental
   law; see *principal*)
print·able
pri·or
prism
pris·mat·ic
pris·on·er
pris·tine
pri·va·cy (–cies)
pri·vate
pri·va·tion
priv·et
priv·i·lege
prize
prob·a·bil·i·ty (–ties)
prob·a·ble
pro·bate
pro·ba·tion·er
pro·ba·tive
pro·bi·ty
prob·lem·at·ic
pro·bos·cis (pro·bos·cises
   or pro·bos·ci·des)
pro·ca·the·dral
pro·ce·dur·al
pro·ce·dure
pro·ceed
pro·cess (pro·cess·es)
pro·ces·sion
pro·claim
proc·la·ma·tion
pro·cliv·i·ty (–ties)
pro·cras·ti·nate
pro·cre·ate
pro·crus·te·an
proc·tor
proc·u·ra·tor
pro·cure·ment
prod·i·gal

pro·di·gious
prod·i·gy (–gies)
pro·duce (noun), pro·duce
   (verb)
pro·duc·tion
pro·fan·i·ty (–ties)
pro·fes·sion
pro·fes·sor
pro·fi·cien·cy (–cies)
pro·file
prof·it (gain; see *prophet*)
prof·li·ga·cy (–cies)
pro·found
pro·fun·di·ty (–ties)
pro·fuse·ly
pro·gen·i·tor
prog·e·ny (–nies)
prog·no·sis
prog·nos·tic
prog·nos·ti·cate
pro·gram, pro·gramme
pro·gres·sion
pro·gres·sive
pro·hib·it
pro·hi·bi·tion
proj·ect (noun), pro·ject
   (verb)
pro·jec·tile
pro·jec·tion
pro·le·gom·e·non (–na)
pro·le·tar·i·at
pro·lif·er·ate
pro·lif·ic
pro·lix
pro·logue, pro·log
pro·long
prom·e·nade
prom·i·nence
pro·mis·cu·ity (–ities)
prom·is·ing
prom·is·so·ry (–ries)
prom·on·to·ry (–ries)
pro·mot·er
pro·mo·tion
prompt·ness
pro·mul·gate
pro·nate
pro·noun
pro·nounce·ment
pro·nun·ci·a·tion

pro·pae·deu·tic
pro·pa·gan·da
prop·a·gate
pro·pane
pro·pel
pro·pen·si·ty (–ties)
prop·er·ly
prop·er·ty (–ties)
proph·e·cy (–cies) (inspired
   declaration; see
   prophesy)
proph·e·sy (to predict; see
   prophecy)
prophet (one who foretells
   the future; see *profit*)
pro·phet·ic
pro·phy·lac·tic
pro·pin·qui·ty
pro·pi·ti·ate
pro·pi·tious
pro·por·tion
pro·pose
prop·o·si·tion
pro·pri·etary (–etar·ies)
pro·pri·etor
pro·pul·sion
pro·rate
pro·sa·ic
pro·sce·ni·um
pro·scribe
pro·scrip·tion
pros·e·cute
pros·e·cu·tor
pros·e·lyte
pros·e·ly·tize
pro·sit, prost
pros·o·dy (–dies)
pro·spec·tive
pro·spec·tus
pros·tate (gland; see
   prostrate)
pros·ti·tute
pros·trate (prone; see
   prostate)
pro·tag·o·nist
pro·te·an
pro·tec·tive·ly
pro·tec·tion
pro·té·gé
pro·tein

pro·tem·po·re (Latin: for
   the present)
pro·test·er, pro·test·or
prot·es·tant
pro·tes·ta·tion
pro·tho·no·ta·ry (–ries)
pro·to·col
pro·ton
pro·to·type
pro·to·zo·an
pro·trac·tor
pro·trude
pro·tru·sion
pro·tu·ber·ant
prove
prov·en·der
pro·ver·bi·al
prov·i·dence
prov·i·den·tial
pro·vin·cial
pro·vi·sion·al
pro·vi·so
prov·o·ca·tion
pro·voc·a·tive
pro·vo·lo·ne (Italian: a kind
   of cheese)
pro·vost
prow·ess
prowl
prox·i·mate
prox·im·i·ty
proxy (prox·ies)
pru·dence
pru·ri·ence
pry·ing
psalm·ist
psal·tery, psal·try
   (psal·ter·ies *or* psal·tries)
pseud·onym
psy·che·del·ic
psy·chi·a·try
psy·chic
psy·cho·anal·y·sis
psy·cho·log·i·cal
psy·chol·o·gist
psy·cho·path
psy·cho·so·mat·ics
psy·cho·ther·a·py
ptar·mi·gan

pto·maine
pu·ber·ty
pu·bes·cent
pu·bic
pub·lic
pub·li·can
pub·lic·i·ty
pub·lic·ly
pub·lish·er
puck·er
pud·ding
pud·dle
pueb·lo (Spanish: village)
pu·er·ile
pu·gi·lism
pu·gi·list
pug·na·cious
puis·sance
pul·chri·tude
pul·let
pul·ley
pul·mo·nary
pul·mo·tor
pulp
pul·pit
pul·sar
pul·sate
pulse
pul·ver·ize
pu·ma
pum·ice
pum·mel
pump·er
pum·per·nick·el
pump·kin
punch
punc·til·io
punc·til·i·ous
punc·tu·al
punc·tu·ate
punc·tu·a·tion
punc·ture
pun·dit
pun·gen·cy
pun·gent
pun·ish·able
pu·ni·tive
pun·ster
punt·er

pup·pet
pup·pe·teer
pup·py·ish
pur·chase
pur·dah
pu·rée (French: to strain
   cooked food)
pur·ga·tive
pur·ga·to·ri·al
pur·ga·to·ry (–ries)
purge
pu·ri·fi·ca·tion
pu·ri·fy
pur·ist
pu·ri·tan·i·cal
pur·lieu (French:
   neighborhood)
pur·loin
pur·ple
pur·port
pur·pose
pur·pose·ly
pur·su·ance
pur·sue
pur·suit
pur·vey·or
pur·view
pushy
pu·sil·lan·i·mous
pussy·foot
pus·tu·lar
pus·tule
pu·ta·tive
pu·tre·fac·tion
pu·tre·fy
pu·trid
put·ter
put·ty (putties)
puz·zling
pyg·my (pygmies)
py·lon
py·or·rhea
pyr·a·mid
pyre
py·ro·tech·nics
pyr·rhic
py·thon
pyx
pyx·ie

Q

quack·ery
quad·ran·gle
quad·rant
qua·dren·ni·al
quad·ri·lat·er·al
qua·drille (French: a type
   of square dance)
qua·driv·i·um
qua·droon
quad·ru·ped
qua·dru·ple
quaff
quag·mire
quail
quaint·ly
quake
qual·i·fi·ca·tion
qual·i·fied
qual·i·fy
qual·i·ta·tive
qual·i·ty (–ties)
qualm
qualm·ish
quan·da·ry (–ries)
quan·ti·fy
quan·ti·ta·tive
quan·ti·ty (–ties)
quan·tum (–ta)
quar·an·tine
quar·rel
quar·rel·some

quar·ry (quar·ries)
quar·ter
quar·ter·back
quar·tet, quar·tette
quar·to
quartz
qua·sar
quash
qua·train
qua·ver
quay
quea·sy, quea·zy
queen
queen-size
queer
quell
quench
quer·u·lous
que·ry (que·ries)
quest
ques·tion
ques·tion·able
ques·tion·naire
queue
quib·ble
quick·en
qui·es·cence
qui·et (free from noise; see
   quite)
qui·etude

qui·etus
quilt
quince
qui·nine
quin·tes·sence
quin·tet, quin·tette
quin·tile
quin·tu·plet
quip
quire (24 sheets of paper;
   variation of *choir*; see
   choir)
quirk
quirky
quis·ling
quit
quite (completely; see
   quiet)
quit·tance
quit·ter
quiv·er
quix·ot·ic
quiz (quiz·zes)
quiz·zi·cal
Quon·set
quo·rum
quo·ta
quot·able
quo·ta·tion
quote
quo·tient

rab·bi
rab·bin·ate
rab·bin·i·cal, rab·bin·ic
rab·bit (rab·bit *or* rab·bits)
rabble
ra·bid
ra·bies (plural also ra·bies)
rac·coon (rac·coon *or*
   rac·coons)
race·way
ra·cial
rac·ism
rack·et, rac·quet
ra·con·teur (French:
   storyteller)
racy
ra·dar
ra·di·al
ra·di·ance
ra·di·ate
ra·di·a·tor
rad·i·cal
rad·i·cal·ly
ra·dio·ac·tive
rad·ish
ra·di·um
ra·di·us (ra·di·us·es *or*
   ra·dii)
raff·ish
raf·fle
raf·ter
rag·a·muf·fin
rag·ged
rag·gle-tag·gle
rag·ing
rag·lan
ra·gout
raid·er
rail·lery (−ler·ies)
rail·road
rai·ment
rain (water falling in drops
   from the atmosphere; see
   reign, rein)
rain·bow
rainy
raise (to lift; see *raze*)
rai·sin
rai·son d'être (French:
   reason for existence)

ra·ja, ra·jah (Sanskrit: type
   of nobility)
rak·ish
ral·ly (rallies)
ram·ble
ram·bunc·tious
ram·i·fi·ca·tion
ram·i·fy
ram·page
ram·pant
ram·part
ram·rod
ram·shack·le
ran·cor·ous
ran·dom
rang·er
ran·kle
ran·sack
ran·som
ra·pa·cious
ra·pac·i·ty
ra·pid
ra·pi·er
rap·ine
rap·port
rar·efy
rar·i·ty (−ties)
ras·cal·i·ty (−ties)
rasp·ber·ry
raspy
ratch·et
rate
rat·i·fy
ra·tio
ra·tion
ra·tio·nal (relating to
   reason; see *rationale*)
ra·tio·nale (underlying
   reason; see *rational*)
ra·tio·nal·ize
rat·tan
rat·tle
rau·cous
raun·chy
rav·age
rav·en·ous
ra·vine
rav·i·o·li
ray·on

raze (destroy to the
   ground; see *raise*)
raz·zle-daz·zle
razz·ma·tazz
reach·able
re·ac·tion
re·ac·tion·ary
re·ac·ti·vate
re·ac·tor
read·able
readi·ly
ready-to-wear
re·align
re·al·is·tic
re·al·iza·tion
re·al·ly
realm
re·al·ty
ream
re·ap·por·tion
re·arm
rea·son·able
re·as·sur·ance
re·bate
re·bel·lious
re·bound
re·buff
re·buke
re·bus
re·but·tal
re·cal·ci·trance
re·ca·pit·u·late
re·cede
re·ceipt
re·ceiv·able
re·ceiv·er
re·cent·ly
re·cep·ta·cle
re·cep·tion·ist
re·cep·tive
re·cess
re·ces·sion
re·cid·i·vist
re·cip·ro·cate
rec·i·proc·i·ty (−ties)
re·cit·al
rec·i·ta·tive
reck·oned
rec·la·ma·tion
re·cluse

R

rec·og·ni·tion
re·cog·ni·zance
re·col·lect
rec·om·men·da·tion
rec·om·pense
rec·on·cil·able
re·con·dite
re·con·nais·sance
re·con·noi·ter
re·con·sti·tute
re·con·struc·tion
re·con·vert
re·cord·er
re·coup
re·course
re·cov·er·able
rec·re·ant
rec·re·a·tion
re·crim·i·nate
re·cru·des·cence
re·cruit
rect·an·gu·lar
rec·ti·fy
rec·ti·lin·ear
rec·ti·tude
rec·tor
re·cum·bent
re·cu·per·ate
re·cur·rent
re·cy·cle
re·dac·tion
red·den
re·deem·er
re·demp·tive
re·de·sign
re·dis·trict
red·o·lent
re·dou·ble
re·dound
red tape
re·duc·ible
re·duc·tion
re·dun·dan·cy (–cies)
re·elec·tion
re·en·act
re·en·try
re·fec·to·ry (–ries)
re·fer·able
ref·er·ee
ref·er·ence

ref·er·en·dum
re·fer·ral
re·fi·nance
re·fine·ment
re·flec·tion
re·flec·tor
re·flex
ref·or·ma·tion
re·for·ma·to·ry (–ries)
re·frac·to·ry (–ries)
re·frain
re·fresh·ment
re·frig·er·a·tor
ref·u·gee
re·fund (noun), re·fund
   (verb)
re·fur·bish
re·fus·al
ref·u·ta·tion
re·gal (royal; see *regale*)
re·gale (to give pleasure;
   see *regal*)
re·ga·lia
re·gard·less
re·gat·ta
re·gen·cy (–cies)
re·gen·er·ate
re·gent
re·gime, ré·gime
reg·i·men (systematic plan;
   see *regiment*)
reg·i·ment (military unit;
   see *regimen*)
re·gion·al
reg·is·ter (to enroll
   formally; see *registrar*)
reg·is·trar (keeper of
   records; see *register*)
reg·is·try (–tries)
re·gres·sion
re·gres·sive
re·gret·ta·bly
reg·u·lar·i·ty (–ties)
reg·u·la·to·ry
re·gur·gi·tate
re·ha·bil·i·tate
re·hears·al
reign (sovereignty; see
   rain, rein)
re·im·burse

rein (part of a bridle; stop
   or check; see *rain, reign*)
rein·deer
re·in·force
re·in·vest·ment
re·is·sue
re·it·er·ate
re·jec·tion
re·join·der
re·ju·ve·nate
re·lapse
re·la·tion
rel·a·tive
rel·a·tiv·i·ty (–ties)
re·lax·ation
re·lease
rel·e·gate
re·lent·less
rel·e·van·cy
re·li·abil·i·ty
re·li·ance
rel·ic
re·lief
re·lieve
re·luc·tant
re·lied
re·lo·cate
re·main·der
re·mark·able
re·me·di·a·ble
re·me·di·al
rem·e·dy (–dies)
re·mem·brance
rem·i·nis·cence
re·mis·sion
re·mit·tance
rem·nant
re·mon·strate
re·morse·ful
re·mote
re·mov·able
re·mu·ner·ate
re·nais·sance, re·na·scence
ren·der
ren·dez·vous
ren·di·tion
ren·e·gade
re·nege
re·ne·go·ti·ate
re·new·al

re·nounce
ren·o·vate
rent·al
re·nun·ci·a·tion
re·open
re·or·ga·ni·za·tion
re·pair·able
rep·a·ra·tion
rep·ar·tee
re·pa·tri·ate
re·peal
re·peat·ed·ly
re·pel·lent, re·pel·lant
re·pen·tance
re·per·cus·sion
rep·er·toire
rep·er·to·ry (–ries)
rep·e·ti·tious
re·place·able
re·plen·ish
re·plete
rep·li·ca
rep·li·cate
re·port·able
re·pose
re·pos·i·to·ry (–ries)
re·pos·sess
rep·re·hend
rep·re·hen·si·ble
rep·re·sen·ta·tive
re·pres·sion
re·prieve
re·pri·sal
re·prise
re·proach
rep·ro·bate
re·pro·duc·tion
rep·tile
re·pub·lic
re·pu·di·ate
re·pug·nance
re·pul·sive
rep·u·ta·ble
re·pute
re·quest
re·qui·em
re·quire·ment
req·ui·site
req·ui·si·tion
re·scind

res·cue
re·search
re·sem·blance
re·sent·ful
res·er·va·tion
res·er·voir
re·shuf·fle
res·i·dence
res·i·den·tial
re·sid·u·al
res·i·due
res·ig·na·tion
re·sil·ience
res·in·ous
re·sis·tance
re·sist·er (one who
    opposes; see *resistor*)
re·sis·tor (electrical device;
    see *resister*)
res·o·lute
re·solve
res·o·nance
res·o·na·tor
re·sound
re·source·ful
re·spect·abil·i·ty (–ties)
re·spec·tive·ly
res·pi·ra·tion
res·pi·ra·tor
re·splen·dent
re·spon·dent
re·spon·si·bil·i·ty (–ties)
re·spon·sive
re·spon·so·ry (–ries)
re·state·ment
res·tau·rant
res·ti·tu·tion
res·tive
res·to·ra·tion
re·strain
re·stric·tion
re·struc·ture
re·sult
re·sume (to begin again;
    see *resumé*)
re·su·mé (short account of
    career; see *resume*)
re·sump·tion
re·sur·gence
res·ur·rec·tion

re·sus·ci·tate
re·tail·ing
re·tain·er
re·tal·i·ate
re·tar·da·tion
re·ten·tive
ret·i·cence
ret·i·cule
ret·i·nue
re·tire·ment
re·tract
re·trench
ret·ri·bu·tion
re·triev·al
ret·ro·ac·tive
ret·ro·grade
ret·ro·gress
re·tro·spect
re·turn·able
re·unite
re·us·able
re·veal
rev·eil·le
rev·e·la·tion
rev·el·er, rev·el·ler
rev·el·ry (–ries)
re·venge·ful
rev·e·nue
re·ver·ber·ate
rev·er·ence
rev·er·en·tial
rev·er·ie, rev·ery
    (rev·er·ies)
re·ver·sal
re·vers·ible
re·vert·ible
re·view (to see again; see
    revue)
re·vile
re·vi·sion
re·vi·tal·ize
re·viv·al
re·vive
re·vo·ca·ble
re·voke
re·volt
rev·o·lu·tion
rev·o·lu·tion·ize
re·volv·er

re·vue (theatrical
  production; see *review*)
re·vul·sion
re·ward
re·write
rhap·so·dy (–dies)
rheo·stat
rhet·o·ric
rheu·mat·ic
rhi·noc·er·os
  (rhi·noc·er·os·es *or*
  rhi·noc·eros *or*
  rhi·noc·eri)
rhu·barb
rhyme
rhythm
rib·ald
rib·bon
rice
rick·ety
rid·dance
rid·dle
ridge
ri·dic·u·lous
ri·fle
rift
rig·ging
right (correct; see *rite*)
righ·teous
ri·gid·i·ty (–ties)
rig·ma·role
rig·or·ous
ring·er
rins·ing
ri·ot·ous
ri·par·i·an
rip·ple
ris·i·ble
risky
ris·qué (French: off-color)
rite (a ceremonial act; see
  right)
rit·u·al

ri·val·ry (–ries)
riv·er·side
riv·et
roach
road
roam
roan
roast
rob·bery (rob·ber·ies)
ro·bot
ro·bust
rock·et
ro·co·co
ro·dent
ro·deo (ro·de·os)
rogue
rogu·ish
rol·lick·ing
ro·man·ti·cize
ron·deau (ron·deaux)
rook·ery (rook·er·ies)
roomy
roost·er
root·less·ness
ro·sa·ry (–ries)
ro·se·ate
ro·sette
Rosh Ha·sha·nah
ros·i·ly
ros·ter
ros·trum
ro·ta·ry (–ries)
ro·ta·tion
rote
ro·tund
ro·tun·da
roué (French: man devoted
  to sensual pleasures)
rouge
rough
rou·lette
round·about

rouse
roust·about
rout (disorderly retreat; see
  route)
route (line of travel; see
  rout)
rou·tine
rou·tin·ize
rov·ing
row·dy
roy·al·ist
roy·al·ty (–ties)
rub·bery
rub·bish
rub·ble
ru·bi·cund
ru·bric
ruck·sack
rud·der
ru·di·men·ta·ry
ruf·fi·an
ruf·fle
rug·by
rug·ged
ru·in·ous
rul·ing
rum·ba
rum·ble
ru·mi·nate
rum·mage
ru·mor
run·ner
rup·ture
ru·ral
ruse
rus·set
rus·tic
rus·ti·cate
rust·i·ness
rus·tle
ru·ta·ba·ga
ruth·less
rye

S

sab·bat·i·cal
sa·ber, sa·bre
sa·ble
sab·o·tage
sab·o·teur
sac·cha·rine
sac·er·do·tal
sa·chem
sa·chet
sac·ra·ment
sa·cred
sac·ri·fice
sac·ri·fi·cial
sac·ri·lege
sac·ris·tan
sac·ris·ty (–ties)
sa·cro·il·i·ac
sac·ro·sanct
sad·den
sad·dle
sa·dism
sa·fa·ri
safe·ty (safeties)
saf·flow·er
sa·ga
sa·ga·cious
sage
sail (canvas used to propel
    ship; see *sale*)
sail·or
sal·able, sale·able
sal·ad
sal·a·ry (–ries)
sale (act of selling; see *sail*)
sales check
sales·clerk
sales tax
sa·lient
sa·line
sa·li·va
sal·i·vate
sal·low
salm·on (sal·mon *or*
    sal·mons)
sa·lon (elegant living room;
    see *saloon*)
sa·loon (place selling
    alcoholic drinks; see
    salon)
sal·ta·to·ry

sa·lu·bri·ous
sal·u·tary
sa·lu·ta·to·ri·an
sa·lute
sal·vage
sal·va·tion
salve
sam·o·var (Russian: an urn
    used to boil water for
    tea)
sam·ple
san·a·to·ri·um
sanc·ti·fi·ca·tion
sanc·ti·mo·nious
sanc·tion
sanc·tu·ary (–ar·ies)
san·dal
sand·wich (–es)
sane
san·guine
san·i·tary
san·i·ta·tion
sap·ling
sap·phire
sar·casm
sar·coph·a·gous,
    sar·co·phag·ic
sar·dine (sar·dines *or*
    sar·dine)
sar·don·ic
sard·onyx
sa·ri, sa·ree (Sanskrit:
    woman's Hindu garment)
sar·sa·pa·ril·la
sar·to·ri·al
sas·sa·fras
sa·tan·ic
satch·el
sate
sa·teen
sat·el·lite
sa·ti·ate
sa·ti·ety
sat·in
sat·ire
sat·is·fac·tion
sat·u·rate
sat·ur·nine
sa·tyr
saucy

sau·er·kraut
sau·na
saun·ter
sau·sage
sau·té
sau·terne
sav·age·ly
sa·van·na, sa·van·nah
sa·vant
sav·able, save·able
sav·ior, sav·iour
sa·voir faire (French:
    sureness in social
    behavior)
sa·vory, sa·voury
sax·o·phone
scab·bard
sca·brous
scaf·fold
scald·ing
scal·lion
scal·lop
scalp·er
scan·dal
scan·dal·ous
scanty
scape·goat
scap·u·lar
scar·ci·ty (–ties)
scarf
scary, scar·ey
scath·ing
scat·o·log·i·cal
scat·ter
scav·enge
sce·nar·io
sce·nar·ist
scen·ery (–er·ies)
sce·nic
scent·ed
scep·ter, scep·tre
sched·ule
sche·mat·ic
scheme
scher·zo (scher·zos *or*
    scher·zi)
schism
schis·mat·ic
schiz·oid
schizo·phre·nia

schnau·zer

schol·ar·ly

scho·las·tic

school

schoo·ner

schwa

sci·at·ic

sci·en·tif·ic

scin·til·late

sci·on

scis·sors

scle·ro·sis

scoff·law

scone

scope

scorch

scor·ing

scorn·ful

scor·pi·on

scoun·drel

scour

scourge

scram·ble

scrap·ing (grate harshly;
see *scrapping*)

scrap·ping (quarreling,
converting to scrap; see
scraping)

scratch

scraw·ny

scream

screech

screen

screen·play

screen test

screw

scrib·ble

scrim·mage

scrim·shaw

script

scrip·ture

scrof·u·lous

scrounge

scruff

scru·ple

scru·pu·lous

scru·ti·nize

scu·ba

scuff

scuf·fle

sculp·tor

sculp·ture

scur·ri·lous

scut·tle

scythe

sea (body of water; see
see)

seamy

sé·ance (French: a session
to receive spirit
communications)

search

sea·shore

sea·son·al

seat

se·cede

se·ces·sion

se·clu·sion

sec·ond·ary

se·cre·cy (–cies)

sec·re·tar·i·at

sec·re·tary (–tar·ies)

se·crete

se·cre·tive

sect

sec·tar·i·an

sec·tion·al

sec·tor

sec·u·lar

se·cu·ri·ty (–ties)

se·dan

se·date

sed·a·tive

sed·en·tary

se·der

sedge

sed·i·ment

se·di·tion

se·duce

se·duc·tive

sed·u·lous

see (perceive by eye; see
sea)

seed·ling

seem·ing·ly

seep·age

seer·suck·er

see·saw

seethe

seg·ment

seg·re·gate

seg·re·ga·tion

se·gue

seine

seis·mic

seis·mo·graph

seize

sei·zure

sel·dom

se·lec·tion

se·lec·tive

self-con·scious

self-de·fense

self-por·trait

sell (to exact a price for;
see *cell*)

sell·er (one who offers for
sale; see *cellar*)

se·man·tics

sema·phore

sem·blance

se·mes·ter

semi·an·nu·al

sem·i·nal

sem·i·nar

sem·i·nary (–nar·ies)

semi·pro·fes·sion·al

sem·pi·ter·nal

sen·a·to·ri·al

se·nes·cence

se·nile

se·nil·i·ty

se·nior·i·ty

sen·sa·tion

sense

sense·less

sen·si·bil·i·ty (–ties)

sen·si·tive

sen·so·ry

sen·su·al

sen·su·ous

sent (past of *send*; see
cent)

sen·tence

sen·ten·tious

sen·tient

sen·ti·men·tal

sen·ti·nel

sen·try (sentries)

sep·a·ra·ble

sep·a·rate
sep·a·ra·tion
sep·ten·ni·al
sep·tu·a·ge·nar·i·an
sep·ul·cher, sep·ul·chre
se·quel
se·quence
se·quen·tial
se·ques·ter
se·quoia
se·ra·pe (Mexican Spanish:
   type of men's woolen
   shawl)
ser·aph, ser·a·phim
   (ser·aphs *or* ser·a·phim)
ser·e·nade
se·ren·i·ty
serge
ser·geant
se·ri·al (arranged in series;
   see *cereal*)
se·ri·a·tim
se·ries (plural also series)
se·ri·ous
ser·mon
ser·pent
ser·rat·ed
se·rum
ser·vant
ser·vice
ser·vice·able
ser·vi·tude
ses·a·me
ses·qui·cen·ten·ni·al
ses·qui·pe·da·lian
ses·sion
ses·tet
set·tle
set·tle·ment
sev·enth
sev·er·al
sev·er·ance
se·ver·i·ty
sew·age
sew·ing
sex·ism
sex·tant
sex·ton
sex·u·al
sexy

shab·by
shack·le
shad·ing
shad·owy
shaft
shag·gy
shaky
shale
shal·low
sham·ble
shame·ful
sham·poo
sham·rock
shank
shan·ty (shanties)
shape
shard
share·crop·per
shark
sharp·en
shat·ter
shav·ing
sheaf (sheaves)
shear (cut off; see *sheer*)
sheath (case for a blade;
   see *sheathe*)
sheathe (to put into a
   sheath; see *sheath*)
sheer (transparent; see
   shear)
sheet
sheikh, sheik
shelf (shelves)
shel·lac
shel·ter
she·nan·i·gan
shep·herd
sher·bet
sher·iff
sher·ry (sherries)
shib·bo·leth
shield
shifty
shin·gle
shin·ing
shiny
ship·ment
shirk·er
shirr
shirt·sleeve

shish ke·bab
shiv·er
shoal
shock
shoe
shop
shor·ing
short·age
short·en·ing
short·hand
short-term
should
shoul·der
shout
shove
shov·el
show·case
show·er
showy
shrap·nel
shrewd
shriek
shrine
shrink
shriv·el
shroud
shrub·bery
shrug
shud·der
shuf·fle
shut·ter
shut·tle
shy
sib·i·lant
sick·le
sick·ly
sick·ness
side·line
si·de·re·al
siege
sieve
sigh
sight·ly
sign
sig·nal
sig·na·to·ry (–ries)
sig·na·ture
sig·nif·i·cant
si·lent
sil·hou·ette

sil·i·con
silky
silver·ware
sil·very
sim·i·an
sim·i·lar
sim·i·lar·i·ty (–ties)
sim·i·le
si·mil·i·tude
si·mo·ny
sim·per
sim·ple
sim·pli·fy
sim·u·la·tion
si·mul·ta·neous
sin·cere·ly
si·ne·cure
sin·ew
singe
singe·ing
sin·gle
sin·gly
sin·gu·lar·i·ty (–ties)
sin·is·ter
sin·u·ous
si·nus
si·phon
si·ren
sis·ter·ly
site (place; see *cite*)
sit·u·at·ed
sit·u·a·tion
six·ty (sixties)
size
siz·zle
skein, skean, skeane
skel·e·ton
skep·ti·cal
sketchy
skied
ski·ing
skil·let
skill·ful, skil·ful
skim·ming
skimpy
skip·per
skirl
skir·mish
skit·tish

skul·dug·gery, skull
  dug·gery (–ger·ies)
skulk
sky
slack·en
sla·lom
slan·der·ous
slaugh·ter
slav·ery
slea·zy
sledge
sledge·ham·mer
sleek
sleeve
sleigh
slen·der·ize
sleuth
slic·ing
slick·er
slide
slight·ing·ly
slime
slip·pery
slip·shod
slith·er
sliv·er
slob·ber
sloe (fruit; see *slow*)
slo·gan
sloop
slope
slop·ing
slop·py
sloth·ful
slouch
slough
slov·en·ly
slow (not hasty; see *sloe*)
sludge
slug·gish
sluice
slum·ber
slushy
sly
small
smart
smat·ter·ing
smear
smelly

smid·gen, smid·geon,
  smid·gin
smile
smirk
smith·er·eens
smoke
smol·der, smoul·der
smooth
smor·gas·bord
smudge
snail
snake
sneak·er
sneer
sneeze
snif·ter
snip·er
snob·bery
snor·kel
snow·flake
snow·mo·bile
snug·gle
soap opera
soapy
soar·ing
so·ber·ly
so·bri·ety
so·bri·quet
soc·cer
so·cia·bil·i·ty (–ties)
so·cial·ism
so·cial·ize
so·ci·etal
so·ci·ety (–et·ies)
so·cio·eco·nom·ic
so·ci·ol·o·gy
so·da·list
so·dal·i·ty (–ties)
sod·den
soft·ware
sog·gy
soil
soi·rée, soi·ree (French:
  evening party)
so·journ
so·lace
so·lar
sol·der
sol·dier

sole (fish *or* bottom of foot;
   see *soul*)
so·le·cism
sol·emn
so·lem·ni·ty (–ties)
so·le·noid
so·lic·it
so·lic·i·tor
so·lic·i·tous
so·lic·i·tude
sol·i·dar·i·ty
so·lid·i·fy
so·lil·o·quize
sol·i·taire
sol·i·tary
sol·i·tude
so·lo·ist
sol·u·ble
so·lu·tion
solv·able
sol·ven·cy
som·ber, som·bre
som·nam·bu·list
som·no·lent
son (male child; see *sun*)
so·nar
son·ic
son·net
so·no·rous
soothe
sooty
so·phis·ti·cat·ed
soph·ist·ry
soph·o·more
so·po·rif·ic
so·pra·no (–nos)
sor·cer·er
sor·did
so·ror·i·ty (–ties)
sor·row·ful
sor·tie (French: type of
   attack)
soul (spiritual essence; see
   sole)
sought
sound
soup du jour (French: soup
   of the day)
sour

source
south·ern
sou·ve·nir
sov·er·eign, sov·ran
so·vi·et
soy·bean
space
spa·cial
spa·cious
spa·ghet·ti
span·gled
span·iel
spar·ing·ly
spar·kle
spar·row
sparse
spasm
spas·mod·ic
spas·tic
spa·tial
spat·u·la
spay
speak·er
spe·cial
spe·cial·ty (–ties)
spe·cies
spe·cif·ic
spec·i·fic·ca·tion
spec·i·fic·i·ty
spec·i·men
spec·ta·cle
spec·tac·u·lar
spec·ta·tor
spec·tral
spec·trum
spec·u·late
speech·less
spend·thrift
sperm
sphag·num
sphere
spher·i·cal
sphinx (sphinx·es *or*
   sphin·ges)
spice
spic·ing
spi·dery
spiel
spig·ot

spill·age
spin·ach
spin·dle
spin·dly
spin·et
spin·ster
spi·ral
spir·i·tu·al
spite·ful
splashy
splen·dor
sple·net·ic
splice
splin·ter
splut·ter
spoil·age
spokes·man
spo·li·a·tion
spon·dee
sponge
spongy
spon·sor
spon·ta·ne·ity
spon·ta·ne·ous
spooky
spoon·ful (spoon·fuls *or*
   spoons·ful)
spo·rad·ic
spore
sport·ive
sporty
spot·light
spot·ty
spouse
spright·ly
spring·time
springy
sprin·kling
sprock·et
sprout
spry
spunky
spu·ri·ous
spurred
spu·tum
spy (spies)
squab·ble
squad·ron
squal·id

squa·lor
squan·der
square
squash
squat·ted
squat·ter
squawk
squeaky
squeal
squea·mish
squeeze
squelch
squint
squire
squirm
squir·rel (squir·rels *or*
   squir·rel)
squirt
sta·bil·i·ty (–ties)
sta·ble
stac·ca·to
stacked
sta·di·um (sta·dia *or*
   sta·di·ums)
staff
stage
stag·ing
stag·nant
staid
stair·case
stake (pointed post; see
   steak)
sta·lac·tite
sta·lag·mite
stale·mate
stalk
stal·lion
stal·wart
stam·i·na
stam·mer
stam·pede
stance
stan·chion
stan·dard·ize
stand·by
stan·za
sta·ple
starchy
star·ry
star·tle

star·va·tion
stash
state
state·ment
stat·ic
sta·tion
sta·tion·ary (immobile; see
   stationery)
sta·tio·nery (materials for
   writing; see *stationary)*
stat·is·ti·cian
sta·tis·tics
stat·ue
stat·ure
sta·tus
stat·u·to·ry
staunch
stead·fast
steak (slice of meat; see
   stake)
steal (to take the property
   of another; see *steel)*
stealthy
steel (a metal; see *steal)*
stee·ple
steer·age
stein
stel·lar
sten·cil
ste·nog·ra·pher
sten·to·ri·an
step (an advance of a foot;
   see *steppe)*
steppe (treeless plain; see
   step)
ste·reo·type
ster·ile
ster·ling
ste·ve·dore
stew·ard
stick·ler
sticky
sti·fle
stig·ma·tize
sti·let·to
stim·u·late
stim·u·lus
stin·gy
sti·pend
stip·u·late

stir·rup
stitch
stock·ade
stock·bro·ker
stodgy
stol·id
stom·ach·ache
stop·page
stor·age
sto·ried
stow·age
strad·dle
strag·gle
straight (free from curves;
   see *strait)*
straight·en
strait (a narrow passageway
   between two bodies of
   water; see *straight)*
strang·er
stran·gle
stran·gu·late
strat·a·gem
stra·te·gic
strat·e·gy (–gies)
strat·i·fy
strato·sphere
stra·tum (stra·ta)
streaky
stream·line
strength
stren·u·ous
stress·ful
stretch·er
stri·at·ed
strick·en
stric·ture
stri·dent
strike
strin·gent
strobe
stroll
strong
struc·tu·ral
struc·ture
strug·gle
strum·pet
strych·nine
stub·ble
stub·by

stuc·co
stu·dent
stu·dio
stu·di·ous
study
stul·ti·fy
stum·bling
stu·pe·fy
stu·pen·dous
stur·dy
stur·geon
stut·ter
sty, stye (sties *or* styes)
style
styl·ish
styl·ized
sty·lus (sty·li *or* sty·lus·es)
suave
sub·com·mit·tee
sub·con·scious
sub·due
sub·ject (noun), sub·ject
  (verb)
sub·ju·gate
sub·lime
sub·lim·i·nal
sub·ma·rine
sub·merge
sub·mis·sion
sub·or·di·nate
sub·orn
sub·poe·na
sub·scribe
sub·scrip·tion
sub·se·quent
sub·ser·vi·ent
sub·side
sub·sid·iary
sub·si·dize
sub·si·dy (–dies)
sub·sis·tence
sub·stance
sub·stan·tial
sub·stan·tive
sub·sti·tute
sub·sume
sub·ter·fuge
sub·tle
sub·trac·tion
sub·ur·bia

sub·ver·sion
suc·ceed
suc·cess·ful
suc·ces·sion
suc·ces·sor
suc·cinct
suc·co·tash
suc·cu·lent
suc·cumb
suck·le
suc·tion
sud·den
sudsy
sue
suede, suède
suf·fer·ance
suf·fice
suf·fi·cient
suf·fo·cate
suf·frage
suf·fuse
sug·ges·tion
sui·cid·al
suit·able
suite
suit·or
sulky
sul·phur, sul·fur
sul·try
sum·ma·ry (abridgment of
  discourse; see *summery*)
sum·mer·time
sum·mery (like summer;
  see *summary*)
sum·mit
sum·mon
sump·tu·ous
sun (celestial body; see
  son)
su·per·an·nu·ate
su·perb
su·per·cil·ious
su·per·fi·cial
su·per·flu·ity (–ities)
su·per·flu·ous
su·per·in·ten·dent
su·pe·ri·or
su·per·la·tive
su·per·nat·u·ral
su·per·sede

su·per·sti·tious
su·per·vi·so·ry
su·pine
sup·plant
sup·ple
sup·ple·men·ta·ry
sup·pli·ant
sup·pli·cate
supply (supplies)
sup·port·ive
sup·po·si·tion
sup·pos·i·to·ry (–ries)
sup·pres·sion
sup·pu·rate
su·prem·a·cy (–cies)
sur·cease
sur·charge
sure·ty (–ties)
sur·face
sur·feit
surge
sur·geon
sur·gi·cal
sur·mise
sur·name
sur·plice
sur·plus
sur·re·al·ism
sur·ren·der
sur·ro·gate
sur·round·ings
sur·tax
sur·veil·lance
sur·vey (noun), sur·vey
  (verb)
sur·viv·al
sus·cep·ti·bil·i·ty (–ties)
sus·cep·ti·ble
sus·pect (noun), sus·pect
  (verb)
sus·pense
sus·pi·cious
sus·te·nance
su·ture
svelte
swad·dling
swag·ger
swampy
swank
swar·thy

swash·buck·ler
swas·ti·ka
swath, swathe
swear
sweaty
sweet·ened
swel·ter
swept
swerve
swin·dle
swing
swirl
swish
switch
swiv·el
swol·len
sword
syb·a·rite

syc·a·more
sy·co·phant
syl·lab·ic
syl·lab·i·fy
syl·la·bus (–bi *or* –bus·es)
syl·lo·gism
sylph
syl·van
sym·bol·ic
sym·met·ri·cal, sym·met·ric
sym·me·try (–tries)
sym·pa·thet·ic
sym·phon·ic
sym·po·sium
symp·tom
syn·a·gogue, syn·a·gog
syn·chro·nize
syn·co·pate

syn·di·cate
syn·ec·do·che
syn·od
syn·onym
syn·op·sis
syn·op·tic
syn·tax
syn·the·size
syn·thet·ic, syn·thet·i·cal
syph·i·lis
sy·ringe
syr·upy
sys·tem·at·ic,
    sys·tem·at·i·cal
sys·tem·atize
sys·tem·ic

T

Ta·bas·co
tab·by
tab·er·na·cle
tab·la·ture
ta·bling
tab·leau (tab·leaux or
　tab·leaus)
ta·ble·spoon·ful
　(ta·ble·spoon·fuls or
　ta·ble·spoons·ful)
tab·let
tab·loid
ta·boo, ta·bu
tab·o·ret, tab·ou·ret
　(French: type of seat or
　stand)
tab·u·lar
tab·u·late
tab·u·la·tor
ta·chom·e·ter
tac·it
tac·i·turn
tack·le
tacky
tact·ful
tac·tic·al
tac·tile
tad·pole
taf·fe·ta
taff·rail
taf·fy
tail (rear end; see *tale*)
tai·lored
taint
tak·ing
talc
tal·cum
tale (story: see *tail*)
tal·ent
tales·man (juror; see
　talisman)
tal·is·man (charm: see
　talesman)
talk·ative
talk·ie (sound motion
　picture; see *talky*)
talky (too much talk; see
　talkie)
tall·ish
tal·low

tal·ly (tal·lies)
tal·ly·ho
tal·on
ta·ma·le
tam·a·rack
tam·bou·rine
tam·ing
tam·per
tan·a·ger
tan·dem
tan·ge·lo
tan·gent
tan·gen·tial
tan·ger·ine
tan·gi·ble
tan·gling
tan·gled
tan·go (tan·gos)
tangy
tan·kard
tan·nery (–ner·ies)
tan·ning
tan·ta·lize
tan·ta·mount
tan·trum
tape
ta·per
tap·es·tried
tap·es·try (–tries)
tap·i·o·ca
tar·an·tel·la
ta·ran·tu·la
tar·di·ly
tar·dy
tare (weed; see *tear*)
tar·get
tar·iff
tar·mac
tar·nish
tar·ot
tar·pau·lin
tar·pon
tar·ra·gon
tar·ry
tar·tan
tar·tar
task
tas·sel
taste·ful
tasty

tat·tered
tat·too
tat·ty
taught
taunt
taupe
taut
tau·tol·o·gy (–gies)
tav·ern
taw·dry
taw·ny
tax·a·tion
tax-ex·empt
taxi·der·my
tax·ied
taxi·ing
tax·on·o·my (–mies)
tax·pay·er
teach·able
tea·ket·tle
teak·wood
team (group; see *teem*)
team·ster
tear (damage from being
　torn; see *tare*)
teas·ing
teat
tech·ni·cal
tech·ni·cian
tech·nique
tech·no·log·i·cal,
　tech·no·log·ic
te·dious
te·di·um
teem (filled to overflowing;
　see *team*)
teen·age
tee·ter
teethe
tee·to·tal·er, tee·to·tal·ler
tele·cast
tele·com·mu·ni·ca·tion
tele·gram
tele·graph
te·le·ol·o·gy
te·lep·a·thy
tele·phon·ing
tele·pho·to
tele·scope
tele·typ·ist

tele·vise
tel·ex
te·mer·i·ty (–ties)
tem·per·a·ment
tem·per·ate
tem·per·a·ture
tem·pered
tem·pes·tu·ous
tem·plate
tem·ple
tem·po (tem·pi *or* tem·pos)
tem·po·ral
tem·po·rar·i·ly
tem·po·rize
tempt
temp·ta·tion
tem·pu·ra
ten·a·ble
te·na·cious
te·nac·i·ty
ten·ant
ten·den·cy (–cies)
ten·den·tious, ten·den·cious
ten·der·ize
ten·der·loin
ten·der·ly
ten·don
ten·dril
ten·e·ment
te·net
ten·or
tense
ten·sile
ten·sion
ten·ta·cle
ten·ta·tive
ten·ter·hook
ten·u·ous
ten·ure
te·pee
tep·id
ter·gi·ver·sa·tion
ter·i·ya·ki (Japanese: spicy meat or shelfish dish)
ter·ma·gant
ter·mi·nal
ter·mi·nate
ter·mi·na·tion
ter·mi·nol·o·gy (–gies)
ter·mi·nus (–ni *or* –nuses)

ter·mite
terp·si·cho·re·an
ter·race
ter·ra-cot·ta
ter·rain, ter·rane
ter·rar·i·um (ter·rar·ia *or* ter·rar·i·ums)
ter·raz·zo
ter·res·tri·al
ter·ri·ble
ter·ri·er
ter·rif·ic
ter·ri·fy
ter·ri·to·ri·al
ter·ri·to·ry (–ries)
ter·ror·ize
ter·ry
terse
ter·tia·ry
tes·sel·late
tes·ta·ment
tes·ta·tor
test·ed
tes·ti·cle
tes·ti·fy
tes·ti·mo·ni·al
tes·ti·mo·ny (–nies)
tes·ty
tet·a·nus
tête-à-tête (French: private conversation between two people)
teth·er
tet·ra·chlo·ride
te·tram·e·ter
text·book
tex·tile
tex·ture
thank·ful
thatch
the·atre, the·ater
the·at·ri·cal
theft
their (relating to them; see *there*)
the·ism
the·mat·ic
theme
thence
the·oc·ra·cy (–cies)

theo·lo·gian
the·ol·o·gy (–gies)
the·o·rem
the·o·ret·i·cal
the·o·rist
the·o·ry (–ries)
the·os·o·phy
ther·a·peu·tic
ther·a·pist
ther·a·py (–pies)
there (in that place; see *their*)
ther·mal
ther·mom·e·ter
ther·mo·stat
the·sau·rus (the·sau·ri *or* the·sau·rus·es)
the·sis
thes·pi·an
thew
they
thick·en·ing
thick·et
thief
thiev·ery (–er·ies)
thigh
thim·ble·ful
think·able
thin·ner
third
thirsty
thir·teenth
this·tle
thith·er
thong
tho·rac·ic
thorny
thor·ough·bred
thor·ough·fare
though
thought
thought·ful
thou·sand
thrash
thread·bare
threat·en
three-di·men·sion·al
thren·o·dy (–dies)
thresh·old
thrift

thrive
throat
throe
throm·bo·sis (–bo·ses)
throne
thronged
throt·tle
through
through·out
thru·way
thug
thumb
thump
thun·der·ous
thwart
thyme
thy·roid
ti·ara
tick·et
tick·ing
tick·le
tid·al
tid·ings
ti·di·ness
tier
tight·rope
tile
till·age
tim·ber (wood; see *timbre*)
tim·bre (quality of sound;
   see *timber*)
time·ly
time·table
tim·id
tim·ing
tim·o·rous
tim·pa·nist
tinc·ture
tin·der
tinge
tin·gle
tin·kle
tin·ny
tin·sel
tint·ing
tip·sy
ti·rade
tire
tis·sue
tithe

tit·il·late
tit·i·vate, tit·ti·vate
ti·tled
tit·tle
toasty
to·bac·co
to·bog·gan
toc·sin
tod·dle
to·ga
to·geth·er·ness
tog·gle
toil
toile (French: type of
   fabric)
toil·worn
to·ken·ism
tole
tol·er·a·ble
tol·er·ance
toll
tom·a·hawk
to·ma·to (–toes)
tomb
to·mor·row
to·nal·i·ty (–ties)
tongue
tongu·ing
to·nic·i·ty
to·night
ton·nage
ton·sil·lec·to·my (–mies)
ton·sil·li·tis
ton·so·ri·al
ton·sure
tool·box
tooth·some
to·paz
top·i·cal
to·pog·ra·phy
to·pol·o·gy (–gies)
top·ple
top·sy·tur·vy
toque
to·re·ador (Spanish:
   bullfighter)
tor·men·tor
tor·na·do (–dos or –does)
tor·pe·do (–does)
tor·pid

tor·por
torque
tor·ren·tial
tor·rid·ly
tor·sion
tor·so (tor·sos or tor·si)
tor·ti·lla
tor·toise
tor·tu·ous
tor·ture
to·tal·i·tar·i·an
to·tal·i·ty (–ties)
to·tal·ly
to·tem
touch
touchy
tough·en
tou·pee (French: wig)
tour de force (French: a
   feat of strength, skill, or
   ingenuity)
tour·ism
tour·na·ment
tour·ney
tour·ni·quet
tou·sle
to·ward
tow·el·ing, tow·el·ling
tow·er·ing
tow·head
town house
tox·ic
toy
tra·chea (tra·che·ae or
   tra·che·as)
trac·ing
trac·ta·ble
trac·tion
trac·tor
trade·mark
tra·di·tion
tra·duce
traf·fic
traf·ficked
tra·ge·di·an (actor in tragic
   roles; see *tragedienne*)
tra·ge·di·enne (actress in
   tragic roles; see
   tragedian)
trag·e·dy (–dies)

trail	tra·verse	trou·ba·dour
train·ing	trav·es·ty (–ties)	trou·bling
trai·tor·ous	trawl·er	trough
tra·jec·to·ry (–ries)	treach·er·ous	troupe
tram·mel	trea·cle	trou·sers
tram·ple	trea·dle	trow·el
tram·po·line	trea·son·able	tru·an·cy (–cies)
trance	trea·sur·er	tru·cu·lence
tran·quil	trea·tise	true
tran·quil·ize, tran·quil·lize	trea·ty	tru·ism
tran·quil·li·ty, tran·quil·i·ty	treble	tru·ly
trans·ac·tion	trek·king	trum·pet·er
trans·at·lan·tic	trel·lis	trun·cat·ed
tran·scen·dence	trem·ble	trun·cheon
trans·scen·den·tal	tre·men·dous	trun·dle
tran·con·ti·nen·tal	trem·or	truss
tran·scribe	trem·u·lous	trust·ee
trans·script	tren·chant	truth·ful
tran·sect	trep·i·da·tion	try
tran·sept	tres·pass	tryst
trans·fer·al	tres·tle	tu·ba
trans·fer·ence	tri·an·gle	tu·ber·cu·lar
trans·for·ma·tion	tri·bal	tu·ber·cu·lo·sis
trans·fu·sion	trib·u·la·tion	tu·ber·ous
trans·gres·sion	tri·bu·nal	tu·bu·lar
tran·sience	trib·u·tary	tu·ition
tran·sient	trick·ery	tum·brel, tum·bril
tran·sis·tor	tri·col·or	tu·mes·cent
tran·sit	tri·cy·cle	tu·mor
tran·si·tion	tri·dent	tu·mul·tu·ous
tran·si·to·ry	tri·fling	tun·dra
trans·la·tion	trig·ger	tung·sten
trans·lu·cent	tril·o·gy (–gies)	tu·nic
trans·mis·si·ble	tri·mes·ter	tun·nel·ing, tun·nel·ling
trans·mit·tance	trin·ket	tur·ban
trans·mute	trio	tur·bid
tran·som	tri·ple	tur·bine
trans·par·en·cy (–cies)	trip·let	tur·bo·jet
tran·spire	trip·li·cate	tur·bo·prop
trans·port·able	trip·tych	tur·bot
trans·pose	trite	tur·bu·lence
trans·verse	tri·umph	tu·reen
tra·peze	tri·um·vir·ate	tur·gid
trashy	triv·et	tur·moil
trau·ma	triv·i·al	turn·key
tra·vail	trol·ley, trol·ly (trol·leys or	tur·pen·tine
trav·eled, trav·elled	trol·lies)	tur·pi·tude
trav·el·er, trav·el·ler	trom·bone	tur·quoise, tur·quois
trav·el·ing trav·el·ling	tro·phy (trophies)	tur·ret·ed
trav·el·ogue, trav·el·og	trop·i·cal	tur·tle

tus·sle
tus·sock
tu·te·lage
tu·te·lary
tu·to·ri·al
tut·ti-frut·ti
tux·e·do (–dos *or* –does)
twain
tweak
tweedy
twee·zers
twelfth
twen·ti·eth
twi·light

twill
twine
twinge
twin·kling
twirl
twist
twitch
twit·ter
two·fer
ty·coon
ty·ing, tie·ing
tym·pa·num (–na *or* –nums)
type·script

type·writ·er
ty·phoid
ty·phoon
ty·phus
typ·i·cal
typ·i·fy
ty·pog·ra·phy
ty·ran·ni·cal, ty·ran·nic
tyr·an·nize
tyr·an·nous
tyr·an·ny (–nies)
ty·ro

ubiq·ui·tous
ubiq·ui·ty
ud·der
ug·li·ness
ukase
uku·le·le
ul·cer
ul·cer·ous
ul·na
ul·ster
ul·te·ri·or
ul·ti·mate
ul·ti·ma·tum (–tums *or* –ta)
ul·tra
ul·tra·vi·o·let
ul·u·late
um·ber
um·bil·i·cal
um·bra (um·bras *or* um·brae)
um·brage
um·brel·la
um·laut
um·pire
un·abat·ed
un·able
un·abridged
un·ac·cept·able
un·ac·com·pa·nied
un·ac·count·able
un·ac·cus·tomed
un·adorned
un·adul·ter·at·ed
un·af·fect·ed
un·aid·ed
un·alien·able
un·aligned
un·al·ter·able
un·am·big·u·ous
una·nim·i·ty
unan·i·mous
un·an·tic·i·pat·ed
un·ap·peal·ing
un·ap·pe·tiz·ing
un·ap·proach·able
un·armed
un·ashamed
un·asked

un·as·sail·able
un·as·sist·ed
un·at·trac·tive
un·avail·able
un·avoid·able
un·awares
un·bal·anced
un·be·com·ing
un·be·known
un·be·liev·able
un·bi·ased
un·bri·dled
un·budg·ing
un·can·ny
un·cer·tain·ty (–ties)
un·change·able
un·char·i·ta·ble
un·cle
un·com·fort·able
un·com·mu·ni·ca·tive
un·com·pli·men·ta·ry
un·con·di·tion·al
un·con·scio·na·ble
un·con·trol·la·ble
un·couth
unc·tion
unc·tu·ous
un·de·bat·able
un·dem·o·crat·ic
un·de·ni·able
un·der·achiev·er
un·der·gird
un·der·grad·u·ate
un·der·priv·i·leged
un·der·signed
un·der·stand
un·der·state·ment
un·der·tak·er
un·de·sir·able
un·de·vi·at·ing
un·due
un·du·lant
un·dy·ing
un·easy
un·em·ployed
un·en·dur·able
un·equiv·o·cal
un·err·ing

un·ex·cep·tion·able
un·fa·mil·iar
un·fash·ion·able
un·fa·vor·able
un·feigned
un·flag·ging
un·flat·ter·ing
un·flinch·ing
un·for·get·ta·ble
un·for·tu·nate·ly
un·fre·quent·ed
un·gain·ly
un·glued
un·gov·ern·able
un·gra·cious
un·gram·mat·i·cal
un·guard·ed
un·handy
un·hes·i·tat·ing
un·hinged
uni·corn
uni·di·rec·tion·al
uni·fi·ca·tion
uni·for·mi·ty (–ties)
uni·fy
uni·lat·er·al
un·imag·in·able
un·im·pas·sioned
un·im·peach·able
un·in·hib·it·ed
un·in·tel·li·gi·ble
un·in·ten·tion·al
un·in·ter·rupt·ed
union
unique
uni·sex
uni·son
unit
uni·tary
unite
uni·ver·sal
uni·ver·si·ty (–ties)
un·kempt
un·know·able
un·known
un·law·ful
un·less
un·lim·it·ed

un·man·ly
un·man·ner·ly
un·men·tion·able
un·mis·tak·able
un·mit·i·gat·ed
un·nec·es·sary
un·oc·cu·pied
un·of·fi·cial
un·or·ga·nized
un·or·tho·dox
un·pal·at·able
un·par·al·leled
un·par·lia·men·ta·ry
un·pleas·ant
un·plumbed
un·prec·e·dent·ed
un·pre·dict·able
un·prej·u·diced
un·pre·ten·tious
un·prof·it·able
un·qual·i·fied
un·ques·tion·ing
un·rav·el
un·re·al·is·tic
un·rea·son·able
un·re·gen·er·ate
un·re·lent·ing
un·re·spon·sive
un·re·strained
un·ri·valed, un·ri·valled
un·ruly
un·sad·dle
un·safe
un·sat·u·rat·ed
un·saved
un·sa·vory
un·scathed
un·sci·en·tif·ic
un·scram·ble
un·scru·pu·lous
un·sea·son·able
un·seat
un·seem·ly
un·seg·re·gat·ed
un·se·lect·ed
un·self·ish
un·set·tle
un·shack·le

un·sheathe
un·shod
un·sight·ly
un·skill·ful
un·snap
un·snarl
un·so·cia·ble
un·so·phis·ti·cat·ed
un·sought
un·sound
un·spar·ing
un·speak·able
un·sports·man·like
un·spot·ted
un·sta·ble
un·steady
un·stop·pa·ble
un·stressed
un·struc·tured
un·stud·ied
un·sub·stan·tial
un·suc·cess·ful
un·suit·able
un·swerv·ing
un·tan·gle
un·tapped
un·taught
un·ten·a·ble
un·think·able
un·ti·dy
un·tie
un·til
un·time·ly
un·ti·tled
un·touch·abil·i·ty
un·touch·able
un·trod·den
un·truth·ful
un·tu·tored
un·twine
un·used
un·usu·al
un·ut·ter·able
un·var·nished
un·veil
un·ver·bal·ized
un·voiced
un·war·rant·able

un·wary
un·whole·some
un·wieldy
un·wise
un·wit·ting
un·wont·ed
un·wor·thi·ness
un·wound
un·writ·ten
un·yield·ing
un·yoke
un·zip
up·beat
up·braid
up·bring·ing
up·com·ing
up·date
up·grade
up·heav·al
up·hol·ster
up·lift
up·on
up·pi·ty
up·right·ness
up·ris·ing
up·roar·i·ous
up·set
up·side down
up·stage
up·stand·ing
up·surge
up·swept
up·tight
up·turn
up·ward, up·wards
up·wind
ura·ni·um
ur·ban (relating to a city;
    see *urbane*)
ur·bane (suave; see *urban*)
ur·ban·ite
ur·chin
ure·mia
ure·ter
ure·thra
urging
ur·gen·cy (–cies)
uric

uri·nal
uri·nary
urine
urn
us·able, use·able
us·age
use·ful
use·ful·ness
ush·er
usu·al

usu·al·ly
usu·fruct
usu·rer
usu·ri·ous
usurp
usu·ry
uten·sil
uter·ine
uter·us (uteri or –us·es)
util·i·tar·i·an

util·i·ty (–ties)
ut·most
uto·pi·an
ut·ter·ance
ut·ter·most
uvu·la (–las or –lae)
ux·o·ri·al
ux·o·ri·ous

va·can·cy (–cies)
va·cant
va·cate
va·ca·tion·ing
vac·ci·nate
vac·cine
vac·il·late
vac·il·la·tion
va·cu·ity (–ities)
vac·u·ole
vac·u·ous
vac·u·um
va·de me·cum (Latin:
    something carried about
    regularly by a person)
va·ga·bond
va·ga·ry (–ries)
va·gi·na (–nae *or* –nas)
vag·i·ni·tis
va·gran·cy (–cies)
va·grant
vague
vain (worthless; see *vane*)
vain·glo·ri·ous
va·lance (drapery: see
    valence)
vale·dic·tion
vale·dic·to·ri·an
vale·dic·to·ry (–ries)
va·lence (combining power
    or chemical element; see
    valance)
val·en·tine
va·le·ri·an
va·let
val·e·tu·di·nar·i·an
val·iant
val·id
val·i·date
va·lid·i·ty
val·late
val·ley (valleys)
val·or
valse
valu·able
val·u·ate
val·u·a·tor
val·ue
val·ued
val·ue·less

va·lu·ta
valve
val·vu·lar
va·moose
vam·pire
va·na·di·um
van·dal·ism
van·dal·ize
vane (weathercock; see
    vain)
van·guard
va·nil·la
van·ish
van·i·ty (–ties)
van·quish
van·tage
va·pid·i·ty (–ties)
va·por
va·por·iza·tion
va·por·iz·er
va·por·ous
vari·abil·i·ty
vari·able
vari·ance
vari·ant
vari·a·tion
vari·col·ored
var·i·cose
var·i·cos·i·ty (–ties)
var·ied
var·ie·gate
va·ri·etal
va·ri·ety (–et·ies)
vari·form
var·i·ous
var·let
var·mint
var·nish
var·si·ty (–ties)
vary
vas·cu·lar
vase
va·sec·to·my (–mies)
Vas·e·line
va·so·mo·tor
vas·sal·age
vast·ly
va·tic·i·na·tion
vaude·ville
vaude·vil·lian

vault
vaunt
veal
vec·tor
veer
vee·ry (–ries)
veg·e·ta·ble
veg·e·tar·i·an
veg·e·tate
veg·e·ta·tive
ve·he·mence
ve·hi·cle
ve·hic·u·lar
veiled
veined
ve·lar
veld, veldt
vel·le·ity (–ities)
vel·lum (leather binding;
    see *velum*)
ve·loc·i·pede
ve·loc·i·ty (–ties)
ve·lo·drome
ve·lour, ve·lours (plural
    also ve·lours)
ve·lum (part of soft palate;
    see *vellum*)
vel·vet
vel·vety
ve·nal
vend
vend·ee
ven·der, ven·dor
ven·det·ta
ve·neer
ven·er·a·ble
ven·er·ate
ven·er·a·tor
ve·ne·re·al
ven·ery
ve·ne·tian blind
ven·geance
venge·ful
ve·nial
ve·ni·re
ve·ni·re·man (–men)
ven·i·son
ven·om
ven·om·ous
ve·nous

vent
ven·ti·late
ven·ti·la·tor
ven·tral
ven·tri·cle
ven·tril·o·quist
ven·ture
ven·ture·some
ven·tur·ous
ven·ue
ve·ra·cious
ve·rac·i·ty (–ties)
ve·ran·da, ve·ran·dah
ver·bal·ly
ver·ba·tim
ver·be·na
ver·biage
ver·bose
ver·dant (French: green)
ver·dict
ver·di·gris
ver·dure
verge
verg·er
verg·ing
ve·rid·i·cal
ver·i·fi·able
ver·i·fi·ca·tion
ver·i·fy
ver·i·ly
veri·si·mil·i·tude
ver·i·ta·ble
ver·i·ty (–ties)
ver·mi·cel·li
ver·mil·ion, ver·mil·lion
ver·min
ver·min·ous
ver·mouth
ver·nac·u·lar
ver·nal
ver·ni·er
ver·sa·til·i·ty
verse
ver·si·cle
ver·si·fi·ca·tion
ver·si·fi·er
ver·sion
ver·sus
ver·te·bra
ver·te·brate

ver·tex
ver·ti·cal
ver·tig·i·nous
ver·ti·go
verve
very
ves·i·cant
ves·i·cle
ves·pers
ves·sel
ves·tal
ves·ti·ary (–ar·ies)
ves·tib·u·lar
ves·ti·bule
ves·tige
vest·ment
ves·try (–tries)
ves·ture
vetch
vet·er·an
vet·er·i·nar·i·an
vet·er·i·nary
ve·to (–toes)
vex·a·tion
vex·a·tious
vi·a·ble
via·duct
vi·al
vi·and
vi·at·i·cum (–cums or –ca)
vibes
vi·brant
vi·brate
vi·bra·tor
vi·bur·num
vic·ar
vic·ar·age
vi·car·i·ate
vi·car·i·ous
vice·roy
vi·chys·soise
vic·i·nage
vi·cin·i·ty (–ties)
vi·cious
vi·cis·si·tude
vic·tim·ize
vic·to·ri·ous
vic·to·ry (–ries)
vict·ual
vict·ual·ler, vict·ual·er

vid·eo·tape
view·ing
vig·i·lance
vig·i·lan·te
vi·gnette
vig·or·ous
vil·i·fi·ca·tion
vil·i·fy
vil·lag·er
vil·lain
vil·lainy (–lain·ies)
vil·los·i·ty (–ties)
vin·ci·ble
vin·cu·lum (–lums or –la)
vin·di·cate
vin·dic·tive
vin·e·gar
vin·ery (–er·ies)
vin·tage
vi·nyl
vi·o·la
vi·o·la·ble
vi·o·late
vi·o·lence
vi·o·let
vi·o·lin
vi·per
vi·ra·go
vir·eo (–e·os)
vir·gin·al
vir·gin·i·ty (–ties)
vir·i·des·cent
vi·rid·i·ty
vir·tu·al·ly
vir·tue
vir·tu·os·i·ty (–ties)
vir·tu·o·so (–sos or –si)
vir·tu·ous
vir·u·lence
vi·rus
vis·age
vis-à-vis (French: face to
    face with)
vis·cer·al
vis·cid
vis·cos·i·ty (–ties)
vis·count
vis·cous
vis·i·bil·i·ty (-ties)
vis·i·ble

vi·sion·ary
vis·i·ta·tion
vis·i·tor
vi·sor
vis·ta
vi·su·al
vi·tal
vi·tal·i·ty (–ties)
vi·ta·min
vi·ti·ate
vit·re·ous
vit·ri·ol
vi·tu·per·a·tive
vi·va·cious
viv·id
viv·i·fy
vi·vip·a·rous
vivi·sec·tion
vix·en
vi·zier
vo·cab·u·lary (–lar·ies)
vo·cal·ist
vo·ca·tion

voc·a·tive
vo·cif·er·ate
vo·cif·er·ous
vod·ka
vogue
voice
void
vol·a·tile
vol·ca·nic
vol·ca·no (–noes *or* –nos)
vo·li·tion
vol·ley (vol·leys)
volt·age
vol·ta·ic
vol·u·ble
vol·u·bil·i·ty
vol·ume
vo·lu·mi·nous
vol·un·tary
vol·un·ta·rism
vol·un·teer
vo·lup·tu·ary (–ar·ies)
vo·lup·tuous

vom·it
voo·doo
vo·ra·cious
vo·rac·i·ty
vor·tex (vor·ti·ces *or* vor·tex·es)
vo·ta·ry (–ries)
vo·tive
vouch
vouch·safe
vow·el
voy·age
voy·eur
vul·gar
vul·gar·i·an
vul·gar·ism
vul·gate
vul·ner·a·ble
vul·pine
vul·ture
vy·ing

wacky

wad·ding (soft mass; see *wading*)

wad·dle

wad·ing (step through water; see *wadding*)

wa·fcr

waf·fle

waft

wage

wag·ging (to be in motion; see *waging*)

wag·gle

wag·ing (to engage in; see *wagging*)

wag·on

waif

wail

wain

wain·scot·ing, wain·scot·ting

waist (narrowed part of body above hips; see *waste*)

wait·er

wait·ress

waive (relinquish voluntarily; see *wave*)

wak·ened

walk·ie-talk·ie

wal·let

wal·lop

wal·low

wall·pa·per

wal·nut

wal·rus

waltz

wam·pum

wan·dered

wan·der·lust

wan·ing

wan·ton

war·bled

war·den

ward·robe

ware·house

war·fare

wari ly

war·mon·ger

warmth

warn

warp

war·rant

war·ran·tee (person to whom warranty is made; see *warranty*)

war·ran·tor

war·ran·ty (–ties) (written guarantee; see *warrantee*)

war·ren

war·ring

war·rior

wash·able

wasp·ish

was·sail

wast·age

waste (refuse from human habitations; see *waist*)

waste·land

wast·rel

watch·ful

wa·ter·proof

wa·tery

watt·age

wat·tle

wave (moving swell on sea surface; see *waive*)

wave·length

wavy

wax·en

waxy

way·far·er

way·lay

way·side

way·ward

weak·ened

weal

wealthy

wean

weap·on

wear·able

wea·ried

wea·sel (–sels)

weath·er (state of atmosphere; see *wether*, *whether*)

weath·er·cock

weave

web·bing

wed·ding

wedg·ing

wed·lock

weedy

weep·ing

wee·vil

weigh

weighty

weir

weird·ly

weirdo

wel·com·ing

weld·er

wel·fare

wel·kin

welsh

welt

wel·ter

wench

were·wolf

west·ern

west·ward

weth·er (castrated sheep; see *weather*, *whether*)

whack

whale

wham·my (–mies)

wharf (wharves *or* wharfs)

what·so·ev·er

wheat·en

whee·dle

wheel·ing

wheeze

whelp

whence

when·ev·er

where·abouts

where·as

where·fore

where·so·ev·er

wher·ev·er

wher·ry (–ries)

whet

wheth·er (alternative condition; see *weather*, *wether*)

whey

which·ev·er
whiff
while
whim·per
whim·si·cal
whim·sy, whim·sey
   (whim·sies *or* whim·seys)
whine
whin·ny
whip·pet
whirl·wind
whis·ker
whis·key, whis·ky
   (whis·keys *or* whis·kies)
whis·pered
whis·tle
whis·tling
whit
whit·en·er
whith·er
whit·tle
whoa
whole·sal·er
whole·some
whol·ly
whoop
whore (prostitute; see *hoar*)
whose
why
wick·er
wide·awake
wid·ow·er
width
wield
wie·ner
wife (wives)
wig·gle
wig·wam
wil·der·ness
wile
will·ful
wil·lies
wil·lowy
wim·ple
wince
winch

wind·ing
wind·lass
win·dow
wind·swept
windy
wined
wing·span
win·ner
win·now
win·some
win·ter·rize
win·ter·time
win·try
winy
wip·ing
wire·less
wir·ing
wiry
wis·dom
wise
wish·ful
wishy-washy
wispy
wist·ful
witch·ery (–er·ies)
with·al
with·drawn
withe
with·er
with·hold
with·out
wit·less
wit·ness
wit·ti·cism
wit·ty
wiz·ard
wiz·ened
wob·ble
woe·be·gone
woe·ful, wo·ful
wold
wolf (wolves)
wolf·ish
wom·an·ish
womb
won·der·ful

won·drous
wont (habit; see *won't*)
won't (will not; see *wont*)
wood·en
woody
woof·er
wool·en, wool·len
woo·zy
wordy
work·able
work·a·day
work·man·ship
world·ly
world·wide
wormy
wor·ri·some
wor·ry (wor·ries)
wors·en
wor·ship·ful
worst
wor·sted
wor·thy
would
wound·ed
wrack
wran·gle
wrap·per
wrath·ful
wreak
wreath (wreaths)
wreathe
wreck·age
wrench
wres·tle
wretch·ed
wrig·gle
wrist·watch
wring
wrin·kle
writ
writhe
writ·ing
wronged
wrought
wry
wurst

X

x-ax·is
xe·non
xe·no·phile
xe·no·pho·bia
xe·rox
Xmas
X-ray
xy·lo·phone

Y

yacht
yachts·man (–men)
ya·hoo
yak
yak·king
yam
Yan·kee
yap·ping
yard·age
yar·mul·ke, yar·mel·ke
yar·row
yawl
yawn·ing
yawp, yaup
year·ling
year·ly
yearn
yeasty
yegg
yel·low·ish
yelp·er
yeo·man (–men)
ye·shi·va, ye·shi·vah
  (ye·shi·vas or
  ye·shi·voth) (Hebrew:
  type of Jewish school)
yes·ter·day
yield
yip·pee
yo·del
yo·ga
yo·gurt, yo·ghurt
y-ax·is
yoke (wooden bar; see
  yolk)
yo·kel
yolk (yellow portion of egg;
  see *yoke*)
Yom Kip·pur
yon·der
yoo-hoo
yore
you
young
young·ster
your (relating to you; see
  you're)
you're (you are; see *your*)
your·self (your·selves)
youth·ful
you've
yowl
yo-yo
yuc·ca
yule
yule·tide
yum·my
yum-yum
yurt
YMCA
YMHA
YWCA
YWHA

Z

za·ba·glio·ne
zag·ging
za·ny (–nies)
zapped
zeal·ot
zeal·ous
ze·bra
zeit·geist (German: cultural
  climate of an era)
ze·nith
zeph·yr
zep·pe·lin
ze·ro (ze·ros or ze·roes)
zesty
zigged
zig·zag
zilch
zil·lion
zinc
zin·nia
Zi·on·ism
zip code
zip·per
zir·con
zith·er
zo·di·ac
zom·bie, zom·bi
zon·al
zone
zonked
zoo (zoos)
zoo·log·i·cal, zoo·log·ic
zo·ol·o·gy
zoom
zoy·sia
zuc·chet·to (–tos)
zuc·chi·ni (–ni or –nis)
zwie·back
zy·gote

The Importance of Spelling

Why Bother to Spell Correctly?

Your spelling can show a great deal about you.

Why Bother to Spell Correctly

We have all made mistakes in spelling, but that is no reason for giving up the attempt to perfect our spelling until we write each word we use correctly. Who would deny that a bad speller reveals his or her mental inefficiency as surely as does the dull or ungrammatical conversationalist? We all know that our futures are often determined by the impressions we make upon important people. We may lose that job, or that raise, or that official position because of something we have said that was not good English usage. Sometimes a slip into bad English may pass unnoticed or be forgotten, with no harm to us. A mistake in spelling, however, is always there to confront the reader. And that error becomes magnified with each reading until all the merits of our letter or article are forgotten and only the misspelling remains to point a forbidding finger at us.

Graphologists are able to deduce many things about your character merely by noting the shape of the letters, the placing of the words, or the slant of the writing. But your misspelled words reveal to the trained observer even more about you; and the revelations are usually unfavorable. Thus, by misspelling certain types of words you can show yourself to be:

- Hard of hearing
- Suffering from weak eyesight
- Inclined to too rapid reading
- Careless in your speech
- Lacking in exactness in thought
- Deficient in the power to associate similar things
- Unable or unwilling to refer to the dictionary

These are pretty serious deficiencies to reveal in your letter of application or invitation before its receiver even sees you. Do you realize the handicap you must overcome if you are ever given a personal interview on the strength of the letter?

There is absolutely no excuse for habitual bad spelling today. Spelling has been studied scientifically by specialists, who have discovered not only the cause for bad spelling, but its cure. You can become an almost perfect speller by applying the proper remedies to your own particular spelling malady. We each suffer from a certain kind of spelling disorder. Having discovered your own particular variety of the disease, you can cure yourself; and you will never suffer from a recurrence of the same indisposition.

When you can spell correctly every word you employ without thinking twice about it, then your life, as far as your writing is concerned, will be much happier. Think of all the time saved in trips to the dictionary or in pondering over this or that spelling! Consider the saving in nervous energy; for you will no longer be uncertain of yourself, and no longer be angry because you realize your weakness and feel that you will never get out of it. You can get out of it! Thousands have discovered that correct spelling can be learned as easily as adding figures or planting flowers. If you will try to discover your special weakness and take the recommended cure you will surely improve and finally recover. But first let us discover why the English language is so difficult to spell.

Why Is Spelling So Difficult?

The *k* in *knave* was not always silent. English pronunciation changed; spelling didn't.

Why Is Spelling So Difficult?

Nearly everybody has difficulty with spelling. Foreign-born speakers have trouble learning English because they see no relationship between the way words are spelled and the way they are pronounced. Native-born speakers of English have trouble for the same reason.

In other languages words are spelled as they are pronounced. If you did not know Italian and came across the Italian word, *inglese*, meaning English, you might pronounce it *ing-gleez*. In Italian, however, the word is pronounced *een-glay-say* because in that language there are no silent vowels such as the silent *e* in English.

There are thousands of English words in which some vowels and consonants are not pronounced. English spelling and pronunciation are often unrelated.

Why?

Linguistic Change

To find the answer we must take a brief look at the development of the English language.

About the middle of the fifth century, three tribes, the Angles, Saxons, and Jutes, who inhabited a section of the North Sea shore which is now Germany and Denmark, invaded Britain, drove the inhabitants into Wales, and established their own kingdoms. They spoke a language which was basically German. Today it is referred to as Old English or Anglo-Saxon.

In 1066 A.D. the Normans, who lived in northwestern France, invaded and conquered Britain. They imposed their language and culture on the conquered land. The common people began to speak a dialect which was a mixture of Anglo-Saxon and Norman French. This dialect is called Middle English.

The most important author to write in this new dialect was Geoffrey Chaucer whose famous book, *The Canterbury Tales*, written about 1387, is still read with enjoyment today.

Chaucer and his contemporaries spelled words as they were pronounced. A final *e* was pronounced like the *a* in *about*; for instance, *nonne* (nun) was pronounced *non-nuh*. All consonants and vowels were pronounced.

Pronunciation began to change about Chaucer's time and continued to change for almost two hundred years, until about 1550. One reason for the change was the French influence because England held large possessions in France. There were other reasons for the shift in pronunciation which we do not fully understand.

At this time printing was introduced into England. The most famous printer of the period, William Caxton, preserved Chaucer's Middle English spelling. Those who came after him followed his example even though most words were no longer pronounced as they had been in Chaucer's time. Pronunciation changed but spelling remained the same. English spelling was no longer phonetic.

The Modern English period began about 1550. From that time until today pronunciation has continued to change, but spelling has remained relatively fixed. There have been spelling changes, of course, but the rate of change has slowed down.

Does this mean that there are no spelling rules? Not at all. There are basic rules, each with exceptions to be sure, but the exceptions are not so numerous as you might think. You can learn these rules with a little effort. By learning them you will greatly improve your spelling ability. In succeeding chapters these rules are stated and explained.

Our Confusing Alphabet

Our alphabet is another cause of spelling difficulties.

A single letter may stand for several different sounds. For example, the letter *a* represents six different sounds and the letter *s* four.

Single Letters with Several Sounds	
A	*S*
p*a*t (ă)	*s*ea (s)
b*a*ke (ā)	no*s*e (z)
c*a*re (â)	*s*ure (sh)
f*a*ther (ä)	plea*s*ure (zh)
*a*ll (a)	
*a*bout (ə)	

At the same time one sound may be represented by several different letters or combinations of letters. For example, the sound of *ā* may be spelled

---

Single Sounds Represented by Several Letters

ā Sound

ay — *as in* say
a — *as in* page
ai — *as in* maid
au — *as in* gauge
e — *as in* fete
ey — *as in* obey
ei — *as in* weigh

The *-ough* words show how many different pronunciations may result from identical spelling.

-OUGH Has Many Sounds

Word	Sound
thr*ough*	(oo)
r*ough*	(uff)
c*ough*	(awf)
pl*ough*	(ow)
thor*ough*	(oh)
hicc*ough*	(up)

To show to what extremes one may go in the strangeness of English spelling, consider the word *potato*. Using some of the unusual combinations in English it is possible to spell the word thus: *ghoughpteighbteau.*

Here is the key:

---

gh	as pronounced in hiccou*gh*
ough	as pronounced in th*ough*
pt	as pronounced in *pt*omaine
eigh	as pronounced in w*eigh*
bt	as pronounced in de*bt*
eau	as pronounced in b*eau*

gh/ough/pt/eigh/bt/eau
(potato)

Try to discover why the word *fish* can be spelled *ghoti.*

Homonyms and Homophones

Words spelled and pronounced alike but differing in meaning are called *homonyms*.

Homonyms

Same Spelling, Same Pronunciation, Different Meaning

pool (a body of water)	pool (a game)
dear (beloved)	dear (high-priced)
fair (light-colored)	fair (a market)

Words pronounced alike but differing in spelling, derivation, and meaning are called *homophones*.

Homophones

Different Spelling, Same Pronunciation, Different Meaning

air	heir
ate	eight
be	bee
beat	beet
berth	birth
compliment (praise)	complement (that which completes)
sum	some
their	there

The abundance of homonyms and homophones in English is a source of difficulty especially to foreign-born students.

Regional Pronunciations

In some regions of our country some words are pronounced differently from common usage. For example, creek is pronounced *crik*; sauce, *sass*; film, *filum*; and draw, *drawr*.

Since we tend to spell words as we hear them pronounced, these and similar regional pronunciations cause spelling difficulties. We must be able to discern dialectal pronunciations to avoid spelling errors.

> ## Remember!
>
> - **Pronunciation has changed rapidly since Modern English began, but spelling has remained relatively stable. As a result, spelling and pronunciation do not always correspond.**
> - **A single alphabetic symbol may stand for several different sounds, and one sound may be represented by more than one symbol.**
> - **There are hundreds of homonyms and homophones in our language. They have brought many a person to despair.**
> - **Local pronunciations may be a source of spelling errors.**

These characteristics of English do not sufficiently explain why misspelling is so widespread. Other factors enter which will be discussed in subsequent pages.

Why You Misspell

Reed·ing kan bee in·tres·ting. And it often improves spelling!

Why You Misspell

We betray our characteristics and feelings in many ways: for example, by the way we behave, speak, sit, and listen. A keen observer like the fictional Sherlock Holmes can learn much about a person by noticing little things.

Your mistakes in spelling tell people many things about yourself. Some of them you may not want people to know. But once the misspelled word is on paper, there is no recall. You have to suffer the consequences, be they social ostracism, failure to get that position or raise, or loss of respect from your reader.

Consider the fate of the secretary in Arnold Bennet's delightful comedy, "The Stepmother."

Christine: Dismiss me, madam?
Gardner: Cora, can you be so cruel?
Mrs. Prout: Alas, yes! She has committed the secretarial sin which is beyond
    forgiveness. She has misspelt.
Gardner: Impossible!

Mispronunciation

We have a tendency to spell words as we hear them. If a word is not pronounced correctly, it will be misspelled. Spelling errors may result from listening to the slovenly enunciation of others or they may result from our own mispronunciations.

Learn to spell by syllables. If you omit syllables when speaking, you are likely to omit them when writing. For example, if you omit a syllable in *incidentally* so that the word comes out as *incidently*, you are likely to write it that way.

Here are some words in which syllables or letters are commonly omitted. The correct number of syllables is indicated in parentheses.

Words with Syllables Commonly Omitted

Correct Word	Mispronounced Word
au·thor·i·ta·tive (5)	au·thor·i·tive (4)
in·ter·est·ing (4)	in·tres·ting (3)
priv·i·lege (3)	priv·lege (2)
hy·gi·en·ic (4)	hy·genic (2)
lic·o·rice (3)	lick·rice (2)
di·a·mond (3)	di·mond (2)
mack·er·al (3)	mack·rel (2)
sar·sa·pa·ril·la (5)	sars·pa·ril·la (4)
lab·o·ra·to·ry (5)	la·bra·to·ry (4)

When practicing spelling aloud, break the word into syllables. Spell by syllables. You will find this method helpful.

Sometimes when you pronounce a word incorrectly you add a syllable where it does not belong, omit a sound, or substitute one sound for another. The following is a list of words that are commonly mispronounced. The correct pronunciation and spelling is as shown. The common mispronunciation and subsequent misspelling is in parentheses. Do you make the mistakes shown in parentheses?

Words Commonly Mispronounced

Correct Word	Mispronounced Word
athletic	athaletic
asked	ast
February	Febuary
government	goverment
kindergarten	kindergarden
library	libery
piggyback, pickaback	pigaback
poinsettia	poinsietta
strictly	strickly

If you have a habit of slurring consonants, omitting syllables, or running syllables together like a verbal accordion player, you make it difficult for your listeners to understand what you are saying. You create an unfavorable impression and raise a barrier to your social and professional success.

One way of improving your speech habits is by listening attentively to individuals who speak clearly. Most radio and television announcers use good American speech. So do most clergymen, statesmen, teachers, and actors and actresses, especially those associated with the legitimate stage. The best speakers speak unaffectedly, pleasantly, and distinctly.

Emotional Disturbance

Everybody has a slip of the tongue now and then. We may be anxious to say something and the words rush out pell-mell. What a mess we make of it! That agitation is revealed when you misspell words whose correct spelling you know. You may not want the reader to think that you are easily aroused. You may be applying for a job where calmness and restraint are prerequisites. But your spelling will give you away.

These are words spelled in a way to reveal your emotional disturbances:

> complete (compelte)
> flies (files)
> applied (appiled)

Suggestion!

After writing a letter or report, read it over carefully. You may find errors committed in haste or agitation. Correct them before your letter application or report leaves your hands.

Hasty Reading

About 10,000 books are published in America each year. If you wanted to read all of them you would have to read about twenty-one a day, every single day in the year. Of course that is impossible. We can't even get around to reading one book a day. This tremendous supply of reading matter (we have not mentioned the morning and evening newspaper, and half a dozen magazines each month) has caused the formation of the habit of hasty reading.

There is a limit to the speed with which you can read. If you go beyond that limit, words become indistinct, blurred, and meaningless. If you boast about finishing the latest novel in two hours, the chances are you misspell many words because you do not have a clear picture of them. You can rarely read more than fifty pages an hour and derive the full benefit of the reading.

Check up on yourself. You will discover that many words which you first met in print, you misspell in your personal writings because you raced over them instead of forming a clear picture of the words in your mind.

This is not to deny the value of rapid reading for a specific purpose which is called *skimming*. When you are not particularly interested in getting every idea and fact from the printed page but only some statistic or date or personal name, it would be a waste of time to read every word slowly. A rapid glance at the entire page will give you the answer you are seeking. However, to read for ideas, beauty of style, or for a detailed explanation requires slow careful reading.

Infrequent Reading

Individuals who read extensively and carefully are usually good spellers. They have learned to spell by reading. Almost unconsciously they observe the spelling of the words they read.

On the other hand poor spellers usually do not have the reading habit. They limit their reading to newspaper headlines or an occasional magazine article.

Read widely, every day if possible. Reading is an excellent means of improving your spelling.

Faulty Observation

A story is told of Toscanini, the great conductor, that illustrates his phenomenal power of observation. Of course, the world knows that he conducted entirely from memory; that he committed to memory the entire score of Respighi's *Pines of Rome* in twenty-four hours. A certain bassoon-player wanted to be excused from a rehearsal because his bassoon needed some repairing. One of the keys would not play the note.

"What note doesn't play?" asked the maestro.
"B-flat," answered the bassoon-player.
"Never mind. Stay for the rehearsal. There are no B-flats for the bassoon parts in tonight's program."

That is careful observation. Infinite pains, hours of concentration and nerve-wracking study went into such perfect knowledge. How many of us will take those pains. How many of us care to observe.

The fault of poor observation is with most of us. The reason is our inertia. Careful observation is too much trouble. By failing to note the correct spelling at first, we fall into the habit of misspelling many words.

Many people, when they are doubtful about the spelling of a word, write it down two or three times. The incorrect forms do not *appear* right. They have a mental picture of the correct word. When they write the correct form, something clicks within them. They recognize they have it right.

You will notice that those who have observed carefully have formed such a vivid picture of the word that they can recall it when they want.

Failure to Consult the Dictionary

There are more than 600,000 words in the English language. Probably no one knows how to spell all of them. Misspellings occur because some words are rare and unusual.

But the spelling of most words is easy because spelling follows established rules. If in doubt, don't guess. Consult the dictionary.

Keep a dictionary at hand when you write. Check on the spelling of unusual words or those words which give you trouble.

Develop the dictionary habit!

Remember!
Misspellings occur because of: • **Mispronunciations** • **Emotional disturbance** • **Hasty reading** • **Infrequent reading** • **Faulty observation** • **Uncertainty or ignorance** **Careful observation pays and pays well.**

4

How To Become A Good Speller

Why is *stAnding* a good memory device for the word *stationAry*? Learn to devise your own spelling shortcuts.

How To Become A Good Speller

Aristotle, the great Greek philosopher, was tutor to the future king, Alexander the Great. One day they were doing a lesson in mathematics which required many calculations. Alexander, always impatient, suddenly threw aside his work and exclaimed:

"Why must I go through all these little steps? Why can't I get the answer immediately? I'm the future king!"
"There is no royal road to knowledge," answered his tutor.

There is no royal road to knowledge. There is no short cut to any branch of learning, and that is especially true for spelling. We had trouble with spelling in America long before Noah Webster published his famous speller. Nobody was ever born a perfect speller. Spellers are *made*; not born. Everyone can become a good speller by following certain scientifically prepared steps. There are some who had to learn the spelling of every word they met painfully and slowly. That was a waste of nervous energy. Time and nerve-power will be conserved, and success will be assured if you will follow the steps enumerated below. This is a prescription for good spelling that has rarely failed. Why not give it a trial?

Learn the Rules and Develop Memory Devices

1. Learn and apply the rules of spelling.
2. Try to discover little devices of your own that will help you to remember the spelling of words that have no rules.

EXAMPLE
PRINCIP*AL* VS. PRINCIP*LE*
Principal: the head of a school or the main thing.
Principle: a rule or a truth.

Much slaughter on the battlefield of spelling has been caused by these two enemies of peace of mind and soul. And yet one simple device will remove forever the confusion caused by them.

A princip*le* is a ru*le*. Both of these end in -*le*. Now you have the whole secret. If it means a ru*le*, spell it with the -*le*.

The other meaning must be spelled princi*pal*. You may remember it another way. If your principal was a fine fellow, he was a *pal* to you. And there you have the second sure way of remembering these two spelling demons.

EXAMPLE
STATION*ARY* VS. STATION*ERY*

Stationary: immobile.

Stationery: materials for writing.

These two have been fighting on our literary battleground ever since we can remember. You think you have the correct spelling when suddenly the other one butts in and then you're lost again.

How can you be certain? Easily. Take a lett*er*; yes, a lett*er*. That's what stationery is used for, and you'll notice that lett*er* ends in -*er*. Now station*ery* ends in -*ery*.

The other word means standing still. Think of the *a* in st*a*nding and you'll remember the -*ary* in station*ary*.

EXAMPLE
SEP*AR*ATE

The word sep*ar*ate has long been a trouble spot.

Think of the word p*art*. When you sep-*ar*-ate, you take things ap-*art*. That will tell you to be sure to spell the word with *ar*.

EXAMPLE
TH*EIR* VS. TH*ERE*

Here is a good way to prevent the confusion in spelling of *their* and *there*.

There is an adverb referring to place. Notice that it contains the word *here*, which also refers to place. For example, The books are *there*.

Their is a personal pronoun referring to ownership. For example, *Their* books.

You will never confuse *there* and *their* if you remember that (t)*here* referring to place always contains *here*. The following sentence uses both words correctly: *Their* possessions are over *there*.

These four devices you may use. But the best of these tricks are the ones you think up yourself. When you discover a way to spell a word that has always given you trouble, you will be so overjoyed at the discovery that you will never forget the spelling. All laws of psychology teach us that we seldom forget anything we learned with pleasure. Therefore, try to be a spelling discoverer; enjoy your latest discovery and one more spelling demon will be eliminated.

Remember!
Form your own memory devices.

Consult the Dictionary

The dictionary is probably the most valuable book in one's library. You should form the habit of consulting it the moment you are confronted with any spelling difficulty. Don't delay. When a word bothers you, and no rule or device will help, look it up while the annoyance is fresh. This is good psychology. The sooner you remove the cause of the annoyance (the doubtful word) the more certain will you be of its disappearance as an annoyance.

A dictionary is more reliable than memory. It will provide the correct spelling of words, indicate the correct pronunciation, and supply the meaning of the words. It will show the difference between *capital* and *capitol*, *strait* and *straight*, and *formerly* and *formally*.

The recommendation made in the previous chapter about consulting the dictionary bears repetition. Keep a dictionary on your desk. You will find it an invaluable tool. If you do not already own a dictionary, purchase one. It will be a good investment.

Remember!
Consult the Dictionary.

Make Your Own Spelling List

Make a list of your difficult words. Try to use these as often as the opportunity presents itself. Mark Twain, who has had no superior in American humor, and whose principles of writing deserve the respect of all who would learn, said, "Use a new word correctly three times, and it's yours." Use a word that has given *you* trouble three times correctly and you should not have any difficulty. The important thing is to use it *correctly*. Misspelling a word a number of times only fixes the misspelling more firmly. There is a popular expression to the effect that "Practice makes perfect." But that should really be "Practice makes permanent." If we always make the same mistake, no amount of practice will do anything to improve our knowledge. Remember to use it correctly the first time.

Listen Attentively

Develop the art of listening carefully. Many people whose hearing shows no organic defect are poor listeners. They do not pay attention and consequently they don't really hear what is being said. The more cultured the topic, the more alert must the listener be. These days there is much talk in the field of economics. Terms like *government, security, conservation* are heard repeatedly. Do you hear *gover-n-ment* or *guvment*? *Scurity* or *security*? *Consivation* or *conservation*?

It is true that sometimes the speaker himself is at fault because his enunciation is not perfect. That does not excuse the listener, however. If a word does not seem quite clear to you, you owe it to yourself to consult the dictionary as soon as you are near one. Thus you will firmly establish that word in your mind.

Remember!
• **Learn the rules and the exceptions.** • **Consult the dictionary if you are in doubt.** • **Make your own spelling list.** • **Listen attentively.**

What has just been said are general instructions. Below are the steps you are to follow in learning any particular word that has given you trouble. Don't take short cuts. Follow the instructions to the letter!

Method for Learning to Spell Any Hard Word!	
	1. *Look* at your word. *Pronounce* each syllable carefully. For example, *in·de·pen·dent.* 2. *Close your eyes* or turn away and form a picture of the word in your mind. If the letters are not clearly before you, look at the word again, until you see it with your eyes closed. 3. *Pronounce* the word and write it at the same time. If you are not sure, try to picture the word. Be certain that you write it correctly the first time. 4. *Write* the word a second time as used in a sentence. 5. The next day write the word as someone else reads it to you.

Rules
for
Spelling

Better Spelling by Ear

Car·bu·ret·or or
Car·bur·e·tor?
**Four simple rules will
take care of all such
words.**

Better Spelling By Ear

Know the Rules!

It is possible, of course, to consult your dictionary every time you are in doubt about the spelling of a word. The knowledge of a few helpful rules, however, will make it unnecessary for you to waste precious time in consulting the dictionary on every occasion when you are in doubt. As is true of almost all rules in English grammar, there are some exceptions to the rules in spelling, too. It is, therefore, necessary to master the exceptions as well as the rules. Study the rules, do the exercises, and try using some of the words you have studied as soon as possible. Remember that your ultimate aim in spelling is to be able to spell every word you want to use without wasting any time trying to figure out the spelling or wasting precious minutes looking up in the dictionary every word of more than two syllables.

Spell by Pronunciation

It has been mentioned before that an impression conveyed by several senses will remain longer in the mind than one coming through only one sense organ. Most human beings are visual-minded. They form only an eye-impression of the things they learn. Some people (musicians especially) are ear-minded. You may discover that you are ear-minded by employing the following spelling devices.

Although English has been rightly accused of not being spelled exactly as it sounds, the fact remains that thousands of words *are spelled* precisely as they are pronounced. If you pronounce these words correctly when you are in doubt about them, you will find no difficulty in spelling them.

You must first understand something about *syllables* and *syllabication*. The late E. L. Thorndike of Columbia University in his *Century Junior Dictionary* defined a syllable as "part of a word pronounced as a unit consisting of a vowel alone or with one or more consonants."

```
do            — word of one syllable
dough·nut — word of two syllables
syl·la·ble  — word of three syllables
```

Divide a Word into Syllables

Rule 1

Begin a syllable with a consonant when the consonant is between two vowels and the first vowel is *long*.

EXAMPLE

ro·man·tic

The consonant *m* begins the second syllable because the vowel *o* is long.

The long vowels are pronounced exactly as they are pronounced when you recite the alphabet.

ā — *as in* hay
ē — *as in* bee
ī — *as in* kite
ō — *as in* note
ū — *as in* mute

Other examples of Rule 1 are:

Mo·hawk   ro·tate   na·ture

Rule 2

End a syllable with a consonant when the consonant is between two vowels and the first vowel is *short*.

EXAMPLE

hab·it

The consonant *b* ends the first syllable because it is between two vowels and the first vowel is short.

The short vowels are present in this line:

Patter, petter, pitter, potter, putter

Syllables with short vowels:

a — *as in* fash·ion, tap·es·try
e — *as in* nec·es·sa·ry
i — *as in* crit·i·cism
o — *as in* prom·i·nent
u — *as in* sub·urb

Other examples of rule 2 are:

proph·et pun·ish ex·ec·u·tive

Rule 3

Adjoining consonants most often separate into syllables.

EXAMPLES

mur·mur can·dy ex·pense

Rule 4

Double consonants are not divided when a suffix is added.

EXAMPLES

mill·er hiss·ing

These rules should help you also in dividing words at the end of a line. Study the syllabication of the following words that are associated with the automobile:

per·for·mance
gas·o·line
man·u·fac·ture
pneu·mat·ic
se·dan

It was one of the principles of the government of Ancient Rome to "divide and conquer." The same rule might apply for long words. Divide them into their component syllables and you can conquer them.

BETTER SPELLING BY EAR

Spell as You Pronounce Syllable by Syllable

Many words appear difficult to spell until we pronounce them carefully. They fall naturally into simple syllables and their difficulty disappears.

Method!

1. **Pronounce the word slowly.**
2. **Spell it aloud** *by syllables*.
3. **Pronounce it slowly twice more, writing as you do so.**
4. **Pronounce it quickly in a sentence, writing the whole sentence.**

Each of the following words will lose its terror if you use this method.

ac·com·mo·date	en·deav·or
mag·nif·i·cent	priv·i·lege
mag·a·zine	dis·ap·pear

Exercise 1

Divide the following words into syllables.

1. bonanza _____
2. repent _____
3. fatigue _____
4. punishment _____
5. ordeal _____
6. rummage _____
7. missing _____
8. gasoline _____
9. excavate _____
10. tyrannical _____

Pay Attention to Troublesome Words

In this section are lists of words that have had their thousands of victims. Have someone dictate these words to you. Spell them. Then compare your spelling with those in the book. The ones you have spelled correctly, you need no longer bother with. Your misspelled words, you must examine. What errors did you make? There is an entire section for each error. Practice the words until you can spell them correctly without the need of thinking twice about them. These words may all be learned by accustoming your ear to hear them correctly.

Difficult "A" Words

Each of the following words has *a* trouble. People forget the existence of *a* and substitute another letter:

captain	certain	calendar
finally	grammar	illegal
maintain	plain	criminal
preparations	probable	dictionary
separate	straight	liberal
usually	villain	justifiable
balance	equivalent	equally
performance	salary	congressional
actually	extravagant	professional
village	capital	temperature
partially	principal	similar

Difficult "E" Words

Each of the words below has an *e* difficulty. Writers frequently forget the *e* and use another letter incorrectly.

apparently	competent	conscience
dependent	coherent	audience
prominent	current	correspondence
machinery	efficient	existence
independent	experience	magnificent
stationery	opponent	patience
privileges	permanent	superintendent
luncheon	cafeteria	description

Difficult "I" Words

In the following words, the *i*'s have it:

acquainted	auxiliary	business
compliment	definite	exhibition
criticized	sympathized	until
participle	peculiar	principle
quantities	quiet	respectively
physical	individual	hosiery
articles	rime	anticipate

Difficult "O" Words

Do you omit these *o*'s? In the words below, the letter *o* comes in for much abuse and neglect. Be kind to these words:

attorney	authorize	competitors
conspicuous	conqueror	editor
favorable	memorial	minor
notorious	organization	senator
society	strenuously	tailor
odor	aviator	capitol
colonel	accustomed	authority
colors	favorite	interior
humorist	memory	motorist
precious	proprietor	successor
surgeon		

Double Letter Problems

Concentrate on the double letters in these words. They are the cause of many common errors:

accommodate	agreed	agreeable
beginning	committee	guaranteed
embarrass	loose	proceed
necessary	parallel	succeed
recommend	speech	too
across	baggage	assistance
dissatisfaction	affirmative	appearance
disappeared	chauffeur	appropriate
disappointed	immigrant	disapproved
illegible	possession	interrupted
occasion		Mediterranean
opposite		professor

Letters Not "Seen"

It used to be said of children that they should be seen and not heard. These words have letters that are often not seen when writing. Don't omit them:

government	promptly	February
indebted	pamphlet	pledged
	condemn	

Exercise 2

Some of the following words are spelled correctly and some are misspelled. Put a check on the blank if a word is spelled correctly. Rewrite it correctly if it is misspelled.

1.	grammar	_____	11.	odor	_____
2.	seperate	_____	12.	accomodate	_____
3.	usally	_____	13.	proffessor	_____
4.	village	_____	14.	goverment	_____
5.	calender	_____	15.	promptly	_____
6.	existence	_____	16.	accross	_____
7.	description	_____	17.	ilegible	_____
8.	untill	_____	18.	equivelent	_____
9.	attorney	_____	19.	precious	_____
10.	senator	_____	20.	accustomed	_____

Reversal Problems

A common type of misspelling occurs when letters are interchanged. For example, *l* and *v* are often reversed in *relevant* so that the word is misspelled *revelant*. This type of error is called *metathesis*. Observe the correct spelling of the following ten words:

Correct	Incorrect
cavalry	calvary
children	childern
hundred	hunderd
jewelry	jewlery
larynx	larnyx
modern	modren
pattern	pattren
*per*spiration	prespiration
relevant	revelant
western	westren

Notice!

The mountain mentioned in the Bible is Calvary. It is spelled with a capital C and should not be confused with cavalry, a troop of horsemen.

Exercise 3

Fill in the missing letters:

1. hund __ __ d
2. mod __ __ n
3. p __ __ spiration
4. west __ __ n
5. re __ e __ ant

6. ca __ a __ ry
7. child __ __ n
8. jew __ __ __ y
9. lar __ __ x
10. patt __ __ n

6

Some Special Difficulties

You too can succeed in handling
IE* vs. *EI
-CEED* vs. *-SEDE
vs. *-CEDE*
It's not hard!

Some Special Difficulties

The *IE* And *EI* Difficulty

The *Saturday Review of Literature* once published the following story:

A neophyte copy editor in a large advertising agency was slowly going out of his mind because his copy chief was constantly taking a small slip of paper from his breast pocket, looking at it, leering, then putting it back. After watching this for months he managed one day, when the copy chief was taking a nap, to steal the secret paper from the jacket in back of the chief's chair. He opened the slip of paper with trembling hands.

It read.
"*I* before *E* except after *C*"[1]

You may be rel*i*eved when you rec*ei*ve this information. Although a great deal of misch*i*ef has been caused by people who were confused about the use of *ie* or *ei*, there is a simple rule that will take care of all cases. Learn this rule!

Rule

**Put i before e,
Except after c,
Or when sounded like *a*,
As in *neighbor* and *weigh*;
And except *seize* and *seizure*
And also *leisure*,
Weird, *height*, and *either*,
Forfeit and *neither*.**

[1] Reprinted by permission of *Saturday Review of Literature*.

> | Remember! |
>
> When the two letters *IE* or *EI* are sounded like ē, then: It is *i* before *e* except after *c*.

IE

Examine the list below.

belief	piece
field	priest
mischief	relieve
yield	

Notice that in no case does a *c* precede the *ie*. It is always a letter other than *c*.

Now examine the additional list.

achieve	befriend	fief	frieze	handkerchief
aggrieve	believe	fiend	frontier	hygiene
alien	besiege	fierce	grief	interview
chief	bier	fiery	grievance	lief
lien	brief	friend	grieve	liege
niece	lieu	mien	mischief	mischievous
quiet	piebald	pied	pierce	piety
review	relief	relieve	reprieve	retrieve
siege	series	shield	shriek	thievery
view	wield	sieve	thief	yield

Exercise 1

Study the list above carefully; notice that never does a c *precede the* ie. *Any other letter in the alphabet may do so, but not the* c. *Write each word once, one word to a line; pronounce it; then write it once in a sentence; follow this scheme.*

Word	Pronounce	Sentence
achieve	a chēē v	I hope to achieve my goal.

Exercise 2

When you feel certain that you know the preceding words, copy and fill in the missing letters in the following:

1. aggr _ _ ve	6. misch _ _ f	11. rel _ _ ve	16. perc _ _ ve
2. br _ _ f	7. sh _ _ ld	12. l _ _ sure	17. gr _ _ f
3. fr _ _ nd	8. shr _ _ k	13. handkerch _ _ f	18. n _ _ ce
4. gr _ _ ve	9. w _ _ ld	14. rec _ _ pt	19. conc _ _ ve
5. front _ _ r	10. spec _ _ s	15. s _ _ ze	20. v _ _ l

Sometimes it will help you to form words into certain groups. Thus if you associate the words with ch*ief* you will get

chief

handker*chief* mis*chief* mis*chie*vous

If you remember the spelling of *chief* (and few ever forget it), the spelling of the other three is easy for you. Think of:

-*ield*	-*ieve*	-*ief*	-*ier*
f*ield*	rel*ieve*	rel*ief*	t*ier*
sh*ield*	repr*ieve*	br*ief*	front*ier*
	bel*ieve*	bel*ief*	

EI

Now we can master the other combinations. Study the following chart:

Handling *EI*

EI follows C	EI because the sound is ā as in HAY	special cases
dec*ei*t	fr*ei*ght	*ei*ther
perc*ei*ve	v*ei*l	h*ei*ght
rec*ei*ve	n*ei*gh	l*ei*sure
		forf*ei*t
		n*ei*ther
		s*ei*ze
		w*ei*rd
		s*ei*zure

EXAMPLE
EI follows C
Read this list carefully and notice that in each case the *ei* follows *c*.

ce*i*ling	dec*ei*tful
conc*ei*t	dec*ei*ve
conc*ei*ted	rec*ei*pt
conc*ei*ve	rec*ei*ve

EXAMPLE
EI Sounds as Ā
The following list has the *ei* because it sounds like *ā* in *bay*.

deign	rein	veil
inveigh	skein	vein
inveigle	sleigh	weigh
reign	surveillance	weight

You have noticed that in *reign*, there is the sound of *ā*. In *foreign*, *sovereign* and *sovereignty* the *eign* is not sounded as *ā*, but spelled *ei*. This sentence will help you to associate these four words:

The *foreign sovereign* resigned when his *sovereignty* was disputed.

EXAMPLES
Special Cases
1. The final *feit* is pronounced *fit*.

> forfeit
> counterfeit
> surfeit

2. These are pronounced *ī* as *kite*. Be sure to put the *e* in.

> height
> sleight

3. A few words have *cie*, but in all cases the *c* is pronounced as *sh*.

ancient	deficient	glacier	species
conscience	efficient	proficient	sufficient

Exercise 3

As a final test of your skill, have someone dictate the following paragraph to you.

A thief tried to deceive a priest. The priest was a friendly soul, but such mischief was beyond belief. Rather than forfeit the night's receipts, he feigned weakness. He waited for an opportunity to seize his attacker and because of his superior height was able to overpower his enemy.

The -*SEDE*, -*CEED* and -*CEDE* Difficulty

Because various letters are pronounced alike in English, difficulties in spelling arise. Originally the letter *c* was pronounced as a *k*. We know that, because the old Romans of 2,000 years ago sounded it that way. They had a word *centum*, which means "one hundred." Today, when a student in high school studies Latin, he says *kentum* (like kennel). But this same word in Italian is pronounced *chento* (cento); in French it is *saunt* (cent). Because it came into English from the French back in the days of the Norman conquest of 1066, our word *cent* is really one-hundredth part of something and is pronounced *sent*. This similarity of pronunciation between *c* and *s* is responsible for the confusion in spelling words ending in -*cede,* -*ceed*, and -*sede*.

-*SEDE*

You should never forget the single word ending in -*sede*. It is *supersede*.

-*CEED*

You can easily remember all the words in -*ceed*. There are only three:

pro*ceed*   ex*ceed*   suc*ceed*

If you want a little device to aid your memory with these words, think of boxer. First, he is a *pro*-fessional. When he is past his prime, he is an *ex*-fighter; then he has a *suc*-cessor.

-*CEDE*

All the other words in this class end in -*cede*. Some are:

accede	recede
precede	secede
concede	

Remember!

   The ending -CEDE is more common than -SEDE or -CEED. Memorize the few words that end in -SEDE or -CEED. All other words end in -CEDE.

Exercise 4

Have the following passage read aloud to you as you spell the italicized words. If you misspell any, study the reason for the error. Follow the procedure outlined on page 111 for mastering difficult words until you have learned all the words in this group.

Little countries no longer like to *accede* to the wishes of large countries. In many parts of the world the old type of imperialism has been *superseded*. Wars over natural resources are *receding* into history, to be *succeeded* by pacts of mutual interest. Although we cannot be *excessively* optimistic about hopes for permanent peace, we must *concede* that the outlook is bright. The *successor* to the old-time viceroy is the new representative of the former colonial power who *intercedes* in his country's interest, but is always willing to listen to the other side. Such mutual respect must *precede* any plan for world-wide disarmament and eventual peace.

Prefixes

**One simple rule is the key
in adding all prefixes.**

Prefixes

This chapter contains only one rule. The rule is simple and easily learned. It will help you avoid many misspellings. It has to do with prefixes.

A prefix is one or more syllables attached to the beginning of a word. Prefixes, as those below, change the meaning of words to which they are attached.

dis + agree	= disagree
il + logical	= illogical
un + kind	= unkind
mis + spell	= misspell
super + vision	= supervision

A List of Common Prefixes

Here is a list of some common prefixes. Become familiar with them to discover the meaning and spelling of words which are new to you.

Common Prefixes

Prefix	Meaning	Examples
a-	on, in	abed
		afire
	not, without	asexual
		achromatic (without color)
ab-	away, from	abject
		abduct
ante-	before	anteroom (a room before another)
		antediluvian (before the flood)
		antecedent (a preceding event)
anti-	against	antiseptic (against poisoning)
		anti-noise (against noise)
circum-	around	circumscribe (to write around)
		circumnavigate (to sail around)
		circumlocution (act of talking around a topic rather than directly)

Prefix	Meaning	Examples
com-, con-	with, together	concelebrate (to celebrate together)
		commingle (to combine)
de-	down	descend
		demote (to put down)
dis-	apart	dismember (to tear from limb to limb)
		dissolve (to fall apart in a liquid)
		disarm (to separate a soldier from his weapons)
hyper-	above, beyond	hyperactive
		hypercritical
hypo-	under, beneath	hypothesis (an assumption under consideration)
il-, im-, in-, ir-	not	illogical
		immoral
		indisposed
		irrelevant
inter-	among, between	interview
		intercollegiate
		international
intra-	within	intracoastal
		intravenous (with a vein)
		intramural (within the walls)
mis-	wrongly, unfavorably	misjudge
		misunderstand
		misappropriate
non-	not	nonsense
		noncombatant
		nonconformist
over-	excessive	overcharge
		overcoat
per-	through	permeate (to penetrate)
		perspire
		persevere
post-	behind, after	post-mortem (after death)
		postpone
		postgraduate
pre-	before	precede
		precipitate
		predecessor
		prevent
pro-	forward, instead of	procession
		provide (to look forward)
		promote
		provisions

Prefix	Meaning	Examples
re-	back, again, against	refer (to bring back to the previous question)
		retaliate (to fight back)
		retract (to take back)
		repel (to hurl back)
sub-	under	subway
		subtract
		subscribe (to write under written material)
super-	above	superintendent
		superficial
		superstructure
trans-	across	transcontinental
		transfer
		transplant
		translucent (permitting the passage of light)
un-	not	unnatural
		unnoticeable
		unoccupied

Adding a Prefix

Armed with a knowledge of these prefixes, you are now ready for the spelling rule relating to them.

Rule

When you add a prefix, do *not* change the spelling of either the prefix or the original word.

EXAMPLES

dis + appear   = disappear
inter + action   = interaction
in + eligible   = ineligible
trans + mit   = transmit
hyper + sensitive = hypersensitive

Simple, isn't it? Yet with this easy rule, you can spell correctly thousands of words.

Caution!

Most errors occur when a prefix ends with the same letter with which the word begins. For example:

un + natural = unnatural (*not* unatural)
dis + satisfied = dissatisfied (*not* disatisfied)
mis + step   = misstep (*not* mistep)

Remember, when you add a prefix, do *not* change the spelling of either the prefix or the original word.

Exercise 1

How many s's in:

1. di ___(?)___ olve _____
2. di ___(?)___ imilar _____
3. mi ___(?)___ pell _____
4. di ___(?)___ appear _____
5. mi ___(?)___ take _____

Exercise 2

Try your skill in building your own words. Take, for example, scribe, *meaning a writer.*

circum—
trans
sub
de
pro
pre—

⟩scribe

Give the meaning of each.

Exercise 3

By adding the proper Latin prefixes to the following italicized words, spell the new formations correctly.

EXAMPLES:

not *satisfied*   *dissatisfied*
not *legible*   *illegible*

1. A *step* wrongly taken   _____
2. not to *understand*   _____
3. not *similar* _____
4. to *echo* again and again _____
5. below the *standard* _____
6. above the speed of *sound* _____
7. before the time of *Columbus* _____
8. he is against *imperialism* _____
9. one who *navigates* around the globe _____
10. complications after an *operation* _____

Pay Attention to *PER-, PRE-, PRO-*

Some difficulties with the spelling of prefixes may be due to carelessness in pronunciation. Thus if you don't pronounce *prescription* properly, you may not spell the prefix with *pre*. The reverse error may come with a word like *pers*piration, in which the initial *per* may be misspelled.

Knowing the meaning of certain prefixes, as indicated earlier in this chapter, will help you to both know the meaning of the word and its spelling.

PER-, PRE-, PRO-

PER- means "through"

Word	Meaning
permeate	to penetrate through and through
perforate	to pierce through
perpetual	through the years
persist	to continue through a project
persecute	to follow through
perspective	to see through

PRE- means "before"

Word	Meaning
precocious	to develop earlier
prefer	to place before
prepare	to make ready beforehand
prejudice	a judgment before the evidence is in
prescribe	to write before

PRO- means "forward"

Word	Meaning
propose	to place before a group
prophecy	something stated before it happens
proceed	to move forward
proclaim	to shout before
produce	to bring forth
prognosis	to forecast the probable outcome of a disease

__Exercise 4__

Underline the correct spelling of the pairs of words in the following sentences.

1. The secret police (persecuted, presecuted) the prisoner.
2. Let us (preceed, proceed) with the trial.
3. This young bright child was obviously (precocious, percocious).
4. We must look at world affairs in the proper (perspective, prospective).
5. The patient asked the doctor to (proscribe, prescribe) something for his cough.
6. The illness was diagnosed as a (perforated, proferated) ulcer.
7. It costs a great deal to (perduce, produce) a musical comedy.
8. We must (persist, presist) in our efforts to find ways to peace.
9. Searching for the truth requires (perpetual, prepetual) effort.
10. Let us (propose, perpose) a toast.

Confusing Suffixes

Some of the most common suffix problems are treated with simple guidelines.

Confusing Suffixes

A suffix is one or more syllables attached to the end of a word.

EXAMPLES

desire + *able* = desirable
move + *ing* = moving
kind + *ly* = kindly
mean + *ness* = meanness
fame + *ous* = famous

Words Ending in -*ABLE*, -*IBLE*

These suffixes are troublesome. When you are able to add them correctly, you are well on your way to becoming a good speller.

Rule 1

The ending -ABLE is more common than -IBLE. If in doubt, use -ABLE and you have more than a fair chance of being correct.

-*ABLE*

1. Our most familiar words add -ABLE to form the adjective.

comfort + *able* = comfortable
drink + *able* = drinkable
eat + *able* = eatable
laugh + *able* = laughable
read + *able* = readable
talk + *able* = talkable
unthink + *able* = unthinkable

139

2. A noun ending in -ATION will have an adjective ending in -ABLE.

abomination	navigation
abomin*able*	navig*able*

-IBLE

1. Words ending in *-ible* are often preceded by a double SS before the -IBLE.

acce*ss*ible	permi*ss*ible
admi*ss*ible	transmi*ss*ible
compre*ss*ible	

2. Words ending in *-ible* often have a noun form ending in *-ion*. Drop the -ION and add -IBLE.

accession
access*ible*

Examine the following words which are all formed the same way:

admission	expansion	extension
admiss*ible*	expans*ible*	extens*ible*
compression	reversion	corruption
compress*ible*	revers*ible*	corrupt*ible*
permission	coercion	division
permiss*ible*	coerc*ible*	divis*ible*
transmission	comprehension	perception
transmiss*ible*	comprehens*ible*	percept*ible*
combustion	digestion	reprehension
combust*ible*	digest*ible*	reprehens*ible*
destruction	collection	conversion
destruct*ible*	collect*ible*	convert*ible*

3. Use -IBLE to keep the soft sound of *g* or *c*. The word *tangent* has the adjective *tangible* because an *-able* would change the pronunciation of *g* from its present *j* sound to the sound of *g* in *gum*. Other words in this class are:

deduc*ible*	produc*ible*	reduc*ible*
conduc*ible*	corrig*ible*	incorrig*ible*
elig*ible*	inelig*ible*	irasc*ible*
intellig*ible*	invinc*ible*	leg*ible*

Remember!

Be sure that you know all the reasons for adding -*ible*.
1. **It follows double *ss* and comes from a noun ending in -*sion* (permission/permiss*ible*).**
2. **It comes from a noun ending in -*ion* (coercion/coerc*ible*).**
3. **It keeps the *c* or *g* soft (deduc*ible*, elig*ible*).**

Exercise 1

Here is a list of words. Add -able *or* -ible.

account	depend	market
avoid	detest	perish
comfort	discount	return
companion	fashion	review
credit	favor	season

Did you add -able *to each of these? Then you were 100% correct.*
Now add -able *or* -ible *to the roots of these words:*
HINT: consol-*a*-tion   consol-*able*

commendation
admiration
conformation
appreciation
consideration

Did you add -able *to the roots of each of these words? You were 100% correct.*
Remember, a noun ending in -ation *will have an adjective in* -able.
As a final task, add the endings -able, *or* -ible *to the roots of the following words.*
HINT: demonstr-*ation*   demonstr-*able*

derivation	exportation	notation
duration	habitation	refutation
estimation	imagination	separation
execration	irritation	taxation
	lamentation	toleration

You should add -able *to the roots of each of the words.*

Exercise 2

Have someone dictate the following passage which contains many words ending in the suffixes -ible *or* -able.

The prosecuting attorney protested that the evidence by the defendant about his *taxable* income was *inadmissible*. In the first place, it was not easily *accessible*. In the second place, although the evidence was originally *acceptable* in a lower court, the decisions in such courts are *reversible*.

The defendant's attorney objected that such reasoning was *unsupportable* and *intolerable* and that it was *reprehensible* on his opponent's part to bring up such a claim. The tension was increasing *perceptibly*. If this continued, the defending attorney might have to be ejected *forcibly*, or be *eligible* for disbarment. However, it took some time for the atmosphere to be cleared and the case proceeded to its *inevitable* conclusion.

The Adverbial Suffix -*LY*

Rule 2

In forming adverbs from adjectives ending in *-al*, **simply add** *-ly* **to the original word.**

adjective + *ly* = adverb

EXAMPLE
verbal + *ly* = verbally

Exercise 3

Form the adverbs of the following adjectives:

1. accidental
2. critical
3. elemental
4. equal
5. exceptional
6. final
7. general (adj.)
8. incidental
9. intentional
10. ironical
11. logical
12. mathematical
13. practical
14. professional
15. real
16. typical
17. usual
18. verbal
19. global

Words Ending in *-OUS*

-OUS before a Consonant

Rule 3

When adding *-ous* to a noun ending in a consonant, do *not* change the spelling of the noun.

-OUS Before a Consonant

Noun	Suffix		Adjective	Noun	Suffix		Adjective
danger	+ *ous*	=	dangerous	mountain	+ *ous*	=	mountainous
hazard	+ *ous*	=	hazardous	murder	+ *ous*	=	murderous
humor	+ *ous*	=	humorous	peril	+ *ous*	=	perilous
libel	+ *ous*	=	libelous	poison	+ *ous*	=	poisonous
marvel	+ *ous*	=	marvelous	riot	+ *ous*	=	riotous
moment	+ *ous*	=	momentous	slander	+ *ous*	=	slanderous

Caution!

Nouns ending in *-f* change the *f* to *v* when *-ous* is added.

EXAMPLES

grief + *ous*   = grievous (*not* grievious)
mischief + *ous* = mischievous (*not* mischievious)

Remember!

Nouns ending in *-y* drop the *y* and add *e* before *-ous*.

EXAMPLES

beauty + *ous* = beauteous
bounty + *ous* = bounteous
duty + *ous*   = duteous
pity + *ous*   = piteous
plenty + *ous* = plenteous

-*OUS* before a Vowel

Rule 4

When adding -*ous* to a noun ending in -*e*, drop the *e*.

EXAMPLES
adventure + *ous* = adventurous
analogue + *ous* = analogous
desire + *ous* = desirous
trouble + *ous* = troublous

Note!

Occasionally the final -*e* is retained before -*ous* for phonetic reasons, as explained on page 181.

EXAMPLES
courage + *ous* = courageous
advantage + *ous* = advantageous
outrage + *ous* = outrageous

Exercise 4

Write the correct adjectives of the following nouns by adding the suffix -ous.

1. advantage _____	11. plenty _____
2. courage _____	12. adventure _____
3. dolor _____	13. bounty _____
4. peril _____	14. danger _____
5. mountain _____	15. grief _____
6. beauty _____	16. humor _____
7. desire _____	17. outrage _____
8. pity _____	18. duty _____
9. trouble _____	19. libel _____
10. mischief _____	20. poison _____

Troublesome Affixes -*AL*, -*EL*, -*LE*

The endings, -*al*, -*el*, and -*le* are called affixes. They are added to the end of words and are a source of many spelling difficulties because they are pronounced in approximately the same way.

Although there are no hard-and-fast rules governing their use, here are some guide lines which will help you spell correctly most of the words in which they occur.

The Affix -*AL*

> **Rule 5**
>
> The affix -*al* is added to nouns and adjectives only.
> The affix -*al* means *of*, *belonging to*, *pertaining to*, or *appropriate to*.

If you remember these meanings, you will scarcely make a mistake.

EXAMPLES
personal — *of* the person
autumnal — *belonging* to autumn
royal — *pertaining* to a king
nautical — *appropriate* to ships

Common Words Ending in -*AL*

Adjectives		*Adjectives*	
additional	fatal	magical	penal
adverbial	fiscal	mechanical	personal
annual	general	medical	regal
brutal	jovial	neutral	several
classical	legal	normal	trivial
clerical	logical	original	
comical		oval	

Nouns	
acquittal	proposal
arrival	recital
betrayal	refusal
capital	rival
denial	signal

> **Caution!**
>
> Do not confuse *capital*, a city, with *capitol*, a building.

The Affix *-EL*

The affix *-el* originally diminished the meaning of a word to which it was attached. For example, tunnel once meant a small barrel or tun, and chapel meant a small church. Nowadays the original significance of *-el* is forgotten.

If you remember that *-el* is used less frequently than *-al* and if you memorize the spelling of the common words below, you will greatly reduce the possibility of misspelling words in which it appears.

Common Words Ending in *-EL*

bushel	jewel	novel	satchel
cancel	kennel	nickel	shovel
channel	kernel	panel	swivel
flannel	model	parcel	travel
funnel	morsel	quarrel	trowel

The Affix *-LE*

The affix *-le* is used far more frequently than *-al* or *-el*. This method will help you to remember the words that end in *-le*.

1. Examine the following list carefully.
2. Form a mental image of each word.
3. Pronounce each word aloud. Then write it in the air with your finger. Underline the *le* after you complete writing the word in the air.
4. Pronounce the word again.

When you perform these steps, you are visualizing, feeling, and hearing. In other words you are employing three senses to help you remember the correct spelling.

> **Note!**
>
> The affixes *-al* and *-le* are never used to make adjectives from nouns. *Nickel* and *little* are adjectives but they were not formed by adding an affix to a noun.

Common Words Ending in -LE

able	double	muffle	scuttle
ample	dribble	muscle	settle
angle	drizzle	muzzle	shuffle
apostle	fable	myrtle	shackle
article	fickle	needle	shuttle
ankle	fiddle	nestle	sickle
baffle	frizzle	nettle	sizzle
battle	gable	nibble	sparkle
beetle	gentle	nuzzle	sprinkle
bottle	giggle	paddle	squabble
brittle	girdle	peaceable	strangle
buckle	gristle	people	subtle
bundle	grizzle	pestle	tackle
bungle	handle	pickle	thimble
cattle	huddle	possible	thistle
chuckle	humble	prattle	treble
circle	hurdle	principle	tremble
couple	jangle	puzzle	trestle
cripple	jingle	raffle	trickle
castle	juggle	rankle	trifle
corpuscle	jungle	riddle	triple
dangle	knuckle	ruffle	trouble
dazzle	ladle	scribble	turtle
disciple	mantle	scruple	twinkle
	miracle	scuffle	

Exercise 5

Select the word in each pair which is correctly spelled.

1. a. brutel   b. brutal   _____
2. a. proposal   b. proposale   _____
3. a. flannel   b. flannal   _____
4. a. dangle   b. dangel   _____
5. a. drizzel   b. drizzle   _____
6. a. corpuscle   b. corpuscel   _____
7. a. fatal   b. fatel   _____
8. a. swivle   b. swivel   _____
9. a. tripel   b. triple   _____
10. a. signel   b. signal   _____
11. a. battle   b. battel   _____
12. a. quarrle   b. quarrel   _____
13. a. rankel   b. rankle

14. a. mechanicle   b. mechanical   _____
15. a. angal   b. angle   _____
16. a. rival   b. rivle   _____
17. a. jewel   b. jewal   _____
18. a. nickel   b. nickle   _____
19. a. girdel   b. girdle   _____
20. a. tragicle   b. tragical   _____
21. a. thimble   b. thimbel   _____
22. a. capital   b. capitle   _____
23. a. knuckel   b. knuckle   _____
24. a. parcle   b. parcel   _____
25. a. regel   b. regal   _____

Words Ending in *-ER* or *-OR*

The suffixes *-er* and *-or* mean *one who* or *that which*. For example, a *visitor* is *one who visits* and an *indicator* is *that which indicates*.

When should you use *-er* and when should you use *-or*?

Caution!
Although there are many words with these suffixes, there is no rule governing their use.

The lack of rule, however, need not disturb you. Simply remember that most words end in *-or*. Then study the list of *-er* words below and pay attention to those you use most often.

Common Words Ending in *-OR, -ER*

-OR			-ER	
actor	contractor	investigator	advertiser	manager
administrator	counselor	operator	beginner	manufacturer
author	editor	radiator	bookkeeper	passenger
aviator	educator	refrigerator	consumer	purchaser
bachelor	elevator	senator	employer	receiver
collector	escalator	spectator	farmer	stenographer
commentator	governor	sponsor	interpreter	treasurer
conductor	indicator	supervisor	laborer	writer
	inventor			

Words Ending in -AR

A relatively small number of words end in -*ar*. The most common are listed below. If you study the list, this ending should never cause you trouble.

Common Words Ending in -AR

---

beggar	dollar	grammar	familiar
calendar	regular	peculiar	liar
collar	singular	similar	

> ### Notice!
>
> Distinguish between *hangar*, a shelter for housing airplanes, and *hanger*, one who hangs or that which hangs.

Exercise 6

Add the suffix -or, -er, *or* -ar *to each of the following words:*

1. begg __ __
2. receiv __ __
3. conduct __ __
4. passeng __ __
5. govern __ __
6. labor __ __
7. operat __ __
8. doll __ __
9. supervis __ __
10. stenograph __ __

Words Ending in -ANCE, -ENCE

There are no simple ways of learning when to add -*ance* or -*ence*. It is best to study each of the following lists, using the words as often as possible until you habitually spell them correctly.

Common -ANCE, -ANCY, -ANT Words

abundant	descendant	inheritance	remembrance
abundance	elegance	irrelevancy	remonstrance
acquaintance	elegant	irrelevant	repentance
appearance	endurance	lieutenant	repentant
assistance	entrance	maintenance	restaurant
assistant	entrant	nuisance	sergeant
balance	grievance	observance	significance
brilliance	guidance	observant	significant
brilliancy	hindrance	pendant	stimulant
brilliant	ignorance	perseverance	tenancy
clearance	ignorant	pleasant	tenant
countenance	importance	preponderant	tolerance
defendant	important		

Common -ENCE, -ENCY, -ENT Words

absence	correspondent	impertinence	permanence
absent	deference	impertinent	permanent
abstinence	(deferential)	imprudence	persistence
abstinent	dependence	imprudent	persistent
adherence	dependent	independence	pestilence
adherent	difference	independent	precedence
antecedent	different	indulgence	preference
apparent	diffidence	indulgent	presence
audience	diffident	inference	present
coherence	diligence	influence	prominence
coherent	diligent	(influential)	prominent
coincidence	divergence	insistence	providence
concurrence	divergent	insolence	provident
concurrent	efficiency	insolent	reference
conference	efficient	intelligence	repellent
confidence	eminence	intelligent	reverence
confident	eminent	intermittent	reverent
conscience	essence	magnificence	residence
consequence	(essential)	magnificent	resident
consequent	equivalent	occurrence	sentence
competence	excellence	opponent	sufficient
competent	excellent	patent	superintendent
compliment (praise)	existence	patience	tendency
convenience	existent	patient	violence
convenient	experience	penitence	violent
correspondence	government	penitent	

Words Ending in -*ENSE*

There are only a few words ending in -*ense*.

Words Ending in -*ENSE*
---

defense or defence (British)
expense
immense
offense or offence
pretense or pretence
suspense

Exercise 7

Insert a *or* e *in the space indicated for the following words:*

1. complim __ nt
2. remembr __ nce
3. consist __ nt
4. superintend __ nt
5. depend __ nt
6. exist __ nce
7. descend __ nt
8. acquaint __ nce
9. griev __ nce
10. perman __ nt
11. magnific __ nt
12. brilli __ nce
13. compl __ mentary
14. conveni __ nce
15. abund __ nce
16. guid __ nce
17. consci __ nce
18. coincid __ nce
19. appar __ nt
20. consequ __ ntial

Words Ending in -*ARY*, -*ERY*

There are more than 300 words ending in -*ary*. There are only two commonly used words ending in -*ery*.

Common Words Ending in -*ERY*

---

cemetery   stationery

Perhaps it may help you to remember that in cemetery only *e*'s are used. Recall that station*ery* is used to write a lett*er*.

Common Words Ending in -*ARY*

---

auxiliary	honorary	secretary
boundary	imaginary	secondary
centenary	infirmary	tertiary
dictionary	library	tributary
elementary	revolutionary	vocabulary
evolutionary		involuntary

Exercise 8

Select the word in each pair which is correctly spelled, and write it in the blank.

1. a. boundery   b. boundary   _____
2. a. revolutionary b. revolutionery   _____
3. a. cemetary   b. cemetery   _____
4. a. imaginery   b. imaginary   _____
5. a. tributery   b. tributary   _____
6. a. corollary   b. corollery   _____
7. a. coronery   b. coronary   _____
8. a. solitary   b. solitery   _____
9. a. militery   b. military   _____
10. a. infirmary   b. infirmery   _____

Words Ending in *-ISE*, *-IZE*

There are no hard and fast rules to differentiate between the words ending in *-ise* and *-ize*. Perhaps the best procedure would be to master the list of *-ise* words and then remember that all others are spelled *-ize*.

Common Words Ending in *-ISE*, *-IZE*

-ISE

advertise	franchise
(advertisement)	merchandise
advise	revise
adviser	(revision)
arise	supervise
chastise	(supervision)
(chastisement)	surmise
compromise	surprise
demise	reprise
despise	(reprisal)
disguise	
enterprise	
exercise	

-IZE

agonize	hypnotize
antagonize	idolization
authorize	itemize
(authorization)	legitimatize
baptize (but baptism)	localize
burglarize	modernize
capsize	neutralize
centralize	ostracize
characterize	patronize
(characterization)	pulverize
demoralize	realize
dramatize	recognize
emphasize (but emphasis)	solemnize
familiarize	specialize
fertilize	symbolize
generalize	tantalize
generalization	terrorize
humanize	visualize

Note!

There are only two words ending in -YZE:

analyze   paralyze

Exercise 9

Add the suffix -ise *or* -ize *to each of the following stems.*

1. agon _____
2. chast _____
3. exerc _____
4. surpr _____
5. visual _____

6. superv _____
7. modern _____
8. enterpr _____
9. fertil _____
10. general _____

9

Plurals
Of
Nouns

S or *ES*? That is the question. Word endings are a basic clue in forming plurals.

Plurals Of Nouns

Regular Plurals

Rule 1

Most English nouns add -*S* to form the plural.

EXAMPLES
cat + *s*   = cats
hat + *s*   = hats
house + *s* = houses

Nouns Endings in a Sibilant Sound

Rule 2

Nouns ending in a sibilant sound (-*s*, -*ss*, -*sh*, soft -*ch*, -*x*, or -*z*) add -ES to form the plural.

156

Nouns Ending in a Sibilant Sound Add -ES for Plural

Sibilant Sound	Plural Nouns	Sibilant Sound	Plural Nouns
-S	bus + *es* = bus*es*	-SH	*fish* + *es* = fish*es*
	gas + *es* = gas*es*		parish + *es* = parish*es*
-SS	kiss + *es* = kiss*es*	-CH	church + *es* = church*es*
	loss + *es* = loss*es*		lunch + *es* = lunch*es*
	pass + *es* = pass*es*		bunch + *es* = bunch*es*
	class + *es* = class*es*		wench + *es* = wench*es*
	mass + *es* = mass*es*		punch + *es* = punch*es*
	business + *es* = business*es*	-X	box + *es* = box*es*
			tax + *es* = tax*es*
		-Z	buzz + *es* = buzz*es*
			quartz + *es* = quartz*es*

Nouns Ending in Long $\bar{O}$

A number of nouns ending in long $\bar{o}$ add -ES for the plural. Learn this entire list.

Nouns Ending in Long $\bar{O}$ with -ES Plural

buffalo*es*	domino*es*	mosquito*es*	tomato*es*
calico*es*	echo*es*	motto*es*	torpedo*es*
cargo*es*	embargo*es*	negro*es*	veto*es*
desperado*es*	hero*es*	potato*es*	virago*es*
			volcano*es*

A few nouns ending in $\bar{o}$, add only an -S. Remember them by groups.

Nouns Ending in Long $\bar{O}$ with -S Plural

Music		*Miscellaneous*
alto*s*		broncho*s*
soprano*s*		studio*s*
contralto*s*	all are borrowed from Italian	tattoo*s*
piano*s*		torso*s*
solo*s*		

Circular Appearance

dynamo*s*   silo*s*

cameo*s*

Nouns Ending in *-F* or *-FE*

Rule 3

Certain nouns ending in *-f* or *-fe* form the plural by changing *f* to *v* and adding *-S* or *-ES*.

Nouns Changing Final *F* or *-FE* to *-V* and Adding *-S* or *-ES* for Plural

Common Nouns

beef	→ beeves
calf	→ calves
elf	→ elves
knife	→ knives
leaf	→ leaves
life	→ lives
loaf	→ loaves
sheaf	→ sheaves
thief	→ thieves
wife	→ wives
wolf	→ wolves

All of the words above except *calf* may be learned in groups according to the sound of the vowel before the *f*.

Nouns with ee̅ Sound

beef	→ beeves
leaf	→ leaves
sheaf	→ sheaves
thief	→ thieves

Nouns with ī Sound

knife	→ knives
life	→ lives
wife	→ wives

Nouns with el Sound

elf	→ elves
self	→ selves
shelf	→ shelves

Nouns Ending in *-F* and Adding Only *-S* for Plural

-IEF

belief	→ beliefs
brief	→ briefs
chief	→ chiefs
grief	→ griefs
handkerchief	→ handkerchiefs

	-OOF	
hoof	→	hoofs (rarely hooves)
proof	→	proofs
roof	→	roofs
	-RF	
dwarf	→	dwarfs
scarf	→	scarfs (*or* scarves)
turf	→	turfs
wharf	→	wharfs (*or* wharves)

Exercise 1

Write plurals for the following words:

1. reproof _____
2. reprieve _____
3. sieve _____
4. halo _____
5. gulf _____
6. coif _____
7. albino _____
8. shelf _____
9. puff _____
10. muff _____

11. slough _____
12. basso _____
13. mambo _____
14. surf _____
15. trough _____
16. stiletto _____
17. sheaf _____
18. radio _____
19. calf _____
20. sylph _____

Nouns Ending in -*Y*

Rule 4

Words ending in *y* preceded by a *vowel* form their plural by adding -*S*.

Ending in -*Y*, Preceded by a Vowel, Adding -*S* for Plural

day	→	days
boy	→	boys
monkey	→	monkeys
valley	→	valleys
volley	→	volleys

Exercise 2

Write the plurals of these words:

1. abbey
2. alley
3. attorney
4. buoy
5. chimney
6. donkey
7. journey
8. key
9. pulley
10. turkey

Rule 5

When the final -*y* is preceded by a *consonant* or *qu,* the -*y* changes to *i* and -*ES* is added to form the plural.

Words Ending in -Y, Preceded by a Consonant, or qu, Changing -Y to -I and Adding -ES for Plural

academy → academ*ies*
actuary → actuar*ies*
ally → all*ies*
army → arm*ies*
caddy → cadd*ies*
cry → cr*ies*
soliloquy → soliloqu*ies*
obloquy → obloqu*ies*

Special Situations

Compound Nouns

Rule 6

Compound nouns add -*S* or -*ES* to only the principal word to form the plural.

EXAMPLES
In the *in-law* series, the principal word is son, brother, etc.

brother*s*-in-law
mother*s*-in-law

Notice!

A few compound words are practically single words and add the -*S* at the end. This explains such cases as

spoonful*s*	**bowlful***s*
cupful*s*	**handful***s*

Old English Plurals

A long time ago the English language had quite a list of words whose plurals ended not in -*S* but in -*EN*. Only a few are left today, but they never give any trouble because they are learned in the very early grades of school. Other variations follow:

Old English Plurals

General Words

child	→	child*ren*
brother	→	breth*ren* (of a congregation)
ox	→	ox*en*
foot	→	*fee*t
tooth	→	t*ee*th
goose	→	g*ee*se
cannon	→	cannon (*or* cannon*s*)
deer	→	deer
sheep	→	sheep
swine	→	swine

Animals

louse	→	l*ice*
mouse	→	m*ice*

The Sexes

man	→	m*e*n
woman	→	w*o*men

French Words

madam	→	m*e*sdam*es*
monsieur	→	m*e*ssieurs

Names of People

> ### Rule 7
> **As a general rule add S to form the plural of names of people.**

EXAMPLES
All the Johns in the school.
All the Jennys in this class.

Letters, Signs, Figures

> ### Rule 8
> **Letters, signs and figures form their plural by adding 'S.**

EXAMPLES
Cross your t's
Mind your P's and Q's
Underline the 3's in the line.
IQ's

Foreign Words

Foreign words act differently when their plurals are formed. Since many of these foreign plurals are from the Latin, the Latin plurals are used. Other foreign plurals are also given.

1. Many **Latin** words ending in *-us* form their plural by changing the *us* to *i*. The most familiar of such words are

Latin Words changing Final *-US* to *I* for Plural

alumnus	→ alumn*i*
fungus	→ fung*i*
focus	→ foc*i*
radius	→ radi*i*
bacillus	→ bacill*i*
terminus	→ termin*i*

2. Some Latin words ending in *-um* change it to *a* to form the plural. A familiar word to us is *datum, data* (the facts in the case).

Latin Words Changing Final *-UM* to *-A* for Plural

medium	→	media (means of doing things)
addendum	→	addenda (things added to a book or program)
bacterium	→	bacteria
candelabrum	→	candelabra
curriculum	→	curricula
desideratum	→	desiderata
erratum	→	errata
maximum	→	maxima
memorandum	→	memoranda
minimum	→	minima
stadium	→	stadia
stratum	→	strata
---

3. **Greek** has a group of nouns ending in *-is* singular, *-es* plural. A familiar case is *crisis, crises*.

Greek Words Changing *-IS* to *-ES* for Plural

analysis	→	analyses
antithesis	→	antitheses (opposite)
axis	→	axes (center)
ellipsis	→	ellipses
hypothesis	→	hypotheses (assumption)
oasis	→	oases
parenthesis	→	parentheses
synopsis	→	synopses
---

4. The Greek language has given us a few words ending in *-on* singular, *-a* plural. These are from the ancient Greeks.

Greek Plurals

automaton	→	automata (mechanical figures working by themselves)
criterion	→	criteria (standard of judgment)
---

5. From the **French** have come these plurals:

French Plurals
---

beau	→ beaux (or beaus)
tableau	→ tableaux (or tableaus)
chateau	→ chateaux
portmanteau	→ portmanteaux (or portmanteaus)

---

6. These familiar words are all **Italian** plural forms:

Italian Plurals
---

spaghetti
confetti
banditti
ravioli

Exercise 3

Plurals of nouns.
Form the plurals of the following nouns:

1. t
2. Mary
3. anniversary
4. dromedary
5. kerchief
6. 4
7. court-martial
8. lieutenant colonel
9. bay
10. tray
11. flurry
12. sulky
13. surrey
14. inequity
15. satellite
16. functionary
17. avocado
18. dynamo

Exercise 4

Have someone dictate the following passage containing many singular nouns for which you will write the plurals.

Mother sent Mary to the Grand Union to purchase some *grocery* ___ for the long week end. Among the *thing* _____ she wanted to obtain were: *tomato* _____ , *potato* _____ , and *avocado* _____ . She also asked for several *quart* _____ of milk, two *pound* _____ of butter, several *piece* _____ of cake, and a pound of caramel-filled *chocolate* _____ .

After making these and several other *purchase* _____ , Mary started to return home. Several interesting *adventure* _____ occurred to her on the way. She met her friend Nancy who was one of the best *soprano* _____ in the church choir. Mary herself was usually placed among the *alto* _____ . After wandering up and down several narrow *alley* _____ , she ended one of the most interesting *journey* _____ by finding a bundle of *key* _____ , which she had lost several *day* _____ before. Such *event* _____ happen too seldom, and Mary will not forget this for a long time.

The Final -Y

**Why should the Final -*Y*
cause so much trouble?**

**Two simple rules will take
care of all such words.**

The Final -Y

Notice these words:

Singular		Plural
abb(ey)	→	abbeys
journ(ey)	→	journeys
monk(ey)	→	monkeys

The -*Y* Preceded by a Vowel

Rule 1

The final -*Y* following a *vowel* remains *Y* when suffixes are added.

These suffixes may be:

1. The letter -*S* to form the plural.

EXAMPLES

attorney + *s* = attorney*s*
chimney + *s* = chimney*s*
donkey + *s* = donkey*s*
medley + *s* = medley*s*
pulley + *s* = pulley*s*
trolley + *s* = trolley*s*
valley + *s* = valley*s*
volley + *s* = volley*s*

2. The suffix **-*ING*** or **-*ED***.

EXAMPLES

allay + *ed*   = allay*ed*
annoy + *ed* = annoy*ed*
buy   *not applicable*
allay + *ing* = allay*ing*
annoy + *ing* = annoy*ing*
buy + *ing*   = buy*ing*

3. The suffix **-*ER*** meaning *one who*.

EXAMPLES

buy + *er*   = buy*er*
employ + *er* = employ*er*

4. The suffix **-*ANCE***.

EXAMPLE

convey + *ance* = convey*ance*

5. The suffix **-*AL***.

EXAMPLE

portray + *al* = portray*al*

Exercise 1

Spell the following words correctly.

1. *tourney* in plural   _____
2. The past tense of *allay*   _____
3. The past tense of *volley*   _____
4. *alley* in plural   _____
5. Past tense of *survey*   _____
6. Present participle of *portray*   _____
7. Past tense of *journey*   _____
8. Past tense of *relay*   _____
9. Plural of *delay*   _____
10. Past tense of *parlay*   _____

The -*Y* Preceded by a Consonant

Rule 2

When a *consonant* precedes the -*Y*, the *Y* changes to *I* when suffixes are added.

Kinds of suffixes:

1. The plural of the noun formed with **-ES**.

    EXAMPLES
    ally + *es*   = all*ies*
    enemy + *es* = enem*ies*
    salary + *es*   = salar*ies*
    tragedy + *es* = traged*ies*

2. The verb form with *he, she,* or *it,* formed by adding **-ES**, or **-ED**.

    EXAMPLES
    carry + *es*   = carr*ies*
    dignify + *es* = dignif*ies*
    marry + *es* = marr*ies*
    carry + *ed*   = carr*ied*
    dignify + *ed* = dignif*ied*
    merry + *ed* = merr*ied*

3. Making an adjective by adding **-FUL**.

    EXAMPLES
    beauty + *ful* = beaut*iful*
    mercy + *ful* = merc*iful*
    pity + *ful*   = pit*iful*

4. Making a noun by adding **-NESS**.

    EXAMPLES
    busy + *ness* = bus*iness*
    cozy + *ness* = coz*iness*
    icy + *ness*   = ic*iness*

5. Making an adverb by adding **-LY**.

    EXAMPLES
    airy + *ly*   = air*ily*
    angry + *ly*   = angr*ily*
    busy + *ly*   = bus*ily*
    clumsy + *ly* = clums*ily*

Caution!

There is only one case in which the *Y* is retained. This is before *-ING*.

EXAMPLES
carry + *ing* = carry*ing*
copy + *ing* = copy*ing*

Exercise 2

In the space to the right put the letter C if the spelling is correct. If it is incorrect, write the proper spelling.

1. merciful _____
2. beautiful _____
3. cozily _____
4. attornies _____
5. valleys _____
6. surveyor _____
7. portraying _____
8. pitying _____
9. busied _____
10. icyly _____

Exercise 3

Write the correct spelling of the following words all of which end in final Y before adding a suffix.

1. pretty + ness _____
2. petty + ness _____
3. steady + ing _____
4. ready + ed _____
5. bully + s _____
6. airy + ness _____
7. pity + ed _____
8. tally + ing _____
9. buy + er _____
10. duty + ful _____
11. ready + ness _____
12. carry + ed _____
13. hurry + ing _____
14. copy + er _____
15. sloppy + ness _____
16. lively + hood _____

Remember!

When adding the present participle (-*ing*) to verbs ending in -*Y*, do not change the *Y*.

EXAMPLES

Word	+ ING	=	Present Participle
accompany	+ ing	=	accompanying
bury	+ ing	=	burying
hurry	+ ing	=	hurrying
study	+ ing	=	studying
worry	+ ing	=	worrying

11

The Final -*E*

DyEing or *Dying*?

One *E* can make a world of difference.

The Final -E

As you know, English has five *vowels:* A, E, I, O, U. The other letters are called *consonants.* Very often a consonant or group of consonants is added to a word and we get a second word. For example, let us consider the letters *-ry.* Add these to the following nouns (names of persons, places, acts, or things).

chemist   — one who analyzes things
chemist*ry* — the science of matter

forest   — the collection of trees
forest*ry* — the study of care of forests

peasant   — worker of the soil
peasant*ry* — the group of peasants

mimic   — one who imitates another
mimic*ry* — the art of imitation

You see that no change occurs in spelling. You simply add the final element to a familiar word and you get a second word of a different meaning.

There are many endings of this character. If you remember that they do not change the spelling of the original word, you will find that they are really old friends with new attachments.

Exercise 1

Write the following words correctly by adding the suffix indicated:

1. pleasant + ry   _____
2. artist + ry   _____
3. portrait + ure   _____
4. clock + wise   _____
5. rocket + ry   _____
6. sophist + ry   _____
7. nation + ality   _____
8. person + ality   _____
9. dialectic + al   _____
10. practical + ity   _____

Few writers have any trouble in spelling words with added parts such as those described. But when a silent *-E* occurs at the end of a word, problems arise. When should you retain the silent *-E* and when should you drop it?

Dropping the Final *-E*

Rule 1

Drop the final *-E* before a suffix beginning with a *vowel* (*a, e, i, o, u*).

Suffixes Beginning with a Vowel

-able	-ence
-ed	-ance
-er	-ing
-est	-ous
-ity	

How to handle these suffixes.

1. Dropping the final *e* before *-ER*.

   EXAMPLES
   large + *er* = larg*er*
   love + *er* = lov*er*
   live + *er* = liv*er*

2. Dropping the final *e* before **-EST**.

EXAMPLES

large + *est* = larg*est*
die + *est* = (thou) di*est*

3. Dropping the final *e* before **-ABLE**.

EXAMPLES
move + *able* = mov*able*
love + *able* = lov*able*
imagine + *able* = imagin*able*
advise + *able* = advis*able*
desire + *able* = desir*able*

4. Dropping the final *e* before **-ING**.

EXAMPLES
come + *ing* = com*ing*
receive + *ing* = receiv*ing*
ache + *ing* = ach*ing*

Note!

When -*ing* is ADDED to words ending in -*ie*, the -*e* is dropped and the *i* changed to *y* to prevent two *i*'s from coming together.
die + *ing* = d*ying*
lie + *ing* = l*ying*

Since many mistakes are made with the -*ing* words, the following list is provided. It contains some of your most useful words.

Handling -*ING*

whine	argue	advise
whin*ing*	argu*ing*	advis*ing*
write	surprise	dine
writ*ing*	surpris*ing*	din*ing*
shine	owe	lose
shin*ing*	ow*ing*	los*ing*
oblige	purchase	fascinate
oblig*ing*	purchas*ing*	fascinat*ing*
judge	pursue	become
judg*ing*	pursu*ing*	becom*ing*
choose	tie	use
choos*ing*	tying	us*ing*

5. Dropping final *e* before **-OUS**.

EXAMPLE

The suffix *-ous* is frequently added to a verb to make an adjective which always has the meaning, *full of*.

desire + *ous* = desir*ous*

EXAMPLE

Sometimes the suffix *-ous* is added to a noun. Again an adjective results also meaning, *full of*.

pore + *ous* = por*ous* full of pores

6. Dropping final *e* before **-ITY**.

EXAMPLE

The suffix *-ity* may be added to an adjective to form a noun. The final *E* before the suffix disappears.

divine + *ity* = divin*ity*

The same thing happens with these words:

Handling -ITY

---

austere	extreme	immense
auster*ity*	extrem*ity*	immens*ity*
dense	facile	intense
dens*ity*	facil*ity*	intens*ity*
docile	grave	oblique
docil*ity*	grav*ity*	obliqu*ity*
opportune	passive	rare
opportun*ity*	passiv*ity*	rar*ity*
scarce	sincere	suave
scarc*ity*	sincer*ity*	suav*ity*

Exercise 2

Form new words by spelling the following:

1. revere + ing
2. love + ly
3. purchase + able
4. extreme + ly
5. pleasure + able
6. large + ly
7. nudge + ed
8. state + ed
9. fete + ed
10. fine + ed
11. dive + ing
12. shove + ed
13. devise + ing
14. deceive + ed
15. relieve + ing
16. procrastinate + ing
17. imagine + ed
18. besiege + ed
19. receive + ing

Caution! ·

Verbs ending in *oe* (canoe) retain the -*E* to preserve the pronunciation.

> **canoeing   hoeing   shoeing   toeing.**

Dye and *singe* **retain the -*E* to differentiate the word from *die* and *sing***

> **dyeing (one's hair)**
> **dying (absence of life)**
> **singeing (one's hair)**
> **singing (a song)**

Exercise 3

Form the present participle (+ -ing) and the past participle (+ -ed) of the following verbs.

Word	Present Participle	Past Participle
1. benefit	_____	_____
2. commit	_____	_____
3. lure	_____	_____
4. refer	_____	_____
5. pine	_____	_____
6. elevate	_____	_____
7. propel	_____	_____
8. fit	_____	_____
9. recur	_____	_____
10. remit	_____	_____
11. open	_____	_____
12. club	_____	_____
13. plunge	_____	_____
14. singe	_____	_____
15. pursue	_____	_____
16. scare	_____	_____
17. throb	_____	_____
18. trot	_____	_____
19. use	_____	_____
20. whip	_____	_____

Retaining the Final -*E*

Rule 2

The final -*E* is retained when the suffix begins with a *consonant*.

Suffixes Beginning with a Consonant

-ness	-ful
-ment	-less

How to handle these suffixes.

1. Adding the suffix *-NESS*.
   Examine the following words which all belong in this class:

Handling -*NESS*

complete	genuine	acute
complete*ness*	genuine*ness*	acute*ness*
expensive	large	appropriate
expensive*ness*	large*ness*	appropriate*ness*
coarse	fierce	vague
coarse*ness*	fierce*ness*	vague*ness*
like	polite	remote
like*ness*	polite*ness*	remote*ness*
rude	wide	white
rude*ness*	wide*ness*	white*ness*

---

2. Adding the suffix *-MENT*.
   Examine the following words which are all formed the same way:

Handling -*MENT*

amuse	discourage	achieve
amuse*ment*	discourage*ment*	achieve*ment*
arrange	enforce	advance
arrange*ment*	enforce*ment*	advance*ment*
atone	engage	advertise
atone*ment*	engage*ment*	advertise*ment*
commence	excite	amaze
commence*ment*	excite*ment*	amaze*ment*
move	require	manage
move*ment*	require*ment*	manage*ment*

Note!

Abridgement, acknowledgement, and *judgement* **may also be spelled** *abridgment, acknowledgment,* **and** *judgment.*

3. Adding the suffix *-FUL*.
The following words belong to this division:

Handling *-FUL*

---

care	tune
care*ful*	tune*ful*
revenge	resource
revenge*ful*	resource*ful*
taste	remorse
taste*ful*	remorse*ful*
grace	hate
grace*ful*	hate*ful*
disgrace	shame
disgrace*ful*	shame*ful*

---

4. Adding the suffix *-LESS*.
Again the silent *E* is preserved because the suffix begins with the consonant *l*.

Handling *-LESS*

---

age	grace	sense	taste
age*less*	grace*less*	sense*less*	taste*less*
care	guide	shape	voice
care*less*	guide*less*	shape*less*	voice*less*
shame	tongue	cease	name
shame*less*	tongue*less*	cease*less*	name*less*
change	noise	smoke	use
change*less*	noise*less*	smoke*less*	use*less*

> ## Caution!
>
> **Some exceptions.**
> - *Due, true, whole,* **drop the *-E* before *-LY*—*duly, truly, wholly.***
> - **Some words ending in *-E*, drop the *-E* before *-MENT* or *-FUL*.**
> **Argument is an instance, as is *awful* (from awe).**

Unusual Situations

Some words retain the final -*E* regardless of the suffix in order to retain pronunciation.

1. When the word ends in double -*EE*, the final -*E* is not dropped. This happens in order to retain the same pronunciation.

    EXAMPLES

agree	see
agree*able*	see*able*
agree*ing*	see*ing*
agree*ment*	

2. Words ending in -*OE* retain the final -*E*.

    EXAMPLES

canoe	shoe
canoe*ing*	shoe*maker*
woe	shoe*string*
woe*ful*	shoe*ing*
woe*begone*	hoe
	hoe*ing*

3. Words ending in -*CE* or -*GE* will retain the final -*E* before a suffix beginning with a vowel. This is necessary to keep the soft pronunciation.

    EXAMPLES

notice	change	outrage
notice*able*	change*able*	outrage*ous*
service	courage	advantage
service*able*	courage*ous*	advantage*ous*

Certain words would lose their hard pronunciation of certain consonants unless a -*K* is added before a suffix beginning with *E*, *I*, or *Y* (used as vowel).

EXAMPLES

mimic + ing = mimicing would not be pronounced with the hard *c* (= to *k*). Hence the *k* is inserted between the final *c* and the beginning vowel of the suffix. Note the following.

colic → colic*k*y
frolic → frolic*king* → frolic*ked*
mimic → mimic*king* → mimic*ked*
panic → panic*king* → panic*ked*
picnic → picnic*king* → picnic*ked*
traffic → traffic*king* → traffic*ked*

Explain why this is not done for *frolicsome* or *panic-stricken* or *traffic-cop*.

Exercise 4

Try your hand at spelling these words containing the final -E and a suffix.

1. agree	+MENT	=	_____
2. amuse	+MENT	=	_____
3. care	+FUL	=	_____
4. canoe	+ING	=	_____
5. come	+ING	=	_____
6. disagree	+ABLE	=	_____
7. engage	+MENT	=	_____
8. excite	+MENT	=	_____
9. immense	+ITY	=	_____
10. like	+LY	=	_____
11. safe	+TY	=	_____
12. sense	+LESS	=	_____
13. shine	+ING	=	_____
14. enlarge	+MENT	=	_____
15. entice	+ING	=	_____
16. perceive	+ED	=	_____
17. escape	+ING	=	_____
18. discharge	+ED	=	_____
19. relieve	+ING	=	_____
20. contrive	+ANCE	=	_____

Exercise 5

Have someone read the following sentences from dictation as you spell the words correctly. There will be many examples of dropping or retaining the final -E.

1. While they were *staring* at the stars, they saw something *stirring* in the bushes.
2. It takes much *planning* to build a house *preferred* by others.
3. The *cannery* used plenty of *cane* sugar with such fruits as *pineapples* and peaches.
4. Dressed *sloppily*, the tramps *plodded* along wearily on the *pitted* country road.
5. By using *scraps* of food, the cook managed to scrape together a fair meal after the *scrapping* of the parents was over.
6. The little *moppet* sat *moping* in her little chair while the mother *mopped* up the food which was lying *sloppily* on the floor.
7. After we *refused* to have anything to do with her, the discharged maid *fumed* and *fussed effusively* and finally stamped out of the room.
8. By *dotting* your *i*'s and *crossing* your *t*'s you can take a small step toward *better spelling*.
9. While a troop of cavalry was *ridding* the woods of the stragglers, a second troop was *riding* into the village.
10. As the giant airliner *hopped* off, my parents were praying and hoping that all would go well.

Exercise 6

Each of the following words has an error in the dropping or retention of final -E. Make the correction in the space to the right.

1. scarcly _____
2. vengance _____
3. truely _____
4. tastey _____
5. noticable _____
6. changable _____
7. perspireing _____
8. retireing _____
9. aweful _____

10. wisedom _____
11. assureance _____
12. insureance _____
13. outragous _____
14. servicable _____
15. couragous _____
16. gorgous _____
17. pronouncable _____

12

Doubling Final Consonants

**Bene*fitt*ing?   Bene*fit*ing?
Ri*d*ing?   Ri*dd*ing?**

Two rules can get the situation under control.

Doubling Final Consonants

Do you know the difference between *riding* a horse and *ridding* the house of undesirable visitors? Do you know when people are *hoping* and when they are *hopping*? These are some examples of words with doubled consonants. There is no reason why anyone should suffer while trying to remember whether to spell a word with one or with two final consonants, for there are rules which will take care of all cases.

How many times have you been puzzled about doubling a consonant?

Does *beginning* have two *n*'s in the middle?

Does *omitted* have two *t*'s?

Why has *benefiting* one *t*, while *admitting* has two?

These and all other questions are easily answered if you will remember these two rules. There are very few rules in English as sure to help you as these.

One-Syllable Words

First you must recall the meaning of the word *syllable*. A syllable is a unit of spoken language forming either a whole word (as *men*) or a division of a word (as *priv* in *priv·i·lege*). Look at these words.

run   *swim*   *hop*

Each of these has a vowel in the middle and a consonant at the end. These make up one syllable and such a word is called a one-syllable word. But look at these:

con·fer   *pre·fer*   *trans·fer*

You notice that we have at least *two* syllables in each word. Now we can proceed to the rules. Notice what happens to our three friends when we add *-ing*.

ru*nn*ing   swi*mm*ing   ho*pp*ing

185

The final consonant (*n, m, p*) has been doubled before a suffix beginning with a vowel. We could have added the suffix *-er*.

ru*nn*er swi*mm*er ho*pp*er

Rule 1

When a one-syllable word ends in one vowel and one consonant, that consonant is *doubled* before a suffix beginning with a vowel.

Now discover for yourself what would happen to the final consonants of these words.

One-Syllable Words Doubling Consonant Before Suffix Beginning with Vowel

Word	+ ER	+ ING
hit →	hi*tt*er →	hi*tt*ing
spin →	spi*nn*er →	spi*nn*ing
wrap →	wra*pp*er →	wra*pp*ing
trim →	tri*mm*er →	tri*mm*ing

These words are easy.

The following words have more than one syllable but they follow the same rule as the words just described. They *double* their final consonant before a suffix beginning with a vowel.

Word	+ ER	+ ING	+ Other Suffix
admit	⟶	admi*tt*ing →	admi*tt*edly
begin	→ begi*nn*er →	begi*nn*ing	
compel	⟶	compe*ll*ing	
confer	⟶	confe*rr*ing	
control	⟶	contro*ll*ing →	contro*ll*able
commit	⟶	commi*tt*ing	
equip	⟶	equi*pp*ing	
omit	⟶	omi*tt*ing	

Words of More Than One Syllable

Rule 2

A word of more than one syllable ending in a single vowel and a single consonant, which has the accent on the final syllable, *doubles* that consonant before a suffix beginning with a vowel. *Remember, the accent must be on the last syllable*.

occ·ur′   ad·mit′   per·mit′

If the final syllable has no accent, there will be no doubling of the consonant. Thus, *benefit* will not double the *t*, because the accent is on the first syllable.

be′·ne·fit·ing   tra′·vel·ed

Note!

Study the suffixes to the following words. Each word satisfies three conditions.
1. It is more than one syllable.
2. The last syllable has the accent.
3. The last syllable ends in *one* vowel and a *single* consonant.

Two-Syllable Words Doubling Consonant Before Suffix Beginning with Vowel

Word	+ ING	+ ED	+ Other Suffix
abet	→ abetting	→ abetted	→ abettor
abhor	→ abhorring	→ abhorred	→ abhorrence
admit	→ admitting	→ admitted	→ admittance
allot	→ allotting	→ allotted	→ allottance
annul	→ annulling	→ annulled	→ annulment
			(one *l* because the suffix begins with a consonant)
confer	→ conferring	→ conferred	→ conference
			(one *r* because the accent is not on *fer* but *con*)
concur	→ concurring	→ concurred	→ concurrence

Word	+ ING	+ ED	+ Other Suffix
defer	→ deferring	→ deferred	→ deference
			(only one *r* because accent is *not* on last syllable)
dispel	→ dispelling	→ dispelled	
excel	→ excelling	→ excelled	
infer	→ inferring	→ inferred	→ inference
			(one *r*. Why?)
occur	→ occurring	→ occurred	→ occurrence
omit	→ omitting	→ omitted	
permit	→ permitting	→ permitted	
rebel	→ rebelling	→ rebelled	→ rebellion
recur	→ recurring	→ recurred	→ recurrence
refer	→ referring	→ referred	→ reference
			(one *r*. Why?)
regret	→ regretting	→ regretted	
transfer	→ transferring	→ transferred	

Special Situations

Rule 3

When adding -*NESS* to a word, use *nn* if the original word ends in *n*.

EXAMPLES
mean + *ness* = mean*ness*
plain + *ness* = plain*ness*
thin + *ness* = thin*ness*

Rule 4

Words ending in -*FUL* have a single *l* unless -*ly* is added.

EXAMPLES

careful + *ly*	= careful*ly*	hopeful + *ly*	= hopeful*ly*
beautiful + *ly*	= beautiful*ly*	useful + *ly*	= useful*ly*
dutiful + *ly*	= dutiful*ly*	youthful + *ly*	= youthful*ly*
wonderful + *ly*	= wonderful*ly*		

Exercise 1

Below is a list of verbs of one syllable. Add -ing to each of them. Some will double their final consonant. Some will not. Why? Remember Rule 1. There must be only one vowel and one consonant.

1. cramp _____
2. drum _____
3. grin _____
4. hit _____
5. look _____
6. nod _____
7. pain _____
8. rest _____
9. rig _____
10. scrub _____

Six out of the ten doubled their consonants. The remaining four did not because they had a vowel and two consonants (cr-a-mp) or two vowels and consonant (l-oo-k)

How Consonants Determine Meaning

Now for a few pairs of words with different meanings, depending upon the doubling of the consonants.

bar	→	He *barred* the door.
bare	→	He *bared* his arm.

din	→	The teacher *dinned* it into John's ear.
dine	→	We *dined* at four.

pin	→	Mary *pinned* her dress.
pine	→	Mary *pined* away.

plan	→	They *planned* a happy life.
plane	→	The carpenter *planed* the wood.

scrap	→	The two dogs *scrapped*.
scrape	→	Walter *scraped* his new knife on the cement floor.

wag	→	He *wagged* his head solemnly.
wage	→	He *waged* a bitter war.

Notice how the meaning is determined by the single or double consonant and why correct spelling is so important to convey your meaning.

Notice these few exceptions to the rule: *chagrined, gaseous, transferable, transference, transferee, facility.*

Exercise 2

Write correctly the words formed as the exercise indicates:

1. defer + ed _____
2. refer + ence _____
3. shop + ing _____
4. disapprove + al _____
5. nine + teen _____
6. hit + ing _____
7. singe + ing _____
8. fame + ous _____
9. control + ing _____
10. repel + ent _____

11. desire + ing _____
12. tire + less _____
13. true + ly _____
14. swim + er _____
15. trim + er _____
16. occur + ence _____
17. move + able _____
18. commit + ed _____
19. equip + age _____
20. excel + ing _____

Exercise 3

Write the present participle *(+ing) and past participle (+ed) of the following verbs. Some will double the final consonant; others will not. When in doubt, refer to the rules on doubling final consonants.*

Word	Present Participle	Past Participle
1. adapt		
2. cramp		
3. design		
4. conceal		
5. congeal		
6. blot		
7. stop		
8. crush		
9. excel		
10. defer		
11. envelop		
12. extol		
13. flutter		
14. happen		
15. hum		
16. level		
17. quarrel		
18. rub		
19. signal		
20. retreat		

Exercise 4

By adding the various endings, make new words. In some instances, the final consonant of the original word will be doubled. When in doubt, refer to the rules about doubling final consonants.

EXAMPLE

Form an adjective of the word *woman* by adding *-ish*.

Word	*Suffix*	*New Word*
woman	-ish	womanish

1. Form an adjective of *wit* by adding *-y*. _____
2. Form a noun from the verb *spin* by adding *-er*. _____
3. Form a noun from the noun *blot* by adding *-er*. _____
4. Form a noun by adding *-er* to *design*. _____
5. Form an adjective by adding *-ical* to *quiz*. _____
6. Form a noun by adding *-er* to *shut*. _____
7. Form a noun by adding *-er* to *slip*. _____
8. Form a noun by adding *-eer* to *profit*. _____
9. Form a noun by adding *-ing* to *meet*. _____
10. Form a noun by adding *-er* to *dry*. _____
11. Add *-able* to *inhabit* to form an adjective. _____
12. Add *-er* to *toil* to form a noun. _____
13. Add *-er* to *put* to form a noun. _____
14. Add *-ment* to *develop* to form a noun. _____
15. Add *-ment* to *defer* to form a noun. _____
16. Add *-er* to *rub* to form a noun. _____
17. Add *-er* to *develop* to form a noun. _____
18. Make the feminine of *god*. _____
19. Name the man who sells you drugs. _____
20. Add *-er* to *trap* to form a noun. _____

Exercise 5

Add the indicated ending to each of the following words.

1. tearful + ly _____
2. careful + ly _____
3. open + ness _____
4. dutiful + ly _____
5. bountiful + ly _____
6. common + ness _____
7. mimic + ed _____
8. picnic + ing _____
9. mimic + ing _____
10. panic + y _____

British and American Spelling

Remember to follow American usage unless there is a compelling reason for adopting a British variant.

British and American Spelling

American spelling does not differ extensively from British spelling, but there are differences. Some of the more important differences are listed below.

British and American Spelling Equivalents

American	versus	British	American	versus	British
-er	*versus*	*-re*	*-or*	*versus*	*-our*
center		centre	color		colour
kilometer		kilometre	labor		labour
theater		theatre	humor		humour
l	*versus*	*ll*	*-se*	*versus*	*-ce*
counselor		counsellor	defense		defence
labeled		labelled	offense		offence
traveled		travelled	pretense		pretence
ll	*versus*	*l*	*-ze/z*	*versus*	*-se/s*
enrollment		enrolment	analyze		analyse
skillful		skilful	criticize		criticise
installment		instalment	organization		organisation

Exercise

The following words are spelled as they are in Great Britain. On the line opposite each word write the American form.

1. candour _____
2. theatre _____
3. labour _____
4. labelled _____
5. traveller _____
6. realisation _____
7. criticise _____
8. skilful _____
9. defence _____
10. analyse _____

English
as a
Second
Language

14

Help for Spanish-Speaking Students

Spanish spelling is more logical than English spelling. The following hints can help you overcome your problems with English.

Help for Spanish-Speaking Students

Spanish words are easy to spell because almost every letter represents only one sound and every letter is pronounced.

Spanish speakers find some English words difficult to spell because some letters represent more than one sound and some letters are not pronounced. Spanish spelling is logical and predictable. English spelling is inconsistent and not always controlled by rules.

If your native language is Spanish, the following hints will help you spell English words correctly.

Different Spellings for the Same Sound

F and PH

Spanish words with an *f* sound are sometimes spelled with a *ph* in English. The sound is the same but the spelling is different.

F and PH Sound Alike

Spanish	English	Spanish	English
catástrofe	catastrophe	geografía	geography
farmacéutico	pharmacist	hemisferio	hemisphere
farmacia	pharmacy	párrafo	paragraph
frase	phrase	teléfono	telephone
filósofo	philosopher	triunfante	triumphant
fotografía	photograph		

Notice!

All the words in the above list are derived from Greek. In such words the sound of *f* is spelled *ph* in English. In most other English words *f* is used; for example, *f*riend, pre*f*er, scar*f*.

CU and *QU*

The sound represented by *cu* in Spanish is spelled *qu* in English, as you may see from the following words:

CU and *QU* Sound Alike

Spanish	English
cuestión	*qu*estion
frecuente	fre*qu*ent
frecuentemente	fre*qu*ently

Spanish *i* and Its Equivalents

The vowel in s*i*, qu*i*, am*i*go is also an English sound. In Spanish this sound is represented by *i*. In English there are ten different ways of representing this sound as shown below.

Spanish *i* and Its Equivalents

Spanish	English
i as in qu*i*, s*i*	ae — as in *Ae*sop, C*ae*sar
	ay — as in qu*ay*
	e — as in *e*ternal, sc*e*nic, conv*e*ne
	ea — as in *ea*ch, b*ea*n, t*ea*
	ee — as in *ee*ry, sl*ee*k
	ei — as in *ei*ther, rec*ei*ve
	eo — as in p*eo*ple
	ey — as in k*ey*
	i — as in mach*i*ne, rav*i*ne, fat*i*gue, cl*i*que
	ie — as in pr*ie*st, ser*ie*s

Exercise 1

Indicate at the right whether the following English words are correctly spelled. Place a C if correct and an X if wrong. If a word is misspelled, spell it correctly.

1. farmacy _____
2. photograf _____
3. philosopher _____
4. geography _____
5. frecuently _____
6. eather _____
7. machene _____
8. triumfant _____
9. peeple _____
10. priest _____
11. recieve _____
12. paragraf _____
13. sereis _____
14. convean _____
15. fatiegue _____

Spanish *u* and Its Equivalents

In Spanish the letter *u* (p*u*ro, C*u*ba) represents a sound which is also used in English but spelled differently. Note that there are several ways of spelling this sound:

Spanish *u* and Its Equivalents

Spanish	English
	oo — as in g*oo*se, al*oo*f, sp*oo*n, r*oo*ster, t*oo*
	ou — as in gr*ou*p, tr*ou*pe, ac*ou*stic, b*ou*quet
u as in p*u*ro, C*u*ba	ough — as in thr*ough*
	u — as in r*u*ler, br*u*tal
	ui — as in fr*ui*t, s*ui*table
	o — as in d*o*, t*o*, two

To, Too, and *Two*

> ### Notice!
>
> The confusion of *to, too*, and *two* is a common error. Be sure you know the difference.

	To	Too	Two
Meaning	a preposition meaning the *opposite of from*; the sign of the infinitive.	an adverb meaning *also* or more than enough.	an adverb meaning *twice* one.
Examples	to the theatre, to go	too late	two friends

Here is a sentence in which the three words are used correctly: The *two* friends wanted *to* go *to* the theatre but they were *too* late.

Exercise 2

Every word below is misspelled. Cross it out and spell it correctly.

1. truip _____
2. brootal _____
3. sootable _____
4. ruster _____
5. throo _____
6. acoostic _____
7. aluf _____
8. ruiler _____
9. booquet _____
10. guis _____

Exercise 3

Compose a sentence in which to, too, *and* two *are used correctly.*

Double Consonants

There are only two double consonants in Spanish, *ll* and *rr*. There are many in English.

Double Consonants

Spanish	English	
ll	cc	mm
rr	ff	pp
	gg	tt
	ll	

Observe that the English words listed below have double consonants while their Spanish counterparts have only one.

English Double Consonants (with Spanish Equivalent)

Consonant	English	Spanish
cc	accent	(el acento)
	accord	(el acuerdo)
	occult	(el oculto)
	occupied	(ocupado)
	occur	(ocurrir)
	accept	(aceptar)
ff	different	(diferente)
	suffer	(sufrir)
	sufficient	(suficiente)
gg	exaggerated	(exagerado)
ll	alliance	(la alianza)
	dollar	(el dólar)
	intelligent	(inteligente)
mm	common	(común)
	grammar	(gramática)
pp	appear	(aparecer)
	appetite	(apetito)
	applaud	(aplaudir)
	apprehend	(aprender)
	approximately	(aproximadamente)
tt	attack	(ataque)
	attention	(atención)
	battle	(batalla)
	bottle	(botella)
	button	(botón)

Exercise 4

*Some of the following words are spelled correctly and some are misspelled.
Put a C on the blank if a word is spelled correctly. Re-write it correctly if
it is misspelled.*

1. acord   _____
2. dollar   _____
3. ocurr   _____
4. appetite   _____
5. aprehend   _____
6. aproximately   _____
7. applaud   _____
8. sufer   _____
9. buton   _____
10. aliance   _____
11. accept   _____
12. ocupied   _____
13. diferent   _____
14. gramar   _____
15. exaggerated   _____
16. apear   _____
17. suficient   _____
18. atention   _____
19. battle   _____
20. occult   _____

Notice!

**Double consonants are more common in English than in Spanish.
Consult the rules on pages 186 – 188 for doubling consonants. You
will find them helpful.**

The English *J* Sound

In Spanish, *j* is pronounced like English *h* in *hello!*, *have*, and *here*. The
English *j* sound does not exist in Spanish. It resembles Spanish *ch* in *muchacho*
except that it is voiced.

To understand the meaning of a voiced consonant, put your fingers on each
side of your voice box (larynx). Say the sounds of *m, n, r*. Can you feel your
vocal cords vibrate? These are called voiced consonants because they are made
with the aid of the vocal cords.

Now say the sound of *ch*. Notice that your vocal cords do not vibrate. A consonant made without vibration of the vocal cords is called a voiceless consonant.

J Sound Spelling Variations

"J" Sound
- di — as in cor*di*al, sol*di*er
- dg — as in bri*dge*, fu*dge*, slu*dge*
- g — as in *g*em, *g*ist, alle*g*e, ma*g*ic, lon*g*itude, lon*g*evity, an*g*el, dan*g*er
- gg — as in su*gg*est
- j — as in *j*ade, *j*ar, *J*apan, *j*ail, *j*eer, *j*ealousy, *j*elly, *j*ingle, *j*ockey, *j*ostle, *j*udge, *j*ury

---

Exercise 5

Each of the following words contains the sound of j. *Insert the missing letter or letters.*

1. alle __ e
2. lon __ evity
3. an __ el
4. __ ostle
5. __ ealousy
6. su __ __ est
7. cor __ __ al
8. sol __ __ er
9. __ ist
10. __ eer

Silent Letters

In many English words there are silent letters. They are written but not pronounced.

Letters Which *May* Be Silent

d — as in We*d*nesday

g — as in *g*narled, *g*nash, *g*nat, forei*g*n, rei*g*n, sovrei*g*n

h — as in *h*eir, *h*erb, *h*onor, *h*our, shep*h*erd, fore*h*ead

k — as in *k*nee, *k*night, *k*nock, *k*now, *k*nowledge

l — as in a*l*mond, a*l*ms, ca*l*f, ca*l*m, cha*l*k, fo*l*k, ha*l*f, Linco*l*n, psa*l*m, so*l*dier, ta*l*k, wa*l*k, yo*l*k n — as in condem*n*, dam*n*, hym*n*, solem*n*

p — as in cor*p*s, cu*p*board, *p*neumonia, *p*sychology, *p*tomaine, ras*p*berry

t — as in chas*t*en, fas*t*en, glis*t*en, has*t*en, lis*t*en, mois*t*en, of*t*en, sof*t*en, epis*t*le, hus*t*le, jos*t*le, nes*t*le, this*t*le

Exercise 6

Replace the silent letter in each of these words:

1. __ night
2. __ salm
3. epis __ le
4. cor __ s
5. sof __ en
6. We __ nesday
7. __ naw
8. fas __ en
9. rei __ n
10. lis __ en
11. hym __
12. ras __ berry
13. __ onor
14. cu __ board
15. mois __ en

The *-OUGH* Combination

The *-ough* combination causes everyone difficulty. There are no rules governing the spelling of words containing it. You must memorize each word individually.

Carefully examine the following words and memorize their spelling:

The *-OUGH* Sound

Word	Pronounced Like:
although, thorough, thoroughfare	oh
through, throughout, slough (a swamp)	you
bought, ought, sought	saw
tough, slough (to shed or cast off)	cuff
cough	awful
hiccough	up
drought	cow

Exercise 7

Fill in each blank with a word selected from the list above.

1. He continued to work _____ he wasn't feeling well.
2. The _____ ran _____ the center of the city.
3. The purchaser _____ some _____ medicine in the drugstore.
4. People who are very ill _____ to see a doctor.
5. Hemp is a _____ fiber.
6. A long severe _____ ruined the crops _____ the countryside.
7. Some snakes _____ off their skins annually.
8. A _____ may be embarrassing.

The -*IGH* and -*EIGH* Combinations

The -*igh* and -*eigh* combinations look frightening but they are really very simple and you can master the spelling of words in which they appear within a few minutes.

The combination -*igh* is always pronounced like the diphthong in Spanish h*ay* and fr*aile*.

Native Spanish speakers tend to spell *might, sight,* and similar words as *mait* and *sait* in accordance with the Spanish pattern. If you carefully study the following list, which contains the most common -*igh* words, you will not make this mistake.

Common *IGH* Words

---

blight	night
bright	playwright
fight	sight
flight	slight
fright	tight
frighten	tighten
might	

The combination *eigh* is pronounced like the diphthong in r*eina* and l*ey*. There are only two exceptions to this rule, *height* and *sleight*, which are pronounced as if they were spelled *jait* and *slait* in Spanish.

Notice!

Usually *i* precedes *e* in English (e.g. *grieve, piece*). However, in *eigh*, *e* precedes *i*.

Common *EIGH* Words

eight   sleigh
freight   weigh
neigh   weight
neighbor

Exercise 8

Fill the blanks with -igh or -eigh:

1. fr _____t
2. w _____t
3. m _____t
4. n _____bor
5. sl _____t
6. t _____t
7. n _____t
8. fr _____t
9. playwr _____t
10. s _____t

The *-TION* Ending

Words which end with *-ción* in Spanish (for example, *habitación*) are spelled with *-tion* in English.

The ending *-ción* does not occur in English. Examine the list below:

-TION and its Spanish Equivalent

Spanish	English	Spanish	English
admiración	admiration	irritación	irritation
atención	attention	preposición	preposition
atracción	attraction	producción	production
construcción	construction	pronunciación	pronunciation
distinción	distinction	tentación	temptation
excepción	exception	tradición	tradition

Words Beginning with *SP-* and *ST-*

Have you noticed that Spanish words beginning with *esp* and *est* drop the initial *e* when they become English? If you are aware of this, you will avoid a common spelling error.

SP-, ST-, and Its Spanish Equivalents

Spanish	English
especial	special
espacio	space
espectáculo	spectacle
espíritu	spirit
establo	stable
estación	station
estado	state
estatua	statue
estilo	style
estómago	stomach
estudio	study
estudiante	student

Exercise 9

Write the English equivalent of each of the following:

1. espectaculo _____
2. atención _____
3. estatua _____
4. construcción _____
5. estudio _____
6. pronunciación _____
7. espacio _____
8. tradición _____
9. estómago _____
10. producción _____

Special Devices

The Hyphen

To save time in consulting your dictionary, learn the basics of compound words and word division.

The Hyphen

English is a language rich in compound words. Sometimes two nouns are combined as in *secretary-treasurer* because the new term combines the functions of both. The hyphen here shows that you are talking about one man or woman. Many compound words are adjectives formed from various parts of speech. For example, to say that a *car is of low price* seems a little archaic. (We might say: *A pearl of great price*.) Hence, we write *low-priced* car.

In describing a suit which you could wear at once after you had bought it, you could write: *a garment that was already made*, or the much shorter, *ready-made* garment.

Many hyphenated words eventually become so familiar, that they are written as one word. Certain magazines like *Time* and *Newsweek*, frequently write as single words those which texts and dictionaries still hyphenate.

Compound Adjectives

When to Hyphenate

There are eight types of such hyphenated adjectives.
1. Noun or adjective + participle.

EXAMPLES
fire-fighting apparatus (noun + participle)
bad-looking apples (adjective + participle)

2. Noun + adjective.

EXAMPLES
city-wide campaign
lily-white hands

209

3. Compound numbers between 21 and 99.

EXAMPLES
twenty-fifth person
the three hundred and *seventy-fifth* bill

4. Number + nouns.

EXAMPLES
the *five-year* plan
thirty-cent seats
twelve *two-year* olds

5. Short adverbs (*best, far, ill, long, much, well*) + participle.

EXAMPLES
best-known author
far-fetched theory
ill-gotten gains
long-needed vacation
well-looking person

6. Adjectives of nationality.

EXAMPLES
Franco-Prussian War
Anglo-Saxon
Anglo-Norman

7. Two nouns forming an adjective.

EXAMPLES
a *father-son* banquet
a *brother-sister* act
a *mother-daughter* outfit

8. Verb plus other elements forming an adjective.

EXAMPLES
The *would-be* actor
The *wait-and-see* plan for peace
A *hit-and-run* driver

When *Not* to Hyphenate

1. When the adjective follows the noun.

   EXAMPLES
   She was an executive well known for her honesty.
   He was a man ill fitted for the job.

2. When two independent adjectives precede the noun and are not combined.

   EXAMPLES
   Napoleon wore his old blue uniform.
   But: *Napoleon wore his sky-blue uniform* (only one adjective).
   She carried the tired old dog.

3. When an adverb modifies an adjective.

   EXAMPLES
   He was a highly paid executive.
   This was a nicely kept room.
   It was a newly born calf.

4. When a comparative or superlative form is one of the two modifiers.

   EXAMPLES
   There was no kinder hearted person in the room.
   The lowest priced car was the compact.
   But: *A low-priced car was desired.*

5. When the compound modifier is a proper noun of two words.

   EXAMPLES
   Thomas Mann was a Nobel Prize winner.
   He was the South American representative in the Security Council.

6. When one word in the compound modifier has an apostrophe.

   EXAMPLES
   The first year's harvest was small.
   The third century's literature was most religious.
   The seventh day's fast was broken.

Exercise 1

Indicate at the right whether the following words are properly hyphenated. Place a C if correct and an X if wrong.

1. well-fed cattle _____
2. redcheeked youngster _____
3. tenday reducing diet _____
4. a three-month delay _____
5. the twenty-second victim _____
6. badly-lit interior of the hut _____
7. state-wide elections _____
8. redeyed Susan _____
9. a seven-day wonder _____
10. the kind-hearted minister _____
11. hornrimmed spectacles _____
12. the legend of the saber toothed tiger _____
13. This was indeed a well kept garden _____
14. His ill-fated story was common knowledge _____
15. My sister was a red-head _____
16. a first class performance _____
17. the silver plated fork _____
18. the sky-blue water _____
19. England's far-flung empire _____
20. the far-off hills of Dune _____

Compound Nouns

By using the hyphen with two or more familiar words, new words have been added to our vocabulary.

1. Use the hyphen when two normally distinct functions are united in one person or thing.

EXAMPLES

secretary-treasurer ⎫ *united*
fighter-bomber ⎬ functions

However, *do not* hyphenate double terms that represent a single office:

EXAMPLES

Major General
Secretary of Defense
General of the Army
Lieutenant Commander
General Manager
Executive Secretary
} *single* office

2. Use the hyphen when two nouns form a new noun. Usually the first acts with the force of an adjective.

EXAMPLES

trade-mark
light-year
foot-pound

3. Sometimes a noun will be combined with another part of speech to form an entirely new noun.

EXAMPLES

passer-by (a noun plus a word meaning direction or motion)
son-in-law
jack-in-the-box (a noun plus a phrase)

4. A verb may be combined with some other part of speech to make a noun.

EXAMPLES

A *know-all*
A *do-nothing*
A *cure-all*
A *know-nothing*
} verb plus object helps make new nouns

A *count-down*
A *flare-up,*   *play-off*
A *lean-to,*   *drive-in*
A *go-between,*   *shake-up*
A *stick-up*
} verb plus preposition helps make new nouns

Compound Numbers and Fractions

1. Use the hyphen in numbers from twenty-one to ninety-nine.
2. In fractions use the hyphen when the fraction is used as an adjective.

   EXAMPLES
   The three and one-half pounds of butter.
   Two and one-eighth quarts of milk.

> | Caution! |
> | :--- |
> | **Do not use the hyphen when the fraction is not a single adjective.** |

   EXAMPLES
   The chairman asked *one third* of the group to stay.
   He drank *one half* of the cup quickly.

Compounds with Certain Particles

1. Most compounds with **self-** use the hyphen.

   EXAMPLES
   self-sacrifice
   self-interest
   self-made man

> | Caution! |
> | :--- |
> | **Do *not* hyphenate the reflexives such as *yourself, himself, herself,* or *self* in such adjectives as *selfless, selfsame*.** |

2. The prefix **RE-** takes the hyphen when it means *again*, especially if necessary to prevent confusion.

   EXAMPLES
   re-form the squad
   re-enact the crime
   re-emerge from retirement

> ## Note!
>
> • **Note the difference between *reform* the drunkard and *re-form* the broken line of infantry.**
> • **To eliminate the hyphen in *re-enact* and *re-emerge* might lead to mispronunciation or misunderstanding.**

3. Use a hyphen with prefixes ending in the same vowel that begins the next word.

   EXAMPLES
   co-owner
   pre-election

4. Use a hyphen when a prefix is added to a word beginning with a capital letter.

   EXAMPLES
   mid-Atlantic
   anti-Russian
   pro-British
   un-American

5. Use a hyphen with titles which are preceded by *VICE-* or *EX-*, or are followed by *-ELECT*.

   EXAMPLES
   Vice-Admiral
   Vice-President
   Senator-elect
   President-elect
   ex-Governor

Used for Clarity

Use a hyphen to avoid confusion of meaning. In the following sentence something is wrong.

Did you ever see a nail polish like this?

Without the hyphen the *nail* appears to be an active agent. With the hyphen the *nail-polish* becomes what it should be.

Here are more boners that result when the hyphen is not used:

    1. The master like pose of John. (Sounds like an Oriental valet speaking.)

    2. The well kept house. (This must be a very versatile well, what with its job as water-producer, and now as house-cleaner.)

Words Which Are NEVER Hyphenated

airman	nevertheless
background	outline
downstairs	pastime
farewell	railroad
headline	semicolon
inasmuch	together
keyboard	warehouse
midday	yourself

Words Which Are ALWAYS Hyphenated

brother-in-law	son-in-law
daughter-in-law	aide-de-camp
father-in-law	man-of-war
mother-in-law	runner-up
sister-in-law	jack-o'-lantern

Used to Divide Words

The hyphen has another use at the end of a line in a page of writing. It is inadvisable as a general principle to divide a word at the end of the line; but if it must be done, then a hyphen is placed at the end of the line, in accordance with the rules of syllabication. See our handy "10,000 Word Ready Reference Spelling List" beginning on page 5.

Words ALWAYS Written Separately

all ready	any day	each other	in fact
all right	any place	*en route*	in order
some way	by and by	every way	in spite
some day	by the bye	every time	*pro tempore*
some place	by the way	*ex officio*	no one

Caution!

Do not confuse *already*, an adverb expressing time, with *all ready*, an adjective meaning fully prepared.

EXAMPLES

The members of the team were *all ready* to go.

He had *already* left.

Exercise 2

Spell the following words correctly by inserting the hyphen where it belongs. If the word is correctly spelled, write C in the space to the right.

1. sisterinlaw _____
2. man of war _____
3. aidedecamp _____
4. runon sentence _____
5. down-stairs _____
6. anti American activities _____
7. ex-husband _____
8. re-emerge _____
9. self-centered child _____
10. one quarter of the population _____
11. runnerup _____
12. drivein theatre _____
13. secretary-treasurer _____
14. Lieutenant General _____
15. tradein _____
16. fire-fighting engine _____
17. pro-European policy _____
18. builtin arch _____
19. The final play-off _____
20. broken-down houses _____

16

The Apostrophe

This little mark of punctuation can show possession and the omission of a letter.

An understanding of it is essential.

The Apostrophe

To Show Contraction

1. Use the apostrophe to indicate a lost vowel.

   EXAMPLES

   do n*o*t = don't   he *is* = he's
   can n*o*t = can't   she *is* = she's
   could n*o*t = couldn't   it *is* = it's
   we *a*re = we're
   you *a*re = you're
   they *a*re = they're

To Show Possession

To Show Possession: Common Nouns

1. Most frequently the apostrophe is used to show possession. A *singular noun* not ending in *-s* adds *'s*.

   EXAMPLES

   The hat of the girl = the girl's hat
   The rights of the man = the man's rights

2. Add *'s* to a *singular noun* which ends in *-s* or an s-sound if a new syllable is formed by pronouncing the possessive.

   EXAMPLES

   The hair of the actress = the actress's hair
   The daughter of the boss = the boss's daughter

219

3. To show possession with a *plural noun*, add *'s* if the noun does not end in *s*.

   EXAMPLES
   men's hosiery
   women's hats
   children's shoes

4. If the *plural noun* ends in -*s* (as most nouns do), add only the apostrophe.

   EXAMPLES
   the doctors' fees
   the dentists' conference
   the teachers' demands

To Show Possession: Proper Nouns

1. To show possession of a *singular proper noun* not ending in -*s*, add *'s*.

   EXAMPLES
   Mr. Mann's library
   Miss Smith's dog
   Dr. Levitt's office

2. When the *proper noun* ends in -*s* and has only one syllable, add *'s*.

   EXAMPLES
   Alger Hiss's case
   Rudolf Hess's escape

3. When the *proper noun* ending in -*s* has two or more syllables, add only the apostrophe.

   EXAMPLES
   Mr. Dickens' readings
   Roger Williams' expulsion

To Show Possession: Compound Nouns

1. The apostrophe is used only after the last noun in the compound.

   EXAMPLES
   my mother-in-law's house
   the man-of-war's deck

To Show Possession: Indefinite Pronouns

1. Use the same rules for indefinite pronouns as those above for common nouns.

   EXAMPLES
   One's honor is at stake. (*singular*)
   The others' hats were soiled while ours were clean. (*plural*)

To Show Possession: Personal Pronouns

1. Personal pronouns *never* use the apostrophe for their possessive case.

   EXAMPLE
   his, hers, its, ours, theirs

2. Be especially careful with *whose*. What is the difference between:

   > Whose house is this?
   > *and*
   > Who's there?

To Avoid Repetition of *S* Sound

1. To avoid the repetition of the *s*-sound, just add the apostrophe.

   EXAMPLE
   for mildness' sake

To Indicate Double Ownership

1. When you wish to indicate *ownership by two or more* persons, use the apostrophe *only* for the last.

   EXAMPLES
   Lewis and Clark's Expedition
   Jim and Joe's locker
   Smith, Kline and French's drugs

2. If you are talking about *separate ownership*, use the apostrophe after each noun.

EXAMPLE
The President's and Secretary of State's reports
This means there were two reports, one by each officer.

| Remember! |

The apostrophe means "belonging to whatever immediately precedes it," *except* **when it is used to indicate a lost vowel.**

EXAMPLES
children's—belonging to children
    men's—belonging to men
    boss's—belonging to a single boss
    bosses'—belonging to more than one boss

Exercise

Rewrite the following phrases in such a way as to use the apostrophe in showing possession:

1. The hat of the young girl
2. The votes of the men
3. The styles of the ladies
4. The paws of the cats
5. The decorations of the sailors
6. The hat of the professor
7. A shoe of a woman
8. The voice of the soprano
9. The tail of the dog

Add the apostrophe in the following sentences to show omission of a letter.

10. They do not vote often.
11. We have not any money.
12. The allies could not agree on the campaign.
13. You are always late.
14. They can not always win.
15. It is too late to go now.
16. Let us wait a little longer.
17. We would not have acted so if we were not hungry.

Capital Letters

These grammatical signposts can be crucial to the meaning of your sentences.

Capital Letters

Basic Principles

What to Begin with a Capital Letter

1. The first word of a sentence.
2. The first word of a quoted sentence.
3. The first word of a line of poetry.
4. The first word, and important words, in titles of books or themes.
5. Proper nouns.
6. The pronoun *I*.
7. The first word of a salutation and complimentary closing of a letter.

Proper Nouns

When to Capitalize

Proper Names
Sioux City
Eastern District High School
State Legislature
United Nations

Definite place names
Madison Avenue

Family relationships
Aunt Jane
Uncle Bill (but when preceded by a possessive: my uncle Bill)

Substitute for person's name (especially in direct address)

"Hurry up, Aunt!"	Dear Sir
"Yes, Mother, I'm hurrying!"	Dear Madam

Definite events
May Day
War of 1870

Races, Languages, Religions

German	Caucasian
Hindu	Mongolian
French	Judaism

Titles

Uncle Don

Dr. Jones

Organization Names

The Odd Fellows (club)

Bethlehem Steel Corporation

Methodist Episcopal Church

The Farmer-Labor Party

Deity (and words associated with Deity)

God

Christ

St. John

Scriptures

Trade names

Hathaway shirt

Revlon's lotion

Note!

Capitalize only the part of the *trade name* that differentiates it from all other brands.

When NOT to Capitalize

Words that are not a specific name

our high school

the cold stream

Point of the compass

four degrees north

The names of the seasons

spring	autumn
summer	winter

Studies other than languages

chemistry

biology

A title after a modifier

my uncle

a doctor

I have two brothers

my cousins arrived

Books, Plays, Music

Remember This Rule in Capitalizing a Title!

Don't cap the "CAPS." The last "CAP" stands for
C—conjunctions (and, but, or, for, nor)
A—articles (the, a, an)
P—prepositions (of, to, for, from)

EXAMPLES

Book: *Moby Dick*
Play: *Hamlet*
"My Fair Lady"
Music: "To a Wild Rose"
"God Bless America"

Exercise

Try your hand at capitalizing the words that need capitals.

1. We stopped at the hotel westover.
2. The buick cars are well advertised.
3. We celebrate decoration day.
4. the north side high school
5. We saw mutiny on the bounty.
6. They sang old french folk songs.
7. In english courts the bible is kissed.
8. Harriet Beecher Stowe's uncle Tom is known wherever the book is read.
9. They walked along fifth avenue.
10. Many people ask for washington coffee.
11. Our vacation to britain lasted six weeks.
12. Bard college is in new york.
13. the taming of the shrew is a play written by shakespeare.
14. My courses in college include mathematics, english, and three years of french.
15. Last spring we visited aunt emily who lives out west.

18

Spelling Abbreviations

F.O.B.   *Esq.*   *R.F.D.*
E.S.T.   *Hon.*   *WY*

Some basics to know when dealing with the business world.

Spelling Abbreviations

The Calendar

Day, Month, Time

Days of the Week

Abbreviation	Weekday
Sun.	Sunday
Mon.	Monday
Tues.	Tuesday
Wed.	Wednesday
Thurs.	Thursday
Fri.	Friday
Sat.	Saturday

Months of the Year

Abbreviation	Month
Jan.	January
Feb.	February
Mar.	March
Apr.	April
Aug.	August
Sept.	September
Oct.	October
Nov.	November
Dec.	December

Time

Abbreviation	Time
A.D.	anno Domini (Latin for "In the year of the Lord")
B.C.	before Christ
A.M.	ante meridiem (Latin for "before noon")
P.M.	post meridiem (Latin for "after noon")
E.S.T.	Eastern Standard Time

Business and Postal Terms

Business Terms

Business Terms

Abbreviation	Term
acct.	account
ad	advertisement
ans.	answer
assn.	association
Ave.	avenue
bldg.	building
Blvd.	boulevard
bros.	brothers
C.O.D.	collect on delivery
dept.	department
Esq.	esquire
etc.	and so forth
F.O.B.	freight on board
Inc.	incorporated
Jr.	junior
Ltd.	limited
mfg.	manufacturing
Mts.	mountains
no.	number
P.O.	post office
P.S.	postscript (written after the letter)
recd.	received

Abbreviation	Term
R.F.D.	rural free delivery
R.R.	railroad
R.S.V.P.	reply, if you please (French: répondez s'il vous plaît)
Sr.	senior
SS	steamship
St.	street
ult.	last month

Postal Terms

When the postal authorities introduced Zip codes some years ago, they drew up a new list of state abbreviations. Each abbreviation consists of two capital letters.

State Abbreviations

Abbreviation	State	Abbreviation	State
AL	Alabama	MT	Montana
AK	Alaska	NE	Nebraska
AZ	Arizona	NV	Nevada
AR	Arkansas	NH	New Hampshire
CA	California	NJ	New Jersey
CO	Colorado	NM	New Mexico
CT	Connecticut	NY	New York
DE	Delaware	NC	North Carolina
DC	District of Columbia	ND	North Dakota
FL	Florida	OH	Ohio
GA	Georgia	OK	Oklahoma
HI	Hawaii	OR	Oregon
ID	Idaho	PA	Pennsylvania
IL	Illinois	PR	Puerto Rico
IN	Indiana	RI	Rhode Island
IA	Iowa	SC	South Carolina
KS	Kansas	SD	South Dakota
KY	Kentucky	TN	Tennessee
LA	Louisiana	TX	Texas
ME	Maine	UT	Utah
MD	Maryland	VT	Vermont
MA	Massachusetts	VA	Virginia
MI	Michigan	WA	Washington
MN	Minnesota	WV	West Virginia
MS	Mississippi	WI	Wisconsin
MO	Missouri	WY	Wyoming

Personal Titles

Titles

Abbreviation	Title
Asst.	Assistant
Capt.	Captain
Com.	commander
	commissioner
	commission
	committee
D.D.S.	Doctor of Dental Surgery
Dr.	Doctor
Gov.	Governor
Hon.	Honorable
Lt.	Lieutenant
M.D.	Doctor of Medicine
Messrs.	Messieurs
Mr.	Mister
Mrs.	Mistress
Ms.	Miss, Mrs.
Ph.D.	Doctor of Philosophy
Pres.	President
Prof.	Professor
Rev.	Reverend
R.N.	Registered Nurse
Supt.	Superintendent
Sec. or Secy.	Secretary
Treas.	Treasurer

Measurement Terms

Standard Measurement

Abbreviation	Term	Abbreviation	Term
in.	inch	bu.	bushel
ft.	foot	doz.	dozen
yd.	yard		
		hr.	hour
oz.	ounce	yr.	year
lb.	pound		

Metric Measurement

Abbreviation	Term
l.	liter
mg.	milligram
kg.	kilogram
cm.	centimeter
mm.	millimeter
km.	kilometer

Exercise 1

In the space to the right, put the correct spelling of the abbreviations of the following words:

1. Secretary _____
2. Treasurer _____
3. Collect on Delivery _____
4. Before noon _____
5. Junior _____
6. dozen _____
7. August _____
8. Doctor of Medicine _____
9. Honorable _____
10. year _____
11. Saturday _____
12. Rural Free Delivery _____
13. Reply if you please _____
14. Esquire _____
15. Department _____
16. pound _____
17. Messieurs _____
18. Dentist _____
19. Reverend _____
20. Boulevard _____

Exercise 2

Write the words for which the following abbreviations are given:

1. Ph.D. _____
2. Ave. _____
3. in. _____
4. etc. _____
5. no. _____
6. Bros. _____
7. P.S. _____
8. R.R. _____
9. Sept. _____
10. F.O.B. _____
11. Prof. _____
12. Asst. _____
13. E.S.T. _____
14. Gov. _____
15. B.C. _____
16. A.D. _____
17. SS _____
18. St. _____
19. recd. _____
20. dept. _____
21. M.D. _____
22. Treas. _____
23. Sat. _____
24. Hon. _____
25. Rev. _____
26. Sec. _____
27. D.D.S. _____
28. Capt. _____
29. Mar. _____
30. P.M. _____

Troublesome Words

Homonyms and Homophones and Other Confusing Pairs of Words

A careful review of these troublemakers can easily clear up some basic usage problems.

Homonyms and Homophones

Earlier in this book we pointed out the necessity of listening carefully. Careless listening may give you a wrong mental picture of a word and thus you take the first step toward misspelling it.

There are many words that are pronounced and spelled alike but differ in meaning. They are called HOMONYMS. *Quail*, meaning a bird, and *quail*, meaning to recoil in dread, are homonyms. So are *pole*, meaning a stake, and *pole*, meaning the end of a magnet.

There are hundreds of other words which are pronounced alike but differ in spelling, derivation, and meaning. They are called HOMOPHONES. *Altar/alter*, *chord/cord*, and *minor/miner* are homophones. So are *awl/all*, *bear/bare*.

Homophones are more likely to cause spelling errors than homonyms.

In the following lists, many of the confusing pairs that cause spelling difficulties are defined and illustrated in sentences. Spelling exercises appear at intervals.

Homonyms and Homophones

Key

n. = noun
v. = verb
adj. = adjective
pp. = past participle
adv. = adverb
pro. = pronoun
prep. = preposition

aisle, n.   a narrow passage.
     The bridal couple walked down the **aisle.**

isle, n.   an island.
     Poets sometimes write about the Golden **Isles.**

already, adv.   by this time.
> We had **already** eaten our lunch.

all ready, adj.   all are ready.
> Mother called the chauffeur when we were **all ready**.

altar, n.   a tablelike structure used for religious purposes in a church or out of doors.
> The bridal couple came toward the **altar**.

alter, v.   to make a change.
> Plastic surgeons can **alter** features.

altogether, adv.   entirely.
> I **altogether** disapprove of such behavior in children.

all together, adj.   all in one place.
> The prisoners were placed **all together** in one room.

berth, n.   a place to sleep.
> We ordered a **berth** on the train.

birth, n.   act of being born.
> The **birth** of the prince caused much joy.

bloc, n.   a combination of persons with a common purpose.
> The radicals voted as a **bloc** in the legislature.

block, n.   a solid piece of material.
> He was pinned under a **block** of concrete.

boarder, n.   one who is provided with meals and lodging.
> The **boarder** paid his rent to his landlady.

border, n.   a boundary.
> The **border** between the U.S. and Canada is not fortified.

born, pp.   that which has been given birth.
> The baby was **born** at dawn.

borne, pp.   carried.
> The countess was **borne** in her sedan chair.

brake, n.   an instrument to stop something.
> Because the **brake** was broken, the car rushed downhill.

break, v.   to smash, cause to fall apart.
> Be careful not to **break** these rare glasses.

bridal, adj.   pertaining to a wedding.
        The **bridal** gown was of taffeta.

bridle, n.   part of a harness.
        The horse pulled at his **bridle.**

bridle, v.   to restrain.
        Some gossips need to **bridle** their tongues.

canvas, n.   a kind of rough cloth.
        The sailor's duffel bag was of **canvas.**

canvass, v.   to solicit.
        Election workers went out to **canvass** the neighborhood.

capital, n.   a major city of a state or nation; also, something of extreme importance; also, stock of wealth.
        Albany is the **capital** of New York.
        Kidnapping in some states is a **capital** offense.
        Liberia welcomes foreign **capital.**

capitol, n.   a building.
        In Washington the **capitol** is popular with visitors.

chord, n.   a pleasant combination of tones.
        The pianist electrified his audience with his opening **chords.**

cord, n.   a rope.
        Can you get me some **cord** to tie these books?

cord, n.   a unit to measure fuel wood.
        He chopped three **cords** of wood today.

coarse, adj.   vulgar.
        Such **coarse** language cannot be permitted.

course, n.   a way to be followed.
        In this emergency, only one **course** was indicated.
        John took the academic **course** in high school.

complement, n. or v.   something that completes another.
        The fresh **complement** of soldiers saved the day.

compliment, n. or v.   something said in praise.
        The president **complimented** the soldier for his bravery.

correspondence, n.   letters exchanged.
        The **correspondence** between the two adversaries was lively.

correspondents, n.   those communicating by letter.
        He had numerous **correspondents** to whom he wrote often.

Exercise 1

Select the correct word in parentheses, and underline:

1. This story cannot (alter, altar) the situation.
2. Some experts think that cargo will soon be (born, borne) in submarines.
3. If you put your foot on the (break, brake) you will stop the car.
4. Many sincere people oppose (capital, capitol) punishment.
5. The center (aisle, isle) of the church was very wide.
6. When the search party arrived, the fire had (all ready, already) died out.
7. Many friends and relatives attended the (bridle, bridal) ceremony.
8. The town drunk was (altogether, all together) beyond help from any social agency.
9. When the attack was sounded, the marines were (all ready, already).
10. Many families have not had to touch their (capitol, capital) for a long time.

council, n.   a deliberative body.
> The city **council** was called into special session.

counsel, n.   advice; also an attorney.
> My **counsel** in this case is to avoid temperature extremes.
> The defendant's **counsel** made a stirring plea.

councilor, n.   one who is a member of a council.
> The newly elected **councilor** was given an ovation.

counselor, n.   an advisor, usually legal.
> In America we use the expression **counselor** whereas in Britain it is solicitor or barrister.

core, n.   a center of fruit.
> The **core** of my apple was rotten.

corps, n.   a unit of people.
> General Smith commanded the Second Army **Corps.**

descent, n.   a going down.
> Poe's "**Descent** into a Maelstrom" is still exciting to read.

dissent, n.   a disagreement.
> Justice Holmes' **dissents** were famous.

desert, v.   to leave behind.
> It is a terrible crime to **desert** one's child.

dessert, n.   the fruit or ice-cream course at the end of a meal.
> We had sliced peaches for **dessert.**

dual, adj.   double.
> Dr. Jekyll and Mr. Hyde were the **dual** personalities of one man.

duel, n.   combat of two men.
> Hamilton was killed in the **duel** with Burr.

feint, v.   to make a pretense of.
> The boxer **feinted** with his left, then struck with his right.

faint, v.   to lose consciousness.
> When she heard the news, the mother **fainted.**

flair, n.   instinctive attraction to.
> The model had a **flair** for style.

flare, v.   to shine with a sudden light.
> A match **flared** in the darkness.

fowl, n.   a bird of any kind.
> The butcher sold freshly killed **fowl.**

foul, adj.   offensive to the senses.
> The air in the dungeon was **foul.**

gate, n.   a means of entrance or exit.
> The rusty **gate** was ajar.

gait, n.   a manner of walking.
> The old man's **gait** was slow and uncertain.

heir, n.   one who inherits property.
> The eldest son was the **heir** to his father's estate.

air, n.   atmosphere.
> The mountain **air** was chilly.

horde, n.   a crowd or throng.
> A **horde** of barbarians once sacked Rome.

hoard, n.   a hidden supply.
> The miser added the coin to his **hoard.**

hostel, n.   an inn.
> The young cyclists stayed overnight at a **hostel.**

hostile, adj.   unfriendly.
> The lawyer cross-examined the **hostile** witness.

instance, n.　　example.
　　　The lawyer gave **instance** after **instance** of good behavior.

instants, n.　　plural, meaning moments.
　　　Pain was stopped for several **instants** before the operation was continued.

its, pro.　　The possessive case of it.
　　　The baby played with **its** finger.

it's,　　abbreviated form of **it is.**
　　　It's too late to go to any restaurant now.

led, v.　　the past tense of **lead.**
　　　The colonel **led** his men to safety.

lead, n.　　(lĕd) a metal.
　　　Plumbers make use of **lead** frequently.

libel, n.　　a defamatory statement.
　　　The politician sued the newspaper for **libel.**

liable, adj.　　likely.
　　　The sidewalk is so icy that you're **liable** to fall.

Exercise 2

Select the correct word in parentheses, and underline.

1. England called its Privy (Council, Counsel) into session.
2. It takes an angle of 40° to (compliment, complement) an angle of 50° to make a right angle.
3. To get out of the swamp, there was only one (course, coarse) to follow.
4. The (desert, dessert) at the end of the banquet was delicious.
5. (It's, Its) amazing how much you can get in a library.
6. The legislature passed the bill without any (dissent, descent).
7. After many skirmishes the captain (lead, led) his company to victory.
8. The witness refused to answer any question without advice from his (counsel, council).
9. Joseph ate his apple down to the (corps, core).
10. The judge said that he had a (dual, duel) responsibility.

miner, n.   one who extracts minerals from the earth.
Mark Twain frequently wrote about **miners** in the Old West.

minor, adj., n.   unimportant; below legal age.
This injury to the skin was a **minor** one.
Alcoholic beverages may not be sold to **minors.**

missal, n.   a prayer book.
He always read a **missal** during church services.

missile, n.   a weapon thrown or projected.
The treaty banned the use of nuclear **missiles.**

peace, n.   a state of quiet; freedom from war.
The U.N. tries hard to keep the **peace.**

piece, n.   a portion.
A **piece** of pie costs fifty cents here.

peddle, v.   to travel about with wares for sale.
He earned a small income by **peddling** vegetables.

pedal, n.   a foot lever.
The bicycle was so high that the child's foot could not reach the **pedal.**

peel, v.   to remove by stripping.
Before you can eat an orange, you must **peel** it.

peal, n.   loud ringing of bells.
He heard the **peal** of bells from the church tower.

plain, adj., n.   *as an adjective,* simple, unadorned.
In this small town we live in **plain** houses.
As a noun, a flat area of land.
Many pioneers perished while crossing this **plain.**

plane, n.   an airplane; a tool; a flat surface.
The **plane** made a forced landing.
To smooth the surface, the carpenter used a new type of **plane.**

principal, adj., n.   *as an adjective,* main, important.
These were the **principal** points in Nixon's speech.
As a noun, the head official in a school.
A **principal** in a modern high school must be a good administrator.

principle, n.   a statement of a rule in conduct or in science or mathematics.
Archimedes discovered the **principle** of buoyancy in liquids.
A candidate for high office must be a man of **principle.**

raise, v.   to help to rise to a standing position.
When the old man fell, several helped to **raise** him.

raze, v.   to destroy to the ground.
The building was **razed** because it was old and unsafe.

review, n.   a reexamination.
The teacher conducted a **review** before the test.

revue, n.   a theatrical production of songs, skits, and dances.
The dramatic society wanted to present a **revue.**

shear, v.   to cut or clip.
With sharp scissors, the tailor was able to **shear** the cloth.

sheer, adj.   straight up and down without a break.
The **sheer** precipice was a hundred feet high.

sight, n.   something that is seen.
The skyline of New York is an impressive **sight.**

site, n.   location of a planned building.
The architect studied the **site** carefully.

soar, v.   to fly high.
The hawk **soared** high in the sky.

sore, adj.   painful.
Unaccustomed to exercise, his muscles were **sore.**

stationary, adj.   fixed, attached.
The old-fashioned schoolroom had **stationary** desks and chairs.

stationery, n.   paper used in correspondence.
Hammerhill is making a new kind of typewriter **stationery.**

straight, adj.   direct.
The path leading to the house was **straight.**

strait, n.   a waterway.
The helmsman steered the ship through the **strait.**

surge, v.   to sweep forward.
The **surge** of the sea hindered the swimmer.

serge, n.   a kind of cloth.
The child wore a blue **serge** suit.

tail, n.   the end of a body of an animal.
The cat's **tail** was accidentally caught in the door.

tale, n.   a narrative.
The prisoner told a long and sorrowful **tale.**

taut, adj.   tightly drawn.
The lines that held the sails were **taut.**

taught, v.   instructed.
The pupils were **taught** the elements of algebra.

team, n.   group on one side.
Our hockey **team** was the best in the league.

teem, v.   to become filled to overflowing.
The mountain lake **teemed** with fish.

there, adv.   an adverb of place.
He placed the package **there.**

their, pro.   a possessive pronoun.
The soldiers opened **their** kits.

they're pro. + v.   contraction of they are.
''**They're** here,'' the colonel shouted.

to, prep.   *preposition with a verb to make an infinitive.*
To err is human; **to** forgive, divine.
Preposition with noun or pronoun.
Please take this book **to** him.
Deliver this package **to** mother.

too, adv.   also, more than enough.
Father arrived late for the ceremony **too.**
Such bad behavior in class was **too** much for the teacher.

two,   numeral, the number 2.
He received **two** dollars an hour.

vain, adj.   conceited.
The **vain** teacher thought her students liked her.

vane, n.   weathercock.
The farmer glanced at the **vane** to see the wind's direction.

vein, n.   blood vessel.
The workman accidentally punctured a **vein** with a knife.

veracious, adj.   truthful.
    The jury believed that the witness's report was **veracious.**

voracious, adj.   having a huge appetite.
    Most large animals are **voracious.**

vial, n.   a small vessel for liquids.
    The druggist gave the customer a **vial** of medicine.

vile, adj.   morally despicable.
    The judge said the criminal's offense was **vile.**

waist, n.   middle section of the body; a garment.
    Every woman admires a narrow **waist.**
    Her **waist** was made of lace.

waste, v., n.   to squander material which is squandered.
    To **waste** food is almost a crime when so many starve.
    Many manufacturers dispose of industrial **wastes** through incineration.

week, n.   a period of seven days.
    There are four **weeks** in a month.

weak, adj.   lacking strength.
    The beggar was **weak** and frail from lack of food.

weight, n.   The amount that an object registers on a scale.
    The child's **weight** was below normal.

wait, n.   a period of waiting.
    The workmen had a long **wait** for the bus.

who's, personal pro.   a contraction of who is.
    "**Who's** there?" she asked.

whose,   possessive of who.
    We should like to know **whose** coat this is.

your,   possessive of you.
    This is **your** hat.

you're,   a contraction of you are.
    "**You're,** elected," the chairman shouted.

Exercise 3

Select the correct word in parentheses, and underline.

1. An appendectomy can hardly be considered (minor, miner) surgery.
2. He was a great admirer of (peace, piece) by friendly negotiation.
3. Because of motor difficulties the (plane, plain) had to make a forced landing on the (plane, plain).
4. The (principle, principal) causes of World War II are not easy to state.
5. The young girl placed the belt around her (waste, waist).
6. The sailors threw (their, there) caps into the air.
7. This insolence was (to, too, two) much to bear.
8. It is not necessary to use expensive (stationery, stationary) on minor occasions.
9. We could never discover (whose, who's) book it was.
10. "(They're, their) here," exclaimed the teacher.

Other Confusing Pairs of Words

There are many other word pairs that are often confused because they sound almost alike, as *illusion* and *allusion*. Strictly speaking, such pairs are not homonyms or homophones. However, they cause spelling difficulties and for that reason are listed and defined below. So, too, are words that resemble one another so closely in spelling that they are a frequent source of trouble, as *moral* and *morale,* and *dairy* and *diary.*

advice, n. counsel.
> We asked the teacher for **advice.**

advise, v. to give counsel.
> Our parents are ready to **advise** us.

affect, v. to influence.
> The piteous plea of the beggar **affected** the passerby.

effect, v. to bring about a result.
> By his skill and knowledge, the doctor **effected** a cure.

ally, v. to join with.
> England can usually be expected to **ally** herself with the United States.

ally, n. one who joins with another.
> France was our **ally** in World War II.

alley, n. a narrow thoroughfare.
> The cat disappeared down the **alley.**

allusion, n.   a reference to.
> The judge made an **allusion** to an old ruling.

illusion, n.   a deception.
> Some people suffer from **illusions.**

angel, n.   a supernatural being.
> Disputes about **angels** are found in medieval thought.

angle, n.   corner; point of view.
> Advertisers are always looking for a new **angle.**

ascent, n.   act of mounting upward.
> The **ascent** of Mount Everest is hazardous.

assent, n.   agreement.
> The father gave his **assent** to his daughter's marriage.

beside, prep.   by the side of.
> The bride stood **beside** her husband.

besides, adv.   in addition to.
> **Besides** a bonus, he received a raise.

breath, n.   an exhalation.
> The **breath** froze in the cold air.

breathe, v.   to take in or let out breath.
> The doctor asked the patient to **breathe** in deeply.

cloths, n.   bits of cloth.
> Try using new wash **cloths.**

clothes, n.   covering for the human body.
> Beau Brummel's **clothes** were the talk of London.

complacent, adj.   self-satisfied.
> When he received the prize he had a **complacent** smile.

complaisant, adj.   inclined to please or oblige.
> He was so **complaisant** that people liked to deal with him.

consul, n.   an official in one country representing another.
> The Russian **consul** in the United States represents his country's interests.

counsel, n.   an attorney.
> The **counsel** for the defense entered a plea of guilty.

corporal, adj.　　relating to the body.
　　Teachers no longer use **corporal** punishment.

corporeal, adj.　　relating to physical rather than immaterial.
　　Ghosts do not have a **corporeal** existence.

credible, adj.　　believable.
　　The witness made her story **credible.**

creditable, adj.　　praiseworthy.
　　The soldier's action was **creditable.**

device, n.　　a contrivance.
　　The inventor showed his new **device** for producing electricity.

devise, v.　　to make a contrivance.
　　The inventor **devised** a new means of producing electricity.

elicit, v.　　to bring out.
　　By patient questioning the investigator **elicited** the truth.

illicit, adj.　　unlawful.
　　The moonshiners operated an **illicit** distillery.

emigrant, n.　　one who leaves a country for another.
　　America welcomes **emigrants** of good character from many lands.

immigrant, n.　　one who comes to another country after leaving his own.
　　Forty million **immigrants** brought many resources to America.

formally, adv.　　done in a formal or regular manner.
　　The bridegroom was dressed **formally.**

formerly, adv.　　earlier.
　　Formerly, soldiers had to wait a long time for promotion.

ingenious, adj.　　clever, tricky.
　　The device for operating the ship was **ingenious.**

ingenuous, adj.　　open, frank, innocent.
　　The **ingenuous** countenance of the pretty witness won over the jury.

later, adv.　　comparative degree of late.
　　It's **later** than you think.

latter, adv.　　of two things, the one mentioned second.
　　Of the two deserts, ice cream or sherbert, I chose the **latter.**

Exercise 4

Select the correct word in parentheses, and underline.

1. He likes to wear brightly colored (clothes, cloths).
2. This development in art comes in a (later, latter) period in history.
3. Refugees in Hong Kong rushed to the American (consul, counsel) for safety.
4. Before signing this contract, you should get legal (advice, advise).
5. He placed the boxes (beside, besides) the wall.
6. During the early part of this century, many (immigrants, emigrants) from England went to Australia.
7. All those who attended the banquet were (formerly, formally) attired.
8. The young child had an (ingenious, ingenuous) countenance.
9. During the last war, the United States was an (ally, alley) of England.
10. The orator's speech was full of literary (illusions, allusions).

loose, adj.   free, unattached.
> The screw was **loose.**

lose, v.   to miss from one's possession.
> I would not like to **lose** any more money at the races.

moral, adj., n.   pertaining to the good and proper.
> Man lives by **moral** law as well as man-made law.

morale, n.   state of well-being of a person or group.
> The **morale** of our troops in the Middle East was high.

personal, adj.   pertaining to a person or individual.
> Our quarrel in the office was not due to a business but to a **personal** argument.

personnel, n.   the body of persons employed in some service.
> Because he had a deep understanding of people, he was appointed **personnel** manager.

quiet, adj.   free from noise.
> In hospital areas, **quiet** must be preserved.

quite, adj.   entirely, completely.
> The patient was **quite** conscious throughout the operation.

respectfully, adv.   showing deference.
> The servant spoke **respectfully** to his employer.

respectively, adv.   in the order given.
> The manager spoke to the bookkeeper, salesperson, and typist **respectively.**

than, a conjunction.
> Gold is heavier **than** silver.

then, adv. an adverb of time.
> We shall await you **then.**

Exercise 5

Select the correct word in parentheses, and underline.

1. Good food cannot always contribute to high (moral, morale) in the army.
2. Such demands are (quiet, quite) impossible to meet.
3. Problems of (personal, personnel) always arise where there are many employees.
4. The (loose, lose) stone caused the scout to slip.
5. Love is more powerful (then, than) hate.
6. I was (formally, formerly) dressed for the occasion.
7. Where did you (lose, loose) the money?
8. Every fable has a (moral, morale).
9. The tree-shaded street was (quite, quiet) deserted.
10. Rather (than, then) take a risk, he put his money in a bank.

Exercises in Word Building

Being familiar with common language families can save you a great deal of time.

Exercises in Word Building

Almost every one of us at least once in his life has wanted to strangle his neighbor's daughter for playing her scale exercises on the piano. The monotony of the same arrangement of notes hour after hour is almost beyond human endurance. Without these scales, however, no virtuoso would ever develop. Spelling, too, has its scales and exercises. They may seem just as boring as the musical exercises, but they are similarly valuable.

Study the following word families. Sometimes you will forget the spelling of one of these words. If you can remember its brother or sister, you will not have to consult the dictionary. A little time spent with these now will mean much time saved later.

Word Families

Words and Variations

Word		Related Words	
abolish	abolished	abolishing	abolition
accomplish	accomplished	accomplishing	accomplishment
account	accounted	accounting	accountant
acknowledge	acknowledged	acknowledging	acknowledgment
advise	advised	advising	adviser (or advisor)
allude	alluded	alluding	allusion
almost	always	already	altogether
appear	appeared	appearing	appearance
arrange	arranged	arranging	arrangement
arrive	arrived	arriving	arrival
assist	assisted	assisting	assistance

252

Word		Related Words	
begin	began	beginning	beginner
believe	believed	believing	believer
busy	busied	busying	business
change	changed	changing	changeable
choose	chose	choosing	chosen
complete	completed	completely	completion
confide	confident	confidence	confidentially
conscience	conscientious	subconscious	unconscious
consider	considered	considerable	consideration
continue	continued	continuation	continually
control	controlling	controller	controllable
critic	critical	criticize	criticism
deceive	deceit	deception	deceiver
decide	decided	decision	deciding
define	definite	definition	definitely
describe	descriptive	describing	description
desire	desirous	desiring	desirable
embarrass	embarrassed	embarrassing	embarrassment
endure	endured	endurable	endurance
equip	equipped	equipping	equipment
every	everybody	everywhere	everyone
exceed	exceeded	exceeding	exceedingly
excel	excelled	excellent	excellence
excite	exciting	excitement	excitable
exist	existed	existing	existence
experience	experienced	experiencing	experiment
extend	extended	extensive	extension
impress	impressed	impressive	impression
intend	intended	intensive	intension
interfere	interfered	interfering	interference
interrupt	interrupted	interrupting	interruption
obey	obedient	obedience	obeisance
occasion	occasioned	occasional	occasionally

Word		Related Words	
peace	peace*ful*	peace*able*	peace*ably*
permit	permit*ted*	permis*sible*	permis*sion*
persist	persist*ed*	persist*ent*	persist*ence*
pity	pit*ied*	pity*ing*	pit*iable*
possess	possess*ed*	possess*ive*	possess*ion*
practice	practic*al*	practic*ed*	practic*able*
prefer	prefer*red*	prefer*ring*	prefer*ence*
recognize	recogniz*ed*	recogni*tion*	recogniz*able*
separate	separa*tion*	*in*separ*able*	separate*ly*
sincere	sincer*ity*	*in*sincere	sincere*ly*
surprise	surpris*ed*	surprisi*ngly*	surprisi*ng*

Exercise

Indicate by the letter C *if the following words are correctly spelled. Correct all errors in the space to the right.*

1. arranger	_____	21. necessarly	_____
2. choosers	_____	22. transferred	_____
3. difinative	_____	23. cancel	_____
4. preferential	_____	24. changable	_____
5. inseparable	_____	25. judgement	_____
6. hypocritical	_____	26. accomadate	_____
7. undefineable	_____	27. gaurantee	_____
8. undesireable	_____	28. reciepts	_____
9. pityless	_____	29. secretary	_____
10. unaccountable	_____	30. business	_____
11. unchangeable	_____	31. choosen	_____
12. incompletely	_____	32. posessed	_____
13. disarrange	_____	33. reconized	_____
14. confiding	_____	34. sincereity	_____
15. confidential	_____	35. existance	_____
16. indecisive	_____	36. embarassed	_____
17. non-existant	_____	37. excellent	_____
18. preferrable	_____	38. exciteable	_____
19. experiential	_____	39. prefered	_____
20. unendureable	_____	40. ocassion	_____

Words Most Frequently Misspelled

Match your skills on commonly misspelled words.

Words Most Frequently Misspelled

The One Hundred Pests

The 100 Pests

ache	dear	instead	raise	too
again	doctor		read	trouble
always	does	just	ready	truly
among	done			Tuesday
answer	don't	knew	said	two
any		know	says	
	early		seems	used
	easy		separate	
been	enough	laid	shoes	
beginning	every	loose	since	very
believe		lose	some	
blue	February		straight	wear
break	forty	making	sugar	Wednesday
built	friend	many	sure	week
business		meant		where
busy	grammar	minute		whether
buy	guess	much	tear	which
			their	whole
can't	half	none	there	women
choose	having		they	won't
color	hear		though	would
coming	heard	often	through	write
cough	here	once	tired	writing
could	hoarse		tonight	wrote
country	hour	piece		

256

Business Terms

The 500 words which follow are those which are most commonly misspelled in business correspondence. If you want to improve your business effectiveness, study these words closely until you can spell every one correctly.

The list was compiled by the National Office Management Association after a comprehensive study of 10,652 letters collected from business concerns and government agencies located throughout the country.

The words are not strange or unusual. They appear frequently in business letters. Many of them appear on other pages of this book. Mastery of this list will insure you against the spelling mistakes committed by many business men and women.

Commonly Misspelled Business Terms

A	aluminum	attractive
accept	analysis	auditor
accommodate	analyze	available
accountant	anniversary	aviation
accumulate	announcement	
acknowledgment	anthracite	
acquainted	anticipating	
acquire	anxiety	B
acquisition	apology	baggage
acquitted	apparatus	balance
actually	appearance	bankruptcy
additionally	applicant	banquet
address	appraisal	barrel
adjustable	appropriation	barter
administration	approval	becoming
advances	argument	beneficiary
advertisement	arrears	benefited
advisability	arrival	biased
advise	articles	bituminous
affects	assessable	bookkeeping
affidavit	assignment	borrower
affirmative	assistance	brief
agency	associate	broadcast
aggravate	assured	brokerage
allotment	attached	budget
allowance	attorney	bulletin
all right	attempt	bureau
alphabetic	attendance	business

C

calculator
calendar
campaign
canceled
candidate
capacity
capitalization
carbon
carrier
cartage
carton
certificate
chattel
circular
clearance
coincidence
collapsible
collateral
collision
column
combination
combustible
commerce
commission
committee
commodity
community
companies
comparative
compel
compensation
competent
complaint
complimentary
concession
condemn
conference
confirmation
congestion
conscientious
consequence
considerable
consignee

consolidated
construction
consumer
container
contemplating
contemporary
contingent
convenience
conveyance
cooperate
corporation
corroborate
corrugated
counterfeit
coupon
courteous
credentials
creditor
curiosity
currency
customer
cylinder

D

decision
defendant
deferred
deficit
definite
defray
demonstration
depreciation
description
desperate
destination
deteriorate
determination
develop
dictionary
director
disappear
disappoint
disastrous
disbursements

discernible
discontinued
discrepancy
discuss
dispatch
dissatisfaction
dissolution
distinction
distinguish
distributor
dividend
document
doubt
duplicate
durable

E

earliest
earnest
easier
economic
eighth
elevator
eligible
embarrass
emergency
enormous
enterprise
envelope
equally
equipped
especially
estimate
essentially
eventually
evidence
exaggerate
examination
exasperate
excellent
except
exchange
executive
exhibition

existence	increment	leisure
expedite	indelible	liabilities
explanation	indemnity	library
extension	indispensable	license
	inducement	likable (*or* likeable)
F	industrial	liquidation
facilitate	inevitable	literature
February	inferred	lucrative
financier	inflation	luscious
foreclosure	infringement	luxury
forehead	initiate	
forfeit	inquiry	**M**
formally	insolvency	machinery
formerly	inspection	maintenance
forty	instance	management
franchise	institution	manila
fundamental	instructor	manufacturer
furniture	insurance	margin
futile	integrity	material
	intelligence	maturity
G	interpretation	mechanical
generally	inventory	medicine
genuine	investigate	memorandum
government	invoice	mercantile
grammar	involved	merchandise
	itemized	merge
	itinerary	middleman
H	its	mimeograph
handkerchief		miniature
hastily		miscellaneous
hazard	**J**	misrepresent
height	jobber	misspelled
hoping	journal	moistener
hosiery		monopoly
humorous	**K**	mortgage
	keenness	movie
I	knowledge	mucilage
illegible		municipal
immediately	**L**	
impracticable	laboratory	**N**
inasmuch	ladies	necessary
inconsistent	latter	ninth
inconvenience	leased	notary
incorporated	ledger	noticeable
incredible	legitimate	

notwithstanding
nowadays

O

obliging
observation
obsolete
obstacle
occasionally
occurred
omission
oneself
opportunity
optimism
option
ordinance
organization
outrageous
overdraw
overhead
oxygen

P

pamphlet
parallel
parenthesis
parliament
particularly
pavilion
peaceable
peculiarities
pecuniary
percent
perforation
performance
permanent
permissible
perpendicular
perseverance
personal
personnel
persuade
perusal
petition

petroleum
photostat
physical
physician
plaintiff
plausible
policy
practically
precedence
precise
preface
preference
prescription
presence
presidency
prestige
primitive
principal
principle
privilege
procedure
process
professional
prominence
promissory
pronunciation
prospectus
psychology

Q

qualification
quantity
questionnaire
quotation

R

readjustment
really
reasonable
rebate
receipt
recognize
recommend
reconstruction

reference
regardless
register
reimburse
reinforcement
relations
remedied
remittance
representative
requisition
resign
respectfully
respectively
responsible
restaurant
ridiculous
rural

S

sacrifice
salary
salutation
sanitary
satisfactory
schedule
scissors
secretarial
security
seize
separate
several
significance
similar
simultaneous
sincerely
sociable
society
solemn
solvent
sometimes
source
southern
souvenir
specialize

specify	surprise	**U**
spectacular	susceptible	unanimous
speculate	syllable	university
statement	syndicate	unmistakable
stationary	systematize	utilities
stationery		utilize
statistics	**T**	
straightened	tangible	**V**
strenuous	tariff	verification
strictly	tendency	vicinity
sublet	testimonials	visible
subsidize	tickler	volume
substantial	together	voucher
substitute	transferred	
subtle	transparent	**W**
successful	treasurer	waive
suggestion	triplicate	warrant
summary	Tuesday	Wednesday
superfluous	turnover	whatever
superintendent	typewriter	wholesale
surplus	typical	wholly
	typographical	women

A National Examination

Exercise

The following words are among those office workers and students frequently misspell. You may notice that some of them have been discussed in previous pages of this book. You should profit from this repetition.

First, study the list carefully. Next, ask a friend to dictate the words to you and write them as dictated. Have your friend check off the words you misspelled. Study these words. Then have your friend dictate these words to you. You can repeat this process until you have mastered all the words.

1. equation
2. bankruptcy
3. partially
4. effect (result)
5. likable (or likeable)
6. reward
7. advantageous
8. nominal
9. certificate
10. campaign

11.	obsolete	56.	obscure
12.	earnest	57.	capacity
13.	excessive	58.	calendar (date)
14.	triumph	59.	erroneous
15.	youthfulness	60.	embarrassed
16.	atomic	61.	ceremony
17.	manufacturer	62.	manageable
18.	jewelry	63.	wholesale
19.	advertisement	64.	replace
20.	believe	65.	magnify
21.	existence	66.	humorous
22.	deductible	67.	noticeable
23.	benevolent	68.	principle (rule)
24.	eighth	69.	tariff
25.	grammar	70.	disagreeable
26.	bargain	71.	durable
27.	visible	72.	precision
28.	offered	73.	malicious
29.	absence	74.	punctuate
30.	deceive	75.	limited
31.	decision	76.	require
32.	fluorescent	77.	illogical
33.	nominate	78.	fulfill
34.	chair	79.	principal (head)
35.	length	80.	its (possessive)
36.	advisable	81.	leniency
37.	beginning	82.	remain
38.	totaling	83.	relay
39.	dropping	84.	where
40.	scissors	85.	agreeable
41.	research	86.	identical
42.	exhaust	87.	likelihood
43.	alliance	88.	guarantee
44.	gesture	89.	opportunity
45.	yield	90.	superintendent
46.	ineligible	91.	loose
47.	license	92.	left
48.	desk	93.	notifying
49.	already	94.	practicable
50.	recede	95.	attorneys
51.	personnel	96.	meantime
52.	labeled	97.	nickel
53.	separate	98.	committee
54.	turnover	99.	negotiate
55.	impel	100.	concede

101.	neutralize	146.	underwrite
102.	forfeit	147.	grasp
103.	omitted	148.	company
104.	installment	149.	sympathy
105.	seize	150.	lose
106.	irreparable	151.	unduly
107.	questionnaire	152.	imperative
108.	familiar	153.	diligent
109.	supersede	154.	messenger
110.	pessimistic	155.	usable
111.	valuable	156.	objectionable
112.	insistent	157.	analysis
113.	ninth	158.	recommend
114.	warehouse	159.	exercise
115.	remittance	160.	mediocre
116.	ambiguous	161.	genuine
117.	letterhead	162.	mailman
118.	salary	163.	equipped
119.	obstruct	164.	insignificant
120.	justified	165.	enforceable
121.	until	166.	knowledge
122.	franchise	167.	prepaid
123.	realize	168.	naive
124.	peculiar	169.	recurrence
125.	exceed	170.	issuing
126.	prescription	171.	surprise
127.	fragile	172.	incredible
128.	diplomatic	173.	testimonial
129.	essential	174.	opponent
130.	infinite	175.	wagered
131.	machinery	176.	illegible
132.	arguing	177.	advocate
133.	nineteenth	178.	impossible
134.	succeed	179.	voluntary
135.	concealed	180.	interpretation
136.	comparable	181.	summarize
137.	obtainable	182.	hindrance
138.	bookkeeper	183.	technical
139.	remind	184.	interfered
140.	impatient	185.	unnecessary
141.	occurrence	186.	generalize
142.	inferred	187.	whether (if)
143.	almanac	188.	indebtedness
144.	occasion	189.	beneath
145.	gauge	190.	indefensible

191. triplicate
192. contribute
193. obstinate
194. confirm
195. travel
196. mileage
197. assistance
198. minimum
199. apologies
200. meanwhile
201. sponsor
202. moreover
203. appointment
204. merchandise
205. athletics
206. aluminum
207. electric
208. maintenance
209. continuous
210. mechanical
211. contain
212. mortgage
213. cooperate
214. literally
215. consistent
216. movable (or moveable)
217. authorize
218. aspirant
219. consensus
220. negative
221. annual
222. procedure
223. dissatisfied
224. remove
225. economical
226. receive
227. expenditure
228. prejudice
229. disappoint
230. relieve
231. equally
232. pamphlet
233. dilemma
234. communicate
235. package

236. effort
237. exhibitor
238. preliminary
239. repair
240. possession
241. employee
242. responsible
243. eligible
244. incidentally
245. balance
246. claim
247. vocabulary
248. colleague
249. vehicle
250. grateful
251. verify
252. grievance
253. commodity
254. mailable
255. sacrifice
256. contrive
257. transferring
258. desolate
259. excusable
260. conferred
261. parallel
262. preference
263. notable
264. earlier
265. excellent
266. amendment
267. expression
268. counsel (advise)
269. efficiency
270. immediately
271. disbursement
272. difficulty
273. literature
274. benefited
275. miscellaneous
276. concur
277. necessarily
278. available
279. leisure
280. criticize

281. oneself
282. deteriorate
283. accumulate
284. devastate
285. marriage
286. office
287. specialize
288. organize
289. controlled
290. dependent
291. statistical
292. envelope
293. formerly
294. liaison
295. secretary
296. dialect
297. schedule
298. diminish
299. encouragement
300. same
301. disappearance
302. scarcely
303. pastime
304. eccentric
305. favorable
306. referring
307. emphasis
308. privilege
309. fourth
310. similar
311. hesitate
312. universal
313. handsome
314. owing
315. development
316. compelled
317. uneasy
318. program
319. percentage
320. desirable
321. distributor
322. eliminate
323. equilibrium
324. lying
325. nevertheless

326. essence
327. allowance
328. adjustable
329. questionable
330. collect
331. enlightenment
332. futurity
333. municipal
334. modify
335. discipline
336. remorse
337. extremely
338. default
339. reimburse
340. revoke
341. multiply
342. financial
343. accustomed
344. executive
345. congenial
346. loneliness
347. dictionary
348. merge
349. record
350. especially
351. penalize
352. memorandum
353. commission
354. environment
355. mutually
356. gratis
357. logical
358. twentieth
359. tracer
360. unfortunately
361. deficient
362. imitation
363. coordinate
364. retainer
365. casualty
366. automatic
367. visualize
368. should
369. evidence
370. equity

371. counterfeit	416. bulletin
372. accommodate	417. exceptional
373. reparation	418. prestige
374. inherent	419. remembrance
375. nuisance	420. abundance
376. tragedy	421. official
377. corridor	422. arrears
378. fortunate	423. unanimous
379. innocence	424. difference
380. auditor	425. censure
381. forgetting	426. depository
382. achievement	427. division
383. exempt	428. victorious
384. ownership	429. fiscal
385. attention	430. destination
386. indicative	431. considerably
387. confidential	432. amount
388. inspection	433. superior
389. legacy	434. pedestrian
390. repetition	435. experience
391. luxury	436. traditional
392. emergency	437. honorable
393. vacation	438. periodical
394. remarkable	439. illiterate
395. reasonable	440. government
396. spacious	441. legislate
397. connect	442. penetrate
398. conduct	443. readily
399. nonchalant	444. proposal
400. reinstate	445. insertion
401. siege	446. perpetrate
402. despair	447. regulation
403. forcibly	448. specimen
404. optimism	449. performance
405. accountant	450. hazard
406. manual	451. quotation
407. announcement	452. suggestion
408. profitable	453. distinction
409. approach	454. studying
410. actually	455. plan
411. serviceable	456. congratulate
412. defendant	457. influence
413. pursuing	458. portrait
414. sufficiency	459. substitute
415. provision	460. frequency

461. misspell
462. integrity
463. unite
464. appropriate
465. currency
466. presentation
467. misfortune
468. strengthen
469. apparently
470. honorary
471. insurable
472. promissory
473. compensate
474. article
475. vacuum
476. warrant
477. diagram
478. recitation
479. beneficiary
480. compromise
481. recuperate
482. acceptance
483. utilize
484. acknowledge
485. constitute
486. number
487. catastrophe
488. liability
489. determination
490. intentionally
491. statute
492. absolutely
493. late
494. competent
495. admittance
496. recreation
497. restitution
498. violence
499. scarcity
500. petition
501. filing
502. tangible
503. prepare
504. diseases
505. ignorant

506. scandal
507. significance
508. circumstances
509. reliable
510. agencies
511. eventually
512. initial
513. addition
514. interrupt
515. ordinarily
516. dominant
517. conviction
518. reservation
519. pronunciation
520. appraisal
521. correct
522. disposition
523. injustice
524. submission
525. amusement
526. improbable
527. reputation
528. opposite
529. serenity
530. skeptical
531. perseverance
532. equivalent
533. applicable
534. typewriter
535. lien
536. assume
537. temporary
538. budgeting
539. inevitably
540. maximum
541. auditorium
542. tax
543. return
544. persuade
545. immovable
546. reduction
547. spontaneous
548. scholastic
549. unconditional
550. handling

551. subtraction	576. minority
552. wrong	577. patience
553. structural	578. security
554. receipt	579. observance
555. engagement	580. personality
556. discuss	581. amateur
557. disability	582. estimate
558. unprofitable	583. changeable
559. ridiculous	584. tolerant
560. ruler	585. examination
561. tentative	586. incentive
562. probability	587. simplicity
563. demonstration	588. collision
564. impediment	589. trivial
565. opinion	590. incurred
566. endowment	591. headache
567. controversy	592. carton
568. resume	593. competition
569. guidance	594. reconciliation
570. departure	595. abbreviate
571. inconvenience	596. illustration
572. variety	597. commerce
573. renewal	598. inadequate
574. acquaintance	599. suspicious
575. texture	600. dismissal

Demons and Superdemons

Now you're ready to deal with some of the most difficult spelling words.

Demons and Superdemons

If you have studied the previous chapters, you are now probably an above-average speller. You spell better than 75 out of 100 randomly chosen persons.

Do you want to spell even better—to rank among the top ten per cent? To reach that exalted level, you must master some well-known spelling demons, words with which even superior spellers like yourself have trouble.

The demons listed below will test your ability. They are difficult and confusing but can be mastered with a little study. Admittedly some are rare, but not unusually so. They turn up in the reading and conversation of cultured people.

To help you master them, two kinds of help are given. First, infrequently used words are defined so that you will not have to run to a dictionary to discover their meaning. Secondly, the spelling difficulty in each word is italicized.

The exercises at the end of the chapter will test your spelling prowess. Don't undertake the exercises, however, without preliminary study. If you score a hundred in any exercise, you are one in ten thousand!

Demons! Demons! Demons!

Demons and Superdemons

abb*eys*

ab*err*ation

alle*l*uia

ap*iary* (a place where bees are kept)

appe*ll*ation

aqu*eo*us

arc*t*ic

a*v*er

baci*llus*

bassin*et*

bes*tial*

bib*ul*ous (inclined to drink)

bou*i*llon

270

cad*uce*us (the insignia of the Medical Corps, U.S. Army)

c*ai*tiff (a mean and wicked person)

calor*ie*

cal*y*x

came*o*s

cance*ll*ation

cant*i*cle (a little song or hymn)

canva*ss* (the act of soliciting votes)

cara*fe* (a glass water bottle for the table)

cata*rrh*

c*au*l (a membrane which sometimes covers the head of a child at birth)

cell*ar*

cell*u*l*ar*

cet*ace*an (a whale)

ch*ai*se

chan*cre* (a venereal sore)

chatt*el*

cheru*b*ic

chi*ffo*n*ier* (a high and narrow chest of drawers)

ch*rysa*lis (the cocoon in which butterflies develop)

clay*ey*

client*ele*

col*e* slaw

coli*c*ky

colo*ss*al

complai*s*ance (disposition to please)

con*dign* (fit, suitable; for example: condign punishment)

co*nn*oi*ss*eur

contract*i*ble

coo*ll*y

corn*u*copia

coro*ll*ary

co*rr*oborate

coun*ci*lor (an advisor)

coun*sel*lor (a lawyer)

co*v*ey

co*x*swain

creva*ss*e (a deep crevice)

cre*w*el (worsted yarn, slackly twisted)

cura*c*y (the office of a curate)

cyn*os*ure (a center of attraction)

dei*gn*

d*ie*re*s*is (two dots placed over a vowel to show that it is pronounced as a separate syllable)

di*phth*eria

distens*i*ble

donk*eys*

do*w*ry

d*y*ne (a unit of force)

dyspeptic

ebu*ll*ient

empyrean (the heavens)

eph*e*meral (lasting only a day)

Eskim*o*s

exce*l*

exe*ge*sis (a critical explanation of a text)

expans*i*ble

exp*i*able (capable of being atoned)

fe*zz*es (felt Turkish hats)

f*ie*ri*e*st (most fiery)

fle*xi*on (a movement of a joint)

fu*l*some

garli*c*ky

garr*ote* (to strangle)

gene*a*logy

*gn*eiss (a kind of rock)

gring*o*s (as used contemptuously by Spanish-speaking people, especially about Americans)

hara–*kiri* (suicide by disembowelment)

hemo*rrh*age

ho*e*ing

impercept*i*ble

infus*i*ble

is*th*mus

*ji*nriki*sha* (a small two-wheeled vehicle
   drawn by a man)

*kh*aki
kil*os*
kimon*o*

labe*l*ed
lary*n*x
ligh*t*ning
ling*oe*s

majordom*os*
me*ll*ifluous (sweetened with honey)
*mn*emonics (the art of improving the
   memory)

penici*ll*in
perfect*i*ble
phleg*m*
picnic*k*ing

*queu*e

refe*rr*er
*rh*eum (a watery discharge from the eyes
   or nose)

sacri*l*egious
sar*s*aparilla
*sc*imitar (a curved sword)
shellac*k*ed
sibilancy
sin*gei*ng
str*ait* jacket

tread*l*e
troll*ey*s

vend*i*ble (salable)

wiry
wr*i*est (most wry)

zw*ei*back

Stump Your Friends!

    At your next party challenge the spelling ability of your friends. Distribute slips of paper and pencils, and dictate the following ten words. Scarcely anyone knows the spelling of all ten, as you will see.

    A score of 7 is commendable; 8 is exceptional; 9 is incredible; and 10 is out of this world.

altos	liquefy
colicky	plague
ecstasy	rarefy
hypocrisy	supersede
inoculate	vilify

Exercise

Some of the following words are spelled correctly and some are misspelled. Put a check on the blank if a word is spelled correctly. Rewrite it correctly if it is misspelled.

1. appelation
2. basinette
3. bouillon
4. calorie
5. cattarrh
6. celler
7. cold slaw
8. connoisseur
9. counsellor
10. dispeptic
11. donkeys
12. Eskimoes
13. excel
14. fulsome
15. garlicky
16. geneology
17. isthmus
18. kimona
19. labelled
20. penicillin
21. queue
22. sacriligious
23. sibbilancy
24. trolleys
25. wiry

Space
Age
Words

These twentieth century words and definitions can make your reading and writing more precise.

Space
Age
Words

Several hundred new words have entered our language to describe space age technology. Some are so recent that they have not yet been included in dictionaries although they frequently appear in newspapers and are part of our daily conversation.

You should know the spelling and meaning of the most common space age words. They are listed below and their spelling difficulties indicated when necessary.

Space Abbreviations

Space Age Abbreviations

Abbreviation	Term
AC	Alternating current
BMEWS	Ballistics Missiles Early Warning System
DOVAP	Doppler Velocity and Positions
G *or* g	Earth's gravity
ICBM	Intercontinental Ballistics Missile
LOX	Liquid oxygen
NASA	National Aeronautics and Space Administration
UHF	Ultra high frequency
VHF	Very high frequency
X	Experimental
Y	Prototype (a model used for operational tests)

Space Terms

Common Space Age Words

Term	Definition

A

abort	To terminate; to cut short
acceleration	Rate of change of speed
aerodynamics	Science dealing with force of air in motion (Note: a singular noun)
air-to-air missile	A missile launched in the air against an air-borne target (Use hyphens because the two nouns form an adjective)
air-to-surface missile	A missile launched in the air against a target on land or sea
antimissile missile	A missile designed to destroy other missiles in flight
antisatellite missile	A missile designed to destroy a satellite in flight
apogee	The point of an orbit which is at the greatest distance from the earth
asteroids	The numerous small planets whose orbits lie between Mars and Jupiter
astronaut	A space flier
avionics system	Navigation instruments

B

ballistic missile	A missile which follows a ballistic trajectory after the force of its initial thrust is ended
booster	An auxiliary rocket

C

Cape Canaveral	Florida launching site
capsule	A sealed cabin in which humans can live during space flight; it contains mechanisms for the return of its occupants to earth
control rocket	A rocket used to guide a space vehicle
cosmic rays	Space radiations
cosmonaut	A space flier; a Soviet astronaut
countdown	The timed events preceding a launching expressed in minus quantities (T minus 5, etc.). After launching, plus time is used (T plus 5, etc.)
crater	A depression formed by the impact of a meteor

D

digital computer	A computer which solves problems by mathematical processes
drone	An unmanned aircraft remotely controlled

Term	Definition

E

elevons	Wing flaps
elliptical	Pertaining to an ellipse
epicycle	Orbit within an orbit

F

fuselage	Airplane body

G

galaxy	A massive collection of stars
gamma ray	A form of electromagnetic radiation
gantry	A structure resembling a crane used to assemble and service large rockets
guided missile	A missile whose flight path can be changed by a mechanism within it

H

hypersonic	Relating to speed faster than sound

I

inclination	The angle formed by two lines or planes
inertia	Tendency of an object at rest to remain at rest
interstellar	Relating to space between stars
ion	An atom minus an outer electron

J

jet propulsion	A form of propulsion in which the propulsion unit obtains oxygen from the air (In rocket propulsion the unit carries its own oxygen-producing material)

L

landing rocket	A rocket used to convey passengers from a spacecraft to the moon or earth
liftoff	The rising of a space vehicle from its launcher (Note that liftoff is not hyphenated)
light-year	The distance traveled by light in a year (Note the hyphen)
Loran	A long-range electrical navigation system (Note capitalization)
lunar	Relating to the moon

M

Mach number	A number expressing the relationship between the speed of a body and the speed of sound (Notice that Mach is capitalized)
maneuvers	Military movements
mare	A lunar sea
microwave	A very short radio wavelength (Note that microwave is not hyphenated)

Term	Definition
	N
nu*clear* rocket	A rocket propelled by nuclear fission
	O
orbit	Path of space vehicle
orbital	Pertaining to an orbit
	P
pad	A launch pad; a base for a launcher
payload	The equipment or cargo carried on a space mission (Not hy-phenated)
peri*gee*	The point of an orbit which is closest to the earth
pi*ck*aback	Carried as one might carry a person on his shoulders or back
planetary	Pertaining to planets
probe	An unmanned space vehicle used for purposes of exploration
prope*ll*ant	Liquid or solid fuel burned in rocket engines to provide thrust
	Q
quark	One of the smallest particles of matter
quasars	Recently discovered radioactive objects billions of light years from the earth
	R
rad*ar*	A device which emits radio energy and receives reflections of that energy from objects
re-entry	The return of a space vehicle to the earth's atmosphere (Note hyphenation)
roger	A word signifying okay
	S
sate*ll*ite	An unpowered space vehicle in orbit around the moon or a planet
scrub	To cancel a launch
shuttle	Re-usable spacecraft
soft landing	A landing on the moon or on a planet without a crash
so*n*ic boom	The roar caused by an aircraft flying at speed faster than sound
spacelab	Experimental station developed by European Space Agency with NASA
	T
tel*em*etry	The radio connection between a missile and a ground station
ter*r*estrial	Relating to the earth
tra*j*ectory	A space vehicle's path through space
tro*po*sphere	The lower layer of the earth's atmosphere

Space Vehicles

Since 1957, when the Soviet Union opened the space age by launching Sputnik I, there have been many space projects and vehicles. They are listed below in alphabetical order for easy reference.

Notice!
All the space vehicle names are capitalized. The italicized letters indicate spelling difficulties.

Space Vehicle Names

Able	Hitch-hiker	San Marco
A*g*ena	(Observe the hyphen)	Saturn
A*l*ouette	In*j*un	Score
Anna	Isis	Scout
A*poll*o	Liberty Bell	Skylab
Ariel	Lofti	Soyuz
Atlas	Luna	Sputni*k*
Beacon	Lunik	Star*ad*
Cent*aur*	Ma*r*iner	S*ur*cal
Columbia	Mars	Surveyor
Composite	Mercury	Sy*n*com
Cosmos	Midas	Telstar
Courier	Mir	Thor
Delta	Nimbus	Ti*ros*
Discoverer	Oscar	Titan
Echo	Pegasus	Tra*ac*
Ele*k*tron	Pion*ee*r	Transit
Explorer	Poly*ot*	Vanguard
Freedom	Radose	Venera
Friendship	Ranger	Venus Probe
Gemini	Redstone	Viking
Greb	Relay	Voskhod
Helios	Salyut	Vosto*k*
	Samos	Voyager

Exercise 1

From each group select the correctly spelled word and place the letter before it in the space at the left.

1. _____ a. Apollo b. Appollo c. Apolo d. Appolo
2. _____ a. nuculear b. nuclaer c. nuclear d. nuc-clear
3. _____ a. trajectory b. tragectory c. tradgectory d. trajerectory
4. _____ a. Sputnick b. Sputtnick c. Sputtnik d. Sputnik
5. _____ a. asteroyds b. astaroids c. astiroids d. asteroids
6. _____ a. hypersonnic b. hypersonic c. hypper-sonic d. hyperssonic
7. _____ a. tropposphere b. troposphere c. tropos-pheer d. troposphear
8. _____ a. astronnaut b. astronaut c. asternaut d. astornaut
9. _____ a. lasser b. lacer c. laser d. laiser
10. _____ a. acceleration b. aceleration c. accellera-tion d. acelleration
11. _____ a. Marriner b. Mariner c. Marinar d. Mar-inner
12. _____ a. apogge b. apoggee c. appoge d. apogee
13. _____ a. rador b. rader c. radar d. raydor
14. _____ a. interrstellar b. intersteller c. intersteler d. interstellar
15. _____ a. missile b. missil c. misile d. misle

Computer Terms

In this computer age you need to know the meaning and spelling of many common computer words.

Computer Terms

The invention of the transistor in 1948 made possible the development of the computer. Today the computer is so widely used that it affects all our lives. It has changed the way we handle government and business, manufacturing products, and operating machines such as the automobile and airplane. It is increasingly employed for the conduct of personal matters.

Computer technology requires many new terms. Some of the more common are listed and defined below. Spelling difficulties are italicized.

Computer Terms

Computer Abbreviations

Abbreviation	Term / Definition
CPU	Central Processing Unit
I/O	Input/Output
K	Kilo or 1000 in decimal notation; unit of measure of capacity of a memory unit. K, written as a capital letter, is one kilobyte or 1024 bytes.
LED	Light Emitting Diode
OS	Operating system controlling overall computer operations
PROM	Programmable Read Only Memory
RAM	Random Access Memory
ROM	Read Only Memory

Computer Programming Languages

Abbreviation	Term / Definition
ALGOL	ALGOrithmic Language used in scientific research
APL	A Programmable Language used often for scientific and business purposes by airlines and insurance companies
BASIC	Beginner's All Purpose Symbolic Instruction Code
COBOL	Common Business Oriented Language
FORTRAN	FORmula TRANslator; often used for scientific and engineering problems
C	A general purpose language designed to save time and memory space
LISP	Non-mathematical language which processes data in the form of LISts
LOGO	Microcomputer language used in education; designed for students and particularly suitable for younger age groups
PASCAL	A language with general application named after mathematician Blaise Pascal
PILOT	Programmed Inquiry Learning OR Teaching. Useful in teaching introductory programming
PL/1	Programming Language 1; designed for scientific and business applications; combines features of Fortran, Cobol, Algol, and other languages
RPG	A relatively simple language to master, helpful for programming many business operations and generating reports
Smalltalk	Adaptable high level language developed by Xerox

Glossary of Computer Words and Phrases

Term	Definition
	A
access	Retrieval of information from a computer
accumulator	A section of the microcomputer in which data is temporarily stored
acronym	A word formed from the first letters of a phrase or name, e.g., BASIC, COBOL
	B
binary system	A number system with base 2
binary digit	Either 0 or 1
bit	Contraction of BInary DigIT
bug	Error in program or system
byte	A group of bits operated on by the computer as a unit; commonly composed of eight binary digits

Term	Definition
C	
cathode ray tube	Electronic tube with screen for displaying information
chip	A silicon semi-conductor containing an integrated electronic circuit
compat*i*bility	The ability of some computers to use programs designed for another computer of different make
counter	A device to record number of occurrences
D	
daisy wheel printer	A circular fan of type bars with raised characters
database	Data stored in computer system; data bank
debug	To remove errors in program
decode	To translate coded information into understandable form
digit*al*	Data in the form of digits
dis*k*	Magnetic surface on which programs are recorded
E	
encode	To translate information into a code
expand*a*ble	Capable of being enlarged
F	
floppy dis*k*	Flexible disk
G	
glitch	An unexpected and often unexplainable electronic surge resulting in a computer problem
graph*ics*	Diagrams and pictures
gulp	Small group of bytes
H	
hardware	Physical equipment including all tangible items such as terminal, printer, etc.
I	
input	Information fed into computer
interface	Hardware connecting computer with peripherals
J	
justify	To align
L	
las*e*r	Narrow beam of light
M	
matr*ix*	Rectangular arrangement of elements into rows and columns
memory	Storage, the capability of a computer to store data; area within computer in which programs and data are stored
megab*y*te	Unit of measure of memory capacity, approximately one million bytes
micro*fiche*	A 4″ x 6″ sheet of film for photography of printed matter
microcomputer	Small computer containing microprocessor

Term	Definition
mod*e*m	A device by which computers are connected by telephone wires; it changes digital signals so that they can be carried over telephone lines
module	A logical part of a program
mon*i*tor	A TY-like display device; a visual display unit
mult*i*process*o*r	Two or more central processors under one control

N

nibb*le*	One-half of a byte

O

o*scillo*graphy	Projection of electrical signals on face of a cathode ray tube
output	Data which has been processed by a computer

P

peri*phe*ral	Accessory attached to a computer; for example, a printer
program	Set of instructions in computer language telling computer what to do
progra*mm*er	An individual who designs programs

R

retr*ie*val	Recovery of stored data

S

software	Computer programs

T

terminal	Unit connected to computer usually containing keyboard

V

var*i*able	A quantity whose value may change when a program is executed

W

word process*o*r	Hardware and software for composing, editing, and printing

Exercise

From each group select the correctly spelled word and place the letter before it in the space at the left.

1. _____ a. didgital b. digitle c. digital d. digatal
2. _____ a. retrieval b. retreival c. retrievle
   d. retreeval
3. _____ a. acronim b. acranym c. acarnym
   d. acronym
4. _____ a. microfishe b. microfich c. microfish
   d. microfiche
5. _____ a. access b. acess c. acces d. acesse
6. _____ a. compatability b. compatibility
   c. commpatability d. compattability
7. _____ a. periferal b. peripheral c. peripherle
   d. peripharal
8. _____ a. osscillography b. oscilography
   c. oscillography d. osscilography
9. _____ a. acumulater b. acummulator c. accumulater
   d. accumulator
10. _____ a. nibble b. nibbel c. nible d. nibel
11. _____ a. expandable b. expandible c. expandabel
    d. expandibel
12. _____ a. varible b. varrible c. varable d. variable
13. _____ a. lasar b. lasir c. laser d. lassar
14. _____ a. programer b. programmar c. programmer
    d. programar
15. _____ a. processer b. proceser c. processor
    d. procesor

Medical Terms

The expansion of medical knowledge and health services has brought many medical terms into common use. You should be aware of their correct spelling.

Medical Terms

Medical science has made great advances in modern times. Diseases which once took a terrible toll in human lives—for example, small pox, tuberculosis, typhoid fever, malaria, scarlet fever, typhus, diphtheria, and infantile paralysis—have been conquered.

The fight against disease continues. Researchers all over the world are striving to find cures for cancer, multiple sclerosis, Alzheimer's disease, and other dread diseases.

The expansion of medical research and services and the discovery of new methods of treatment have made hundreds of medical terms commonplace. Once known and used only by specialists, they are now household words.

In this chapter some of the most common abbreviations and terms are briefly defined and spelling difficulties are italicized.

Medical Terms

Medical Abbreviations

Abbreviation	*Term / Definition*
CATSCAN	Computerized Axial Tomography Scan. A radiological diagnostic technique in which a series of x-rays are computerized to show a scan (picture) of the body
Chol.	Cholesterol
DOA	Dead on arrival
ECG or EKG	Electrocardiogram
EEG	Electroencephalogram
IUD	Intrauterine device
IV	Intravenously
LPN	Licensed practical nurse
MRI	Magnetic resonance imaging
PT	Physical therapist
RN	Registered nurse
RPH	Registered pharmacist

Medical Terms

Term	Definition

A

Term	Definition
aborti*facient*	Drug or agent that causes abortion
abra*sion*	Superficial tearing of the skin
ab*scess*	Localized buildup of pus
a*cne*	Inflammation of oil glands
a*cupuncture*	Puncture of skin by needle to relieve pain
a*llergy*	Hypersensitive reaction to certain substances
ambul*ance*	Vehicle equipped for transportation of ill or wounded to hospital
ambulatory	Able to walk about
a*mnesia*	Loss of memory
anal*gesic*	Substance providing relief from pain
anesthesia	Loss of sensation or feeling
an*eurism*	Abnormal widening of vein or artery
antib*iotic*	Antibacterial substance
a*orta*	Artery carrying blood from the heart
arter*io*sclerosis	Hardening of the arteries

B

Term	Definition
be*nign*	Harmless
biop*sy*	Examination of small sample of tissue
bo*ny*	Relating to bone

C

Term	Definition
cal*cify*	To make stony by deposit of lime salts
calor*ie*	Measure of energy (heat) in nutrition
cap*illary*	Thin-walled blood vessel
car*cinoma*	Type of cancer
car*ies*	Tooth or bone decay
cartil*age*	Elastic tissue
cholesterol	Fatlike substance found in blood
co*agulant*	That which produces clotting
col*icky*	Pertaining to paroxysmal pain in abdomen
convale*scent*	Recovering from illness
cuti*cle*	Dead skin at base of fingernail or toenail
c*yst*	Abnormal cavity enclosing fluid or gas

D

Term	Definition
denti*frice*	Powder, paste, or liquid used to clean teeth
diaphra*gm*	Large muscle between chest and abdomen
dia*rrhea*	Profuse discharge from intestines

E

Term	Definition
ec*zema*	Skin rash characterized by itching
emb*ryo*	Fetus in first 8 weeks after conception
en*ema*	Fluid injected through rectum to lower bowel
epi*lepsy*	Disease of nervous system characterized by convulsive seizures

Term	Definition
F	
fl*uoro*scope	X-ray that projects images on screen
G	
gl*au*coma	Disease of the eye caused by increased pressure within the eye
gy*ne*cologist	Specialist in women's diseases
H	
hemo*rrh*age	Abnormal bleeding caused by rupture of a blood vessel
he*pa*titis	Inflammation of the liver
hyg*ie*ne	Science of health preservation
h*y*pnosis	Trancelike state
hypo*ch*ondriac	One who is excessively anxious about supposed ill health
h*y*sterectomy	Surgical removal of uterus
I	
indigest*i*ble	Not easily digested
infec*tious*	Capable of being easily diffused or spread
i*n*oculate	To insert a virus into the skin or tissues
intra*venous*	Into or within a vein
J	
jug*u*lar	Pertaining to throat or neck
K	
*kera*tosis	An overgrowth of horny tissue
ki*n*etic	Pertaining to motion
L	
*lary*nx	Voicebox
le*u*kemia	Malignant disease of the white blood cells
l*ymph*	Transparent yellowish fluid containing cellular elements
M	
mas*tec*tomy	Surgical removal of breast
mens*trua*tion	Monthly discharge of blood and tissue from the uterus
mi*graine*	Periodic severe headaches
mu*cus*	Viscous fluid produced by certain glands in the body
N	
nau*sea*	Desire to vomit
neuralg*ia*	Sharp pain produced by nerve stimulation
ne*u*ritis	Inflammation of nerve
O	
o*phthal*mologist	Specialist in diseases of the eye
opi*ate*	Narcotic containing opium
osteo*porosis*	Disease in which bones become porous

Term	Definition
P	
paraplegic	One who is paralyzed in both legs
paro*xysm*	Sudden, temporary attack of disease
pe*tit* mal	Form of epilepsy
*phleb*itis	Inflammation of a vein
ph*legm*	Mucus produced by the lungs
*ph*obia	Abnormal fear
*pn*eumonia	Inflammation of lung tissue
pro*phyl*axis	Prevention of disease
psy*chia*try	Branch of medical science dealing with mental health
R	
rab*ies*	Hydrophobia
re*gimen*	A systematic course of procedure
S	
sa*cch*arin	Sugar substitute
sa*liv*a	Secretion of salivary glands
si*ckle* cell anemia	Heriditary form of anemia
*syph*ilis	Contagious venereal disease
*syr*inge	Device for injecting liquids
T	
testi*cle*	Male sex gland
tho*rac*ic	Pertaining to the chest
tonsi*llec*tomy	Surgical removal of tonsils
tourni*quet*	Device for stopping bleeding
to*xic*ity	State of being poisonous
U	
ulcer*ous*	Pertaining to loss of tissue
ure*mia*	Condition in which toxic substances are not removed from the blood by the kidneys
urin*ary*	Pertaining to urine
V	
va*cc*ination	Inoculation to stimulate immunity to disease
va*cc*ine	Altered microorganisms that stimulate immunity
ver*tebr*a	Roundish bone in spinal column
vi*a*ble	Capable of survival
vir*al*	Pertaining to a virus
W	
*wh*ooping cough	Children's disease characterized by violent, compulsive cough

Exercise

From each group select the correctly spelled word and place the letter before it in the space at the left.

1. _____ a. diarhea b. diahea c. dierrhea d. diarrhea
2. _____ a. innoculate   b. inocculate   c. inocullate
   d. inoculate
3. _____ a. anisthesia   b. anesthesia   c. anessthesia
   d. annesthesia
4. _____ a. calory b. calorie c. calore d. callorie
5. _____ a. hemorrhage b. hemorhage c. hemmorhage
   d. hemorrage
6. _____ a. rabes b. rabies c. rabeis d. rabbies
7. _____ a. tonsilectomy b. tonsilecimy c. tonsillectimy
   d. tonsillectomy
8. _____ a. abscess b. absess c. abses d. absces
9. _____ a. capillary   b. capilary   c. cappilary
   d. capillery
10. _____ a. colicy b. colicky c. collicky d. collichy
11. _____ a. larnyx b. larinx c. larynx d. larinks
12. _____ a. arterosclerosis   b. artiriosclerosis
   c. arteriosclerosis   d. arterioslerosis
13. _____ a. indigestable b. indigestible c. indegestible
   d. indegistible
14. _____ a. diafram   b. diaphram   c. diraphragm
   d. diaphragm
15. _____ a. sacharin   b. saccarin   c. saccharin
   d. saccharrin

Measuring Your Progress

Achievement Tests

An overall chapter-by-chapter review so that you can test yourself.

SCORE _____

Achievement Test 1

Chapters 1–4

Indicate by writing T or F to the right whether the following statements about English spelling are true or false.

1. English spelling is difficult because it is not phonetic. _____
2. At one time in the history of English the endings in *through, thorough, plough* were pronounced. _____
3. The element *pt* in *ptomaine, pterodactyl*, and *ptarmigan* is pronounced in Modern English. _____
4. *Spaghetti, toreador, echelon*, and *sputnik* are derived from Italian, Spanish, French, and Russian respectively. _____
5. Such words as *birth—berth, air—heir* are called antonyms. _____
6. Many poor spellers do not hear words correctly. _____
7. Nervous tension never interferes with ability to spell. _____
8. There are no rules in spelling that are worth learning. _____
9. The most reliable source of information for spelling is in the dictionary. _____
10. Occasionally there are differences between British and American spelling. _____
11. The sounds of English vowels have not changed through the centuries. _____
12. The *k* in *knowledge*, and the *k* in *knee* were at one time pronounced in English. _____
13. Good examples of homonyms are *fright—freight; sleigh—sleight; tray—trait*. _____
14. Spelling *antidote* as *anecdote* may indicate poor or careless listening. _____
15. Dictionaries vary their spelling in accordance with the areas of the country. _____
16. To become a better speller you must read everything very slowly. _____
17. Many good spellers can tell that a word is misspelled by its appearance (or configuration). _____
18. All good spellers inherit this ability. _____
19. Sometimes you can discover your own spelling devices to help you. _____
20. A good way to recall the spelling of *stationary* is to think of *station*. _____

21. The British prefer to add an extra *u* in such words as *labour, favour,* and *armour*. ____

22. The section on correct spelling in a good dictionary is entitled *Orthography*. ____

23. The words *center* and *centre* are examples of *homonyms*. ____

24. The words *theater* and *theatre* are examples of *antonyms*. ____

25. There is little value in compiling your own list of misspelled words. ____

26. In learning how to spell the word *superintendent* it is advisable to pronounce each syllable distinctly. ____

27. The letter *b* in *debt* and *doubt* is not pronounced in Modern English. ____

28. In learning how to spell a new word it is helpful to write it several times correctly. ____

29. The trouble with English spelling is that there are no rules. ____

30. The ancient Sumerians used a language that was called hieroglyphics. ____

31. There is no difference in pronunciation between *trough* and *through*. ____

32. *Tough* and *rough* are homonyms. ____

33. *Through* and *true* have the same final sound. ____

34. The final sound in *knight* and *tight* is pronounced *īt*. ____

35. Many English words derived from ancient Greek have silent letters as in *psyllium* and *pseudonym*. ____

36. *Moat* and *mote* are examples of homophones. ____

37. Words like *privilege* and *government* are frequently misspelled by omitting a letter. ____

38. Skimming will make one a better speller. ____

39. Careful observation helps one to become a better speller. ____

40. It is possible to train your eyes so they can recognize misspelled words by their appearance. ____

41. You can fix the correct spelling of the word *principle* by associating it with ru*le*. ____

42. To fix the correct spelling of *separate*, think of *sepa* plus *rate*. ____

43. By recalling the spelling of *where*, you may spell *there* correctly. ____

44. The words *hair* and *heir* are pronounced the same. ____

45. Though "practice makes perfect" many professional writers are sometimes plagued by misspellings. ____

46. The ultimate aim of learning to spell is to avoid consulting the dictionary. ____

47. If you read a printed article containing the words *savour* and *connexion* you might conclude that the article was printed in England. ____

48. Some people might learn to spell *their* correctly by associating it with *heir*. ____

49. The words *rough* and *ruff* are true homophones. ____
50. The words *sough* and *rough* are identical in sound. ____
51. Words in English derived from ancient Greek are pronounced exactly as they were in Greece. ____
52. English words are spelled exactly as they sound. ____
53. The best way to study spelling is memorize all the words you need.
54. *Beet* and *beat* are true antonyms. ____
55. Because there are *gh* in *night* and *sight*, they should be pronounced.
56. A person writing *litature* instead of *literature* has probably not heard the word correctly.
57. Because the *b* in *debt* is silent, therefore the *b* in *debit* should also be silent. ____
58. An error in spelling *magazine* and *temperament* is that the middle *a* is frequently omitted. ____
59. To pronounce *scrambled* as *skwambled* may be due to infantile speech. ____

_____ SCORE _____

Achievement Test 2

Chapter 6

Underscore the word spelled correctly in the parentheses.

1. The agent signed the (receipt, reciept) for the rent.
2. It was a great (relief, releif) to go home at last.
3. Mary gave a loud (shriek, shreik) and ran.
4. The marines refused to (yeild, yield) their positions.
5. He was a perfect (fiend, feind) in his behavior.
6. His (acheivement, achievement) was remarkable.
7. Once we have lost our reputation, it is difficult to (retreive, retrieve) it.
8. It takes a good (freind, friend) to make one.
9. The slain leader was carried to the (beir, bier).
10. He was (chief, cheif) of the whole island.
11. We were (receiveing, receiving) visitors all day.
12. It is difficult to (deceive, decieve) people all the time.
13. Strenuous efforts are required to (achieve, acheive) a scholarship.
14. Astronomers can now (percieve, perceive) stars that are quite small.
15. Our (neighbors, nieghbors) to the south were angry at our behavior.
16. Careless training may lead to such (mischievious, mischievous) behavior in childhood.
17. The last (frontier, fronteir) is now in space.
18. Although the (ceiling, cieling) was low, he bought the house.

SCORE _____

Achievement Test 3

Chapters 7–8

In the following sentences the italic words are sometimes correctly spelled; sometimes misspelled. In the spaces to the right, place C if the spelling is correct. Write the correct spelling for all misspelled words.

1. Our lighter team was at a *dissadvantage*. _____
2. Park all *disabled* cars here. _____
3. Any *mistatement* of fact will be punished. _____
4. The old man could not *reccollect* anything that had happened. _____
5. The doctor *recommended* an aspirin. _____
6. This procedure was an *inovation*. _____
7. Let us *rennovate* your apartment. _____
8. Actions such as these are *unatural*. _____
9. This apartment had been *unoccupied* for a month. _____
10. Congress tried to *overide* the veto. _____
11. For misbehaving the sergeant was *dimoted*. _____
12. Sugar will easily *disolve* in water. _____
13. As a lawyer Clarence Darrow was *preminent*. _____
14. One should always have some *anteseptic* handy for unexpected cuts. _____
15. His behavior under fire was *degrading*. _____

Select the correct choice of the two in parentheses:

16. By crossing the state border they ran into difficulty with the (intra-state, interstate) commission. _____
17. Do not (interrupt, interupt) an older person. _____
18. At the end of his letter he added a (poscript, postscript). _____
19. Many (suburban, subburban) communities are growing. _____
20. When the lights blew out we called the (superrintendent, superintendent). _____
21. Quite a few hotels here welcome (transient, transent) guests. _____
22. The judge ruled that this evidence was not (admissible, admissable). _____

23. Such arguments are (laughible, laughable). _____
24. It was (unthinkable, unthinkible) that he could lose the game. _____
25. For many years he was the most (eligible, eligable) bachelor in town. _____
26. England has always been (invincible, invincable) in a crisis. _____
27. (Legible, legable) handwriting is a delight for the reader. _____
28. Make yourself (comfortable, comfortible). _____
29. Many foods are (perishible, perishable) unless properly refrigerated. _____
30. Evidence of the disease was not yet (demonstrable, demonstrible). _____

In the following sentences the italic words are sometimes correctly spelled; sometimes misspelled. In the spaces to the right, place C if the spelling is correct. Write the correct spelling for all misspelled words.

31. The debater made a *mistake*. _____
32. I don't *reccolect* what happened. _____
33. *Professional* ball-players receive high salaries. _____
34. His sleight of hand was *unoticeable*. _____
35. That player is vastly *overated*. _____
36. Sometimes it is better if one doesn't know his *antice-dents*. _____
37. Iodine is still a popular *antiseptic*. _____
38. "Don't *interrupt* me," she exclaimed. _____
39. Lincoln was not very happy when several states *seseded* from the Union. _____
40. The doctor diagnosed the disease as a *preforated* ulcer. _____
41. We must look at things in their proper *prespective*. _____
42. Let us *proceed* with the business. _____
43. Many a *percocious* child can learn how to play chess well. _____
44. This water is hardly *drinkible*. _____
45. Some mountains are *inaccessable*. _____
46. The *combustible* materials were placed in fire-proof bins. _____
47. Many an *eligable* bachelor has been attracted by a pretty young girl. _____
48. There are some schools for *incorrigible* youngsters. _____
49. "Such language is *detestable*," said the teacher. _____
50. He was an old *acquaintence*. _____

51. The face of the *defendent* became pale as the verdict was read. _____
52. Sometimes little things turn out to have great *significence*. _____
53. The mechanics overhauled the airplane motor in a *hanger*. _____
54. The *collar* of his shirt was frayed. _____
55. The businessman advertised in a local newspaper for an experienced *stenographer*. _____
56. Most department store customers prefer to use an *escalator* when they wish to ascend to another floor. _____
57. The *radiater* of the car started to boil over in the hot weather. _____
58. Readers who disagree with a newspaper's editorial position should write a letter to the *editor*. _____
59. One of the duties of a *superviser* is to train employees. _____
60. The *purchaser* is protected by a money-back guarantee. _____

_____ SCORE _____

Achievement Test 4

Chapters 9–11

Underscore the word spelled correctly in the parentheses.

1. All the (buffaloes, buffalos) were killed in this territory.
2. The President sent through his two (vetoes, vetos) to Congress.
3. All the (tomatoes, tomatos) had ripened.
4. We examined six (pianos, pianoes) before we selected one.
5. Cowboys learn how to do many stunts with their (lassoes, lassos).
6. Among the (calfs, calves) were some spotted ones.
7. All the (leafs, leaves) fell down.
8. Many old (beliefs, believes) must be disregarded.
9. Napoleon crushed many (armies, armys) in his time.
10. This farm still made use of (oxes, oxen).
11. Hailstones fell down several (chimneys, chimnies).
12. In this machine there were many levers and (pulleys, pullies).
13. The soldiers shot several (volleys, vollies) at their fleeing enemies.
14. The (salaries, salarys) of his employees were frequently raised.
15. The Greeks composed the greatest dramatic (tragedeys, tragedies).
16. The judge pronounced his sentence (angrily, angryly).
17. It is advisable occasionally to be (mercyful, merciful).
18. The band-leader played several (medleys, medlies).
19. A public (conveyance, conveyence) was supplied to the general.
20. Good carriage always (dignifies, dignifys) the person.
21. My father reminded us that we would be (dineing, dining) at six.
22. It was the loveliest sight (imagineable, imaginable).
23. (Judging, Judgeing) from the attendance, the play was a hit.
24. Her success in college was (surpriseing, surprising).
25. Thoreau was (writeing, writing) a great deal while staying at Walden Pond.
26. The wounded dog was (whining, whineing) all night long.
27. All those (desireous, desirous) of success must work hard.
28. The (density, denseity) of the atmosphere is being studied.
29. The lecturer spoke clearly and (sincerely, sincerly).
30. Certain traits sometimes run in (families, familys).
31. We both like (dining, dineing) out frequently.
32. This trail is not for the birds but for (donkeys, donkies).

33. Much (encouragment, encouragement) was required before the baby would walk.
34. Space travel is no longer (unimagineable, unimaginable).
35. This line had the fewest (casualties, casualtys).
36. We noticed that all the ants seemed (busily, busyly) engaged in building a new home.
37. Jascha Heifetz was (accompanied, accompanyed) by an accomplished pianist.
38. When her son did not return the mother was (worried, worryed).
39. Reynolds frequently (portrayed, portraied) the English nobility of the 18th Century.
40. His sermons frequently seemed touched with (sublimity, sublimeity).
41. Such actions at this time seemed (inadvisable, inadviseable).
42. By careless handling, she seemed to be (singing, singeing) her hair.
43. In expository writing (vagueness, vaguness) is not tolerated.
44. "Stop (argueing, arguing) and come away," the wife shouted to her husband.
45. Considering everything, it was a (lovely, lovly) wedding
46. Such (couragous, courageous) action was rarely seen.
47. Dinner at this late hour was (tastless, tasteless).
48. Working long on the (contriveance, contrivance) made him a bit fanatic about it.
49. (Anniversaries, anniversarys) should be celebrated properly.
50. A pair of (oxes, oxen) is a rarity on a farm today.
51. The printer corrected the (proofs, prooves) of the new book.
52. My friend liked all his (brothers-in-law, brother-in-laws).
53. The castle was (beseiged, besieged) for ten days.
54. Mary's (likeness, likness) was obvious in the portrait.
55. After many lessons he learned to dance (gracfully, gracefully).
56. This celebration was (truly, truely) magnificent.
57. The comic made his living by (mimicing, mimicking) others.
58. Some ranches have as many as 10,000 (sheeps, sheep).
59. All the (alumni, alumnuses) of Fairweather College returned on Founder's Day.
60. Before the American public high schools, there were many (academies, academys).
61. It is very difficult to discover a single (curricula, curriculum) which can satisfy all people.
62. Ehrlich stained many (bacilli, bacilluses) in his career.

SCORE _____

Achievement Test 5

Chapters 12–15

Underscore the word spelled correctly in the parentheses.

1. He wanted to buy a (low-priced, low priced) car.
2. This author was (best known, best-known) for his characterization.
3. She was the (thirty-first, thirty first) queen to be chosen.
4. This hypothesis was a little (far-fetched, far fetched).
5. The ewe was (newly-born, newly born).
6. It was the (highest priced, highest-priced) dress in the store.
7. It was a successful (pre-election, preelection) bet.
8. To get this loan, you must have a (coowner, co-owner).
9. They cheered the (exGovernor, ex-Governor).
10. (Vice-Admiral, Vice Admiral) Rooney was promoted.
11. The doctors (conferred, confered) for two hours.
12. We had no (preference, preferrence) in this matter.
13. After many trials, he was (transferred, transfered) to another prison.
14. The girl quickly tore the (wrapings, wrappings) from the package.
15. Many new bills are thrown into the legislative (hoper, hopper).
16. Mulvaney was the best (hitter, hiter) in the league.
17. Turkey, plus all the (trimings, trimmings) was served yesterday.
18. The Dupont Company had a (controlling, controling) interest in the firm.
19. Our graduates (excelled, exceled) all others at Yale.
20. The prisoner never (regretted, regreted) his misdeeds.
21. The house had a (low-ceiling, low ceiling).
22. (One half, one-half) of the audience left at the end of the first act.
23. All night the tune kept (dining, dinning) in her head.
24. The duchess wore a (low necked, low-necked) gown at the party.
25. The employer demanded several (references, referrences).
26. We are all (hoping, hopping) for permanent peace.
27. Such freak accidents (occured, occurred) seldom.
28. The guilty culprit wore a (hangdog, hang-dog) look.
29. America at that time had (unparalleled, unparaleled) prosperity.
30. It was the (twenty ninth, twenty-ninth) celebration of the ending of the war.
31. The (pre-dawn, predawn) flight was a success.

32. My cousin was the (high scorer, high-scorer) in the game.
33. My mother always (prefered, preferred) to save rather than spend everything.
34. The (ex policeman, ex-policeman) was found guilty of perjury.
35. The judge and the attorneys (conferred, confered) for three hours.
36. The athlete (chined, chinned) thirty times on the horizontal bar.
37. The (Pro-Temperance, Pro Temperance) Party won few votes.
38. The poor little bird (flaped, flapped) her wings feebly and then remained still.
39. The (red-cheeked, red cheeked) youngster seemed shy.
40. Some of the guests at the home were over (eighty eight, eighty-eight) years old.
41. Television has been accused of (sub-liminal, subliminal) advertising.
42. The soldier seemed (regretful, regrettful) of his actions.
43. This rouge seems to be the (lowest priced, lowest-priced) in the entire shop.
44. Adolescents are frequently (smitten, smiten) with puppy love.
45. His appearance at the trial was (well-timed, well timed).
46. He was (hiting, hitting) well in that game.
47. The boy kept (running, runing) despite the cries of his mother.
48. Many guards (patroled, patrolled) the prison on the day of the execution.
49. Passengers should be (already, all ready) at 10 P.M.
50. A (run-on, run on) sentence contains more than enough for one complete sentence.
51. We greeted the (Senator-elect, Senator elect).
52. Rescue boats went back and forth in the (mid Atlantic, mid-Atlantic) area.
53. Her praises were (extoled, extolled) for her amazing performance.
54. Eisenhower's (aide-de-camp, aidedecamp) was later decorated for his contributions.
55. After a little encouragement the guitarist (regaled, regalled) the picnickers with many songs.
56. Mary won first prize; but Susan was (runner up, runner-up).
57. Mills for (spining, spinning) cotton have long supported the town.
58. A few parts of the story were (omitted, omited) by the defendant.
59. Children frequently (scraped, scrapped) their elbows at the corner.
60. Periods of prosperity have (recurred, recured) with regularity in this state.
61. Their marriage was (annuled, annulled) by mutual consent.
62. The nurse (scrubed, scrubbed) the baby's face until it was gleaming.
63. The crowd (paniced, panicked) after the accident.
64. South America (rebeled, rebelled) against the mother country.
65. Judge Harmon (deferred, defered) sentence until Friday.

SCORE _____

Achievement Test 6

Chapters 16–17

Underscore the word spelled correctly in the parentheses.

1. Many college freshmen (don't, dont) know how to study.
2. This salesman specialized in (mens', men's) hosiery.
3. It was (his, his') greatest victory.
4. (Who'se, Who's) there?
5. Dot all the (i's, is) and cross the (ts, t's).
6. "(Youve, You've) won your battle," said the trainer.
7. The shopper specialized in (lady's, ladies') shoes.
8. This was my (brother-in-law's, brother's-in-law's) house.
9. It was the (children's, childrens') ward to which we hurried.
10. This (couldn't, could'nt) have happened to a nicer chap.
11. It was once more a conflict between (East, east) and (West, west).
12. The young artists admired the works of (grandma Moses, Grandma Moses).
13. At the Sorbonne, he specialized in the (hindu, Hindu) languages.
14. My uncle belonged to the (elks, Elks).
15. The hit of the week was ("For my Beloved," "For My Beloved").
16. A popular novel in high school is (*A Tale of two Cities*, *A Tale of Two Cities*).
17. They traveled (North, north) for twenty miles.
18. On (Columbus Day, Columbus day), many stores are closed.
19. One of the greatest musical hits is (*My fair Lady*, *My Fair Lady*).
20. He was recently elected to the (house of representatives, House of Representatives).
21. The (boy's, boys') hat was on crooked.
22. ("They're, theyr'e) here," the Captain shouted.
23. The conference passed a resolution against all high (doctor's, doctors') fees.
24. The numerous (teacher's, teachers') contributions were finally rewarded.
25. Count all the (7's, 7s) in this line!
26. We enjoyed (Harrigan and Hart's, Harrigan's and Hart's) humor.
27. The sale took place in the (women's, womens') hosiery department.
28. "I never want to touch a penny of (their's, theirs)," she shouted.
29. All the (ts, t's) in this word are left uncrossed.

30. He admired his (lawyer's, lawyers') integrity.
31. The "Ivy League" colleges are situated mostly in the (east, East).
32. After studying (french, French) literature he began to appreciate Moliere.
33. Higher (Mathematics, mathematics) fascinated Einstein at an early age.
34. (Governor, governor) Rockefeller attempted to balance the state budget.
35. Several (captains, Captains) won their promotions in this campaign.
36. The fiftieth state in the union is (hawaii, Hawaii).
37. Mrs. Morrow wrote *North to the* (*Orient, orient*).
38. There are one hundred members of the U.S. (Senate, senate).
39. On (arbor day, Arbor Day) an interesting ceremony took place.
40. Of all the novels read in high school (*Silas Marner, Silas marner*) seems to be most popular.
41. Great praise has come recently to (admiral, Admiral) Rickover.
42. A famous radio personality years ago was (uncle Don, Uncle Don).
43. This store had good bargains in (boys', boy's) shoes.
44. There are many fine students from the (south, South) in the colleges today.

SCORE _____

Achievement Test 7

Chapter 19

Select the correctly spelled word from the two in parentheses:

1. Teachers frequently give good (advice, advise) to their students. _____
2. England and the U.S. have long been (alleys, allies). _____
3. There is nothing as beautiful as a happy bride walking down the (isle, aisle). _____
4. My parents said that they were (already, all ready). _____
5. Frequently one can have an optical (illusion, allusion) after eyestrain. _____
6. The judge refused to (altar, alter) his decision. _____
7. (Altogether, All together) there were twelve cents in his pocket. _____
8. The casket was (borne, born) on the shoulders of the pallbearers. _____
9. There were several (angles, angels) in this picture by Raphael. _____
10. We ordered an upper (berth, birth) on the train to Chicago. _____
11. Father was almost (besides, beside) himself with grief. _____
12. (Break, Brake) the news gently. _____
13. The baby's (breath, breathe) came in short spasms. _____
14. The cowboy grasped the horse by the (bridal, bridle). _____
15. Ward leaders tried to (canvass, canvas) the district. _____
16. In Washington we visited the beautiful (Capital, Capitol). _____
17. The angry principal began to (censure, censor) the students for misbehavior. _____
18. He could chop several (cords, chords) of wood each day. _____
19. The salesmen showed me several suits of (clothes, cloths). _____
20. In college, my brother took the pre-medical (course, coarse). _____
21. Don't forget to (complement, compliment) him on his good grades. _____

22. The German (consul, council) telegraphed to his ambassador in Washington. _____
23. The cook removed the (corps, core) of the apple. _____
24. Scientists are often (incredulous, incredible) of new theories. _____
25. Many authors like to keep (diaries, dairies) when they are young. _____
26. Justice Oliver Wendell Holmes frequently would (dissent, descent) from his colleagues. _____
27. After the meat course, we had a delicious (dessert, dissert). _____
28. Da Vinci invented a (devise, device) to hurl cannonballs. _____
29. Hamilton and Burr fought a (duel, dual) in New Jersey. _____
30. This spot was (formally, formerly) a cemetery. _____
31. For several (instance, instants) he remained quiet. _____
32. Through an (ingenious, ingenuous) trick the prisoner escaped. _____
33. Actresses like to receive (complements, compliments) for their performances. _____
34. There were thirteen delicious (deserts, desserts) on the menu. _____
35. The Dutch (consul, counsel) in New York helped us to obtain a visa. _____
36. The new President was (formally, formerly) inaugurated. _____
37. Good food in the barracks will help produce good (moral, morale). _____
38. A graduate of Harvard was the (personal, personnel) manager of the store. _____
39. Avogadro's (principal, principle) led to many other important discoveries. _____
40. This company advertises a fine quality of (stationery, stationary). _____
41. Standing in line for a token is often a (waste, waist) of valuable time. _____
42. New inventions (supersede, supercede) old customs. _____
43. It was an (excedingly, exceedingly) hot day. _____
44. Nothing (succeeds, suceeds) like success. _____
45. The parade (proceded, proceeded) without further interruption. _____
46. The magician created an optical (allusion, illusion) for us. _____

47. The West will not (accede, acede) to these demands. _____
48. After the waters (receeded, receded), we returned to _____
    our home.
49. The (corps, corpse) was taken to the morgue. _____
50. The baby liked (it's, its) finger. _____
51. "It's (later, latter) than you think," the preacher said. _____
52. Four black-robed monks (led, lead) the way yesterday. _____
53. After the battle, the general called his (council, counsel) _____
    together.
54. Several (lose, loose) shingles fell down. _____
55. Liquor is not permitted to (minors, miners). _____
56. A world at (peace, piece) is a world of security. _____
57. It was as (plane, plain) as the nose on his face. _____
58. After the hike, the boys were (quite, quiet) starved. _____

27

Answer Key

Answer Key

For Chapters 5–23

CHAPTER 5

Exercise 1/Page 119
1. bo·nan·za
2. re·pent
3. fa·tigue
4. pun·ish·ment
5. or·deal
6. rum·mage
7. miss·ing
8. gas·o·line
9. ex·ca·vate
10. ty·ran·ni·cal

Exercise 2/Page 122
1. grammar
2. separate
3. usually
4. C
5. calendar
6. C
7. C
8. until
9. C
10. C
11. C
12. accommodate
13. professor
14. government
15. C
16. across
17. illegible
18. equivalent
19. C
20. C

Exercise 3/Page 123
1. hundred
2. modern
3. perspiration
4. western
5. relevant
6. cavalry
7. children
8. jewelry
9. larynx
10. pattern

CHAPTER 6

Exercise 1/Page 126
No answers are needed for this exercise since the correct spellings are given.

Exercise 2/Page 127

1. aggrieve
2. brief
3. friend
4. grieve
5. frontier
6. mischief
7. shield
8. shriek
9. wield
10. species
11. relieve
12. leisure
13. handkerchief
14. receipt
15. seize
16. perceive
17. grief
18. niece
19. conceive
20. veil

Exercise 3/Page 128
The answers to this exercise are incorporated in the sentences.

Exercise 4/Page 130
The answers to this exercise are found in the passage.

CHAPTER 7

Exercise 1/Page 135

1. dissolve
2. dissimilar
3. misspell
4. disappear
5. mistake

Exercise 2/Page 135
circumscribe—draw limits
transcribe—write a copy
subscribe—sign one's name
describe—represent by words
proscribe—denounce and condemn
prescribe—dictate directions

Exercise 3/Page 136

1. misstep
2. misunderstood
3. dissimilar
4. re-echo
5. substandard
6. supersonic
7. pre-Columbian
8. anti-imperialist
9. circumnavigates
10. postoperative

Exercise 4/Page 137

1. persecuted
2. proceed
3. precocious
4. perspective
5. prescribe
6. perforated
7. produce
8. persist
9. perpetual
10. propose

CHAPTER 8

Exercise 1/Page 141
The answers are contained in the exercise.

Exercise 2/Page 142
The answers are contained in the exercise.

Exercise 3/Page 142
1. accidentally
2. critically
3. elementally
4. equally
5. exceptionally
6. finally
7. generally
8. incidentally
9. intentionally
10. ironically
11. logically
12. mathematically
13. practically
14. professionally
15. really
16. typically
17. usually
18. verbally
19. globally

Exercise 4/Page 144
1. advantageous
2. courageous
3. dolorous
4. perilous
5. mountainous
6. beauteous
7. desirous
8. piteous
9. troublous
10. mischievous
11. plenteous
12. adventurous
13. bounteous
14. dangerous
15. grievous
16. humorous
17. outrageous
18. duteous
19. libelous
20. poisonous

Exercise 5/Page 147
1. b
2. a
3. a
4. a
5. b
6. a
7. a
8. b
9. b
10. b
11. a
12. b
13. b
14. b
15. b
16. a
17. a
18. a
19. b
20. b
21. a
22. a
23. b
24. b
25. b

Exercise 6/Page 149
1. beggar
2. receiver
3. conductor
4. passenger
5. governor
6. laborer
7. operator
8. dollar
9. supervisor
10. stenographer

Exercise 7/Page 151
1. compliment
2. remembrance
3. consistent
4. superintendent
5. dependent
6. existence
7. descendant
8. acquaintance
9. grievance
10. permanent
11. magnificent
12. brilliance
13. complimentary or complementary, depending upon meaning
14. convenience
15. abundance
16. guidance
17. conscience
18. coincidence
19. apparent
20. consequential

Exercise 8/Page 152
1. b
2. a
3. b
4. b
5. b
6. a
7. b
8. a
9. b
10. a

Exercise 9/Page 154
1. agonize
2. chastise
3. exercise
4. surprise
5. visualize
6. supervise
7. modernize
8. enterprise
9. fertilize
10. generalize

CHAPTER 9

Exercise 1/Page 159
1. reproofs
2. reprieves
3. sieves
4. halos or haloes
5. gulfs
6. coifs
7. albinos
8. shelves
9. puffs
10. muffs
11. sloughs
12. bassos or bassi, (Italian)
13. mambos
14. surfs
15. troughs
16. stilettos or stilettoes
17. sheaves
18. radios
19. calves
20. sylphs

Exercise 2/Page 160
1. abbeys
2. alleys
3. attorneys
4. buoys
5. chimneys
6. donkeys
7. journeys
8. keys
9. pulleys
10. turkeys

Exercise 3/Page 164

1. t's	7. courts-martial	13. surreys
2. Marys	8. lieutenant colonels	14. inequities
3. anniversaries	9. bays	15. satellites
4. dromedaries	10. trays	16. functionaries
5. kerchiefs	11. flurries	17. avocados
6. 4's	12. sulkies	18. dynamos

Exercise 4/Page 165

1. groceries	7. pounds	13. altos or alti (Ital.)
2. things	8. pieces	14. alleys
3. tomatoes	9. chocolates	15. journeys
4. potatoes	10. purchases	16. keys
5. avocados	11. adventures	17. days
6. quarts	12. sopranos or soprani (Ital.)	18. events

CHAPTER 10

Exercise 1/Page 168

1. tourneys	5. surveyed	8. relayed
2. allayed	6. portraying	9. delays
3. volleyed	7. journeyed	10. parlayed
4. alleys		

Exercise 2/Page 170

1. C	5. C	8. C
2. C	6. C	9. C
3. C	7. C	10. icily
4. attorneys		

Exercise 3/Page 170

1. prettiness	7. pitied	13. hurrying
2. pettiness	8. tallying	14. copier
3. steadying	9. buyer	15. sloppiness
4. readied	10. dutiful	16. livelihood
5. bullies	11. readiness	
6. airiness	12. carried	

CHAPTER 11

Exercise 1/Page 174

1. pleasantry	5. rocketry	8. personality
2. artistry	6. sophistry	9. dialectical
3. portraiture	7. nationality	10. practicality
4. clockwise		

Exercise 2/Page 177

1. revering
2. lovely
3. purchasable
4. extremely
5. pleasurable
6. largely
7. nudged
8. stated
9. feted
10. fined
11. diving
12. shoved
13. devising
14. deceived
15. relieving
16. procrastinating
17. imagined
18. besieged
19. receiving

Exercise 3/Page 178

1. benefit — benefiting — benefited
2. commit — committing — committed
3. lure — luring — lured
4. refer — referring — referred
5. pine — pining — pined
6. elevate — elevating — elevated
7. propel — propelling — propelled
8. fit — fitting — fitted
9. recur — recurring — recurred
10. remit — remitting — remitted
11. open — opening — opened
12. club — clubbing — clubbed
13. plunge — plunging — plunged
14. singe — singeing — singed
15. pursue — pursuing — pursued
16. scare — scaring — scared
17. throb — throbbing — throbbed
18. trot — trotting — trotted
19. use — using — used
20. whip — whipping — whipped

Exercise 4/Page 182

1. agreement
2. amusement
3. careful
4. canoeing
5. coming
6. disagreeable
7. engagement
8. excitement
9. immensity
10. likely
11. safety
12. senseless
13. shining
14. enlargement
15. enticing
16. perceived
17. escaping
18. discharged
19. relieving
20. contrivance

Exercise 5/Page 183

The answers to this exercise are contained in the sentences among the words italicized.

Exercise 6/Page 183

1. scarcely	7. perspiring	13. outrageous
2. vengeance	8. retiring	14. serviceable
3. truly	9. awful	15. courageous
4. tasty	10. wisdom	16. gorgeous
5. noticeable	11. assurance	17. pronounceable
6. changeable	12. insurance	

CHAPTER 12

Exercise 1/Page 189

1. cramping	5. looking	8. resting
2. drumming	6. nodding	9. rigging
3. grinning	7. paining	10. scrubbing
4. hitting		

Exercise 2/Page 190

1. deferred	8. famous	15. trimmer
2. reference	9. controlling	16. occurrence
3. shopping	10. repellent	17. movable
4. disapproval	11. desiring	18. committed
5. nineteen	12. tireless	19. equipage
6. hitting	13. truly	20. excelling
7. singeing	14. swimmer	

Exercise 3/Page 190

1. adapt	adapting	adapted
2. cramp	cramping	cramped
3. design	designing	designed
4. conceal	concealing	concealed
5. congeal	congealing	congealed
6. blot	blotting	blotted
7. stop	stopping	stopped
8. crush	crushing	crushed
9. excel	excelling	excelled
10. defer	deferring	deferred
11. envelop	enveloping	enveloped
12. extol	extolling	extolled
13. flutter	fluttering	fluttered
14. happen	happening	happened
15. hum	humming	hummed
16. level	leveling	leveled
17. quarrel	quarreling	quarreled
18. rub	rubbing	rubbed
19. signal	signaling	signaled
20. retreat	retreating	retreated

Exercise 4/Page 191
1. witty
2. spinner
3. blotter
4. designer
5. quizzical
6. shutter
7. slipper
8. profiteer
9. meeting
10. dryer
11. inhabitable
12. toiler
13. putter
14. development
15. deferment
16. rubber
17. developer
18. goddess
19. druggist
20. trapper

Exercise 5/Page 191
1. tearfully
2. carefully
3. openness
4. dutifully
5. bountifully
6. commonness
7. mimicked
8. picnicking
9. mimicking
10. panicky

CHAPTER 13

Exercise/Page 193
1. candor
2. theater
3. labor
4. labeled
5. traveler
6. realization
7. criticize
8. skillful
9. defense
10. analyze

CHAPTER 14

Exercise 1/Page 198
1. pharmacy
2. photograph
3. C
4. C
5. frequently
6. either
7. machine
8. triumphant
9. people
10. C
11. receive
12. paragraph
13. series
14. convene
15. fatigue

Exercise 2/Page 199
1. troop
2. brutal
3. suitable
4. rooster
5. through
6. acoustic
7. aloof
8. ruler
9. bouquet
10. goose

Exercise 3/Page 199
Example: The *two* boys took *too* long *to* get dressed.

Exercise 4/Page 201

1. accord
2. C
3. occur
4. C
5. apprehend
6. approximately
7. C
8. suffer
9. button
10. alliance
11. C
12. occupied
13. different
14. grammar
15. C
16. appear
17. sufficient
18. attention
19. C
20. C

Exercise 5/Page 202

1. allege
2. longevity
3. angel
4. jostle
5. jealousy
6. suggest
7. cordial
8. soldier
9. gist
10. jeer

Exercise 6/Page 203

1. k
2. p
3. t
4. p
5. t
6. d
7. g
8. t
9. g
10. t
11. n
12. p
13. h
14. p
15. t

Exercise 7/Page 204

1. although
2. thoroughfare—through
3. bought—cough
4. ought
5. tough
6. drought—throughout
7. slough
8. cough

Exercise 8/Page 205

1. fright or freight
2. weight
3. might
4. neighbor
5. slight
6. tight
7. night
8. freight or fright
9. playwright
10. sight

Exercise 9/Page 206

1. spectacle
2. attention
3. statue
4. construction
5. study
6. pronunciation
7. space
8. tradition
9. stomach
10. production

CHAPTER 15

Exercise 1/Page 212

1. C	6. C	11. X	16. X
2. X	7. C	12. X	17. X
3. X	8. X	13. X	18. C
4. C	9. C	14. C	19. C
5. C	10. C	15. X	20. C

Exercise 2/Page 217

1. sister-in-law	8. C	15. trade-in
2. man-of-war	9. C	16. C
3. aide-de-camp	10. C	17. C
4. run-on	11. runner-up	18. built-in
5. downstairs	12. drive-in	19. C
6. anti-American	13. C	20. C
7. C	14. C	

CHAPTER 16

Exercise/Page 222

1. The young girl's hat	10. don't
2. The men's votes	11. haven't
3. The ladies' styles	12. couldn't
4. The cats' paws	13. You're
5. The sailors' decorations	14. can't
6. The professor's hat	15. It's
7. The woman's shoe	16. Let's
8. The soprano's voice	17. wouldn't
9. The dog's tail	

CHAPTER 17

Exercise/Page 226

1. Hotel Westover	9. Fifth Avenue
2. Buick	10. Washington coffee
3. Decoration Day	11. Britain
4. North Side High School	12. Bard College, New York
5. *Mutiny on the Bounty*	13. *The Taming of the Shrew*, Shakespeare
6. Old French	
7. English, Bible	14. English, French
8. Uncle	15. Aunt Emily, West

CHAPTER 18

Exercise 1/Page 232

1. Sec. or Secy.	8. M.D.	15. Dept.
2. Treas.	9. Hon.	16. lb.
3. C.O.D.	10. yr.	17. Messrs.
4. A.M.	11. Sat.	18. D.D.S.
5. Jr.	12. R.F.D.	19. Rev.
6. doz.	13. R.S.V.P.	20. Blvd.
7. Aug.	14. Esq.	

Exercise 2/Page 233

1. Doctor of Philosophy	16. anno Domini
2. Avenue	17. Steamship
3. inch	18. Street
4. et cetera (and so forth)	19. received
5. number	20. department
6. Brothers	21. Doctor of Medicine
7. Postscript	22. Treasurer
8. Railroad	23. Saturday
9. September	24. Honorable
10. Freight on Board	25. Reverend
11. Professor	26. Secretary
12. Assistant	27. Doctor of Dental Surgery
13. Eastern Standard Time	28. Captain
14. Governor	29. March
15. before Christ	30. post meridiem (after noon)

CHAPTER 19

Exercise 1/Page 239

1. alter	5. aisle	8. altogether
2. borne	6. already	9. all ready
3. brake	7. bridal	10. capital
4. capital		

Exercise 2/ Page 241

1. Council	5. It's	8. counsel
2. complement	6. dissent	9. core
3. course	7. led	10. dual
4. dessert		

Exercise 3/ Page 246

1. minor	5. waist	8. stationery
2. peace	6. their	9. whose
3. plane—plain	7. too	10. They're
4. principal		

Exercise 4/ Page 249

1. clothes
2. later
3. consul
4. advice
5. beside
6. emigrants
7. formally
8. ingenuous
9. ally
10. allusions

Exercise 5/ Page 250

1. morale
2. quite
3. personnel
4. loose
5. than
6. formally
7. lose
8. moral
9. quite
10. than

CHAPTER 20

Exercise/ Page 254

1. C
2. C
3. definitive
4. C
5. C
6. C
7. undefinable
8. undesirable
9. pitiless
10. C
11. C
12. C
13. C
14. C
15. C
16. C
17. non-existent
18. preferable
19. C
20. unendurable
21. necessarily
22. C
23. C
24. changeable
25. judgment or
     judgement
26. accommodate
27. guarantee
28. receipts
29. C
30. C
31. chosen
32. possessed
33. recognized
34. sincerity
35. existence
36. embarrassed
37. C
38. excitable
39. preferred
40. occasion

CHAPTER 22

Exercise/ Page 273

1. appellation
2. bassinet
3. C
4. C
5. catarrh
6. cellar
7. cole slaw
8. C
9. C
10. dyspeptic
11. C
12. Eskimos
13. C
14. C
15. C
16. genealogy
17. C
18. kimono
19. labeled
20. C
21. C
22. sacrilegious
23. sibilancy
24. C
25. C

CHAPTER 23

Exercise/Page 280

1. a	6. b	11. b
2. c	7. b	12. d
3. a	8. b	13. c
4. d	9. c	14. d
5. d	10. a	15. a

CHAPTER 24

Exercise/Page 286

1. c	6. b	11. a
2. a	7. b	12. d
3. d	8. c	13. c
4. d	9. d	14. c
5. a	10. a	15. c

CHAPTER 25

Exercise/Page 292

1. d	6. b	11. c
2. d	7. d	12. c
3. b	8. a	13. b
4. b	9. a	14. d
5. a	10. b	15. c

For Achievement Tests 1–7

ACHIEVEMENT TEST 1

Chapters 1–4/ Page 295

1. T	16. F	31. F	46. T
2. T	17. T	32. F	47. T
3. F	18. F	33. T	48. T
4. T	19. T	34. T	49. T
5. F	20. T	35. T	50. F
6. T	21. T	36. T	51. F
7. F	22. T	37. T	52. F
8. F	23. F	38. F	53. F
9. T	24. F	39. T	54. F
10. T	25. F	40. T	55. F
11. F	26. T	41. T	56. T
12. T	27. T	42. F	57. F
13. F	28. T	43. T	58. T
14. T	29. F	44. F	59. T
15. F	30. F	45. T	

ACHIEVEMENT TEST 2

Chapter 6/ Page 298

1. receipt	7. retrieve	13. achieve
2. relief	8. friend	14. perceive
3. shriek	9. bier	15. neighbors
4. yield	10. chief	16. mischievous
5. fiend	11. receiving	17. frontier
6. achievement	12. deceive	18. ceiling

ACHIEVEMENT TEST 3

Chapters 7–8/ Page 299

1. disadvantage	21. transient	41. perspective
2. C	22. admissible	42. C
3. misstatement	23. laughable	43. precocious
4. recollect	24. unthinkable	44. drinkable
5. C	25. eligible	45. inaccessible
6. innovation	26. invincible	46. C
7. renovate	27. legible	47. eligible
8. unnatural	28. comfortable	48. C
9. C	29. perishable	49. C
10. override	30. demonstrable	50. acquaintance
11. demoted	31. C	51. defendant
12. dissolve	32. recollect	52. significance
13. pre-eminent	33. C	53. hangar
14. antiseptic	34. unnoticeable	54. C
15. C	35. overrated	55. C
16. interstate	36. antecedents	56. C
17. interrupt	37. C	57. radiator
18. postscript	38. C	58. C
19. suburban	39. seceded	59. supervisor
20. superintendent	40. perforated	60. C

ACHIEVEMENT TEST 4

Chapters 9–11/ Page 302

1. buffaloes, buffalos, buffalo	8. beliefs	17. merciful
	9. armies	18. medleys
	10. oxen	19. conveyance
2. vetoes	11. chimneys	20. dignifies
3. tomatoes	12. pulleys	21. dining
4. pianos	13. volleys	22. imaginable
5. lassos, lassoes	14. salaries	23. judging
6. calves	15. tragedies	24. surprising
7. leaves	16. angrily	25. writing

26. whining
27. desirous
28. density
29. sincerely
30. families
31. dining
32. donkeys
33. encouragement
34. unimaginable
35. casualties
36. busily
37. accompanied

38. worried
39. portrayed
40. sublimity
41. inadvisable
42. singeing
43. vagueness
44. arguing
45. lovely
46. courageous
47. tasteless
48. contrivance
49. anniversaries

50. oxen
51. proofs
52. brothers-in-law
53. besieged
54. likeness
55. gracefully
56. truly
57. mimicking
58. sheep
59. alumni
60. academies
61. curriculum
62. bacilli

ACHIEVEMENT TEST 5

Chapters 12–15/ Page 304

1. low-priced
2. best-known
3. thirty-first
4. far-fetched
5. newly born
6. highest priced
7. pre-election
8. co-owner
9. ex-Governor
10. Vice-Admiral
11. conferred
12. preference
13. transferred
14. wrappings
15. hopper
16. hitter
17. trimmings
18. controlling
19. excelled
20. regretted
21. low ceiling
22. one half

23. dinning
24. low-necked
25. references
26. hoping
27. occurred
28. hangdog
29. unparalleled
30. twenty-ninth
31. predawn
32. high scorer
33. preferred
34. ex-policeman
35. conferred
36. chinned
37. Pro-Temperance
38. flapped
39. red-cheeked
40. eighty-eight
41. subliminal
42. regretful
43. lowest priced
44. smitten

45. well-timed
46. hitting
47. running
48. patrolled
49. all ready
50. run-on
51. Senator-elect
52. mid-Atlantic
53. extolled
54. aide-de-camp
55. regaled
56. runner-up
57. spinning
58. omitted
59. scraped
60. recurred
61. annulled
62. scrubbed
63. panicked
64. rebelled
65. deferred

ACHIEVEMENT TEST 6

Chapters 16–17/ Page 306

1. don't
2. men's
3. his
4. who's
5. i's, t's
6. you've
7. ladies'
8. brother-in-law's
9. children's
10. couldn't
11. East, West
12. Grandma Moses
13. Hindu
14. Elks
15. "For My Beloved"
16. *A Tale of Two Cities*
17. north
18. Columbus Day
19. My Fair Lady
20. House of Representatives
21. boy's
22. They're
23. doctors'
24. teachers'
25. 7's
26. Harrigan and Hart's
27. women's
28. theirs
29. t's
30. lawyer's
31. East
32. French
33. mathematics
34. Governor
35. captains
36. Hawaii
37. Orient
38. Senate
39. Arbor Day
40. *Silas Marner*
41. Admiral
42. Uncle Don
43. boys'
44. south

ACHIEVEMENT TEST 7

Chapter 19/ Page 308

1. advice
2. allies
3. aisle
4. all ready
5. illusion
6. alter
7. altogether
8. borne
9. angels
10. berth
11. beside
12. break
13. breath
14. bridle
15. canvass
16. Capitol
17. censure
18. cords
19. clothes
20. course
21. compliment
22. consul
23. core
24. incredulous
25. diaries
26. dissent
27. dessert
28. device
29. duel
30. formerly
31. instance
32. ingenious
33. compliments
34. desserts
35. consul
36. formally
37. morale
38. personnel
39. principle
40. stationery
41. waste
42. supersede
43. exceedingly
44. succeeds
45. proceeded
46. illusion
47. accede
48. receded
49. corpse
50. its
51. later
52. led
53. council
54. loose
55. minors
56. peace
57. plain
58. quite

MOVE TO THE HEAD OF YOUR CLASS

THE EASY WAY!

Barron's presents THE EASY WAY SERIES—specially prepared by top educators, it maximizes effective learning, while minimizing the time and effort it takes to raise your grades, brush up on the basics and build your confidence.

Comprehensive and full of clear review examples, THE EASY WAY SERIES is your best bet for better grades, quickly! Each book is only $9.95, Can. $13.95. (Except titles marked with one or two asterisks: * $8.95, Can. $11.95 ** $10.95, Can. $14.95.)

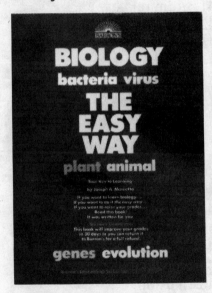

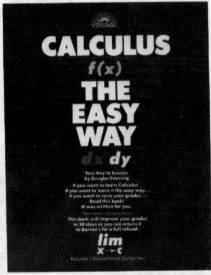

Accounting the Easy Way, 2nd Ed.
Algebra the Easy Way, 2nd Ed.
Arithmetic the Easy Way, 2nd Ed.
Biology the Easy Way, 2nd Ed., NEW
Bookkeeping the Easy Way, 2nd Ed., NEW
Business Letters the Easy Way
* Business Mathematics the Easy Way
Calculus the Easy Way, 2nd Ed.
Chemistry the Easy Way, 2nd Ed.
Computer Programming In Basic the Easy Way, 2nd Ed.
* Computer Programming In Cobol the Easy Way
Computer Programming In Fortran the Easy Way
Computer Programming In Pascal the Easy Way
* Data Processing the Easy Way
Electronics the Easy Way, 2nd Ed.

English the Easy Way, 2nd Ed.
French the Easy Way, 2nd Ed.
* French the Easy Way, Book 2
Geometry the Easy Way, 2nd Ed., NEW
German the Easy Way
Italian the Easy Way
Mathematics the Easy Way, 2nd Ed.
Physics the Easy Way
Spanish the Easy Way, 2nd Ed.
Spelling the Easy Way, 2nd Ed.
Statistics the Easy Way, 2nd Ed.
Trigonometry the Easy Way
** Typing the Easy Way, 2nd Ed.
Writing the Easy Way

BARRON'S EDUCATIONAL SERIES
250 Wireless Boulevard
Hauppauge, New York 11788
In Canada: Georgetown Book Warehouse
34 Armstrong Avenue
Georgetown, Ontario L7G 4R9

Prices subject to change without notice. Books may be purchased at your bookstore, or by mail from Barron's. Enclose check or money order for total amount plus sales tax where applicable and 10% for postage and handling (minimum charge $1.50; Canada $2.00). All books are paperback editions.